Thank you for
your interest and
support.
Linda

Every Fourth Girl

Linda Dell Moore

Every Fourth Girl

Copyright © 2017 by Linda Dell Moore

All rights reserved. No part of this book may be reproduced or transmitted in any form or by any means, electronic or mechanical, including photocopying, recording, or any information storage and retrieval system, without permission in writing from the author.

Library of Congress Case Reference Number:
1-5826673323
ISBN – 13: 978-1974207886
ISBN – 10:1974207889

Printed by CreateSpace, An Amazon.com Company Available from Amazon.com, CreateSpace.com, and other retail outlets. Available on Kindle and other devices.

Cover design: Brandi Myszkowski

Dedicated to my family, Brandi, Brian, and Marley,
To my first true therapist, Kate
And to my healing partners at
New Horizons of the Treasure Coast

Foreword

As a survivor of years of traumatic sexual abuse, I lived my life in the, "Third Person," as if I were on the outside looking in. The cruelty I suffered was at the hands of my parents. My memoir, *Every Fourth Girl* describes how their upbringing affected me. How their lives nearly destroyed mine. I tell two-thirds of my own life story from the perspective of an observer. Finally, I relate personally, the last third of my life after having recovered my own memories.

Sexual, physical, and psychological trauma consumed my childhood and much of my adult life. The abuse was chronic, most often violent. I detached from myself through the mental processes of dissociation. The abuse began when I was just a toddler. I was too young to defend myself. My young mind developed a defense mechanism to protect me from the pain and injuries inflicted on me.

This coping skill became the strongest part of my self-preservation instincts, and indeed saved me from life-threatening circumstances. Dissociation creates the effects of "lost time" and "out of body" experiences. My own mind worked to protect my sanity and my life. I was either unconscious during the abuse, or an ephemeral outside witness of the mistreatment.

Until my mind reclaimed my experiences, I lived without recollection of most of my life. However, the memories were there—safeguarded by the parts of me that preserved my rationality in a life of constant dysfunction and deliberate brutality.

I titled my memoir as I did, because one out of every four female children becomes the victim of sexual exploitation or abuse by the age of 18 years old. *Every Fourth Girl* is my story, and the story of 25 percent of girls and women in the United States today.

Prologue

Fugue State: An altered state of consciousness in which a person may move about purposely and even speak but is not fully aware. A fugue state is usually a type of complex partial focal seizure; also referred to as dissociative fugue.
Medterms Dictionary, Dr. Martin Zipster, M.D. Board certified

Tuesday, March 4, 1997—Linda drove along the shore on Lake Washington Boulevard heading home from work. As a consultant, she set her own hours and worked from her office, but today she had spent four hours at her client's site processing payroll for 150 employees. It was a typical Seattle day for early March wispy rain, slate skies, forty-five degrees—as Linda drove her sad misty eyes, gray mood, and age pressing against the middling forties were a match for the day. She pulled into the parking lot of the grocery store down the hill from home; at noon, the lot was nearly empty. Linda was planning a quick twenty minutes to grab a few things for a weeknight dinner.

Walking into the store, she experienced a moment of light-headedness and reached for a grocery cart to steady her balance. Steering her way toward the produce aisle she took a couple of slow deep breaths remembering that she'd had nothing except black coffee. Linda stepped away from the cart to get a couple of plastic produce bags, her vision dimmed forcing her back to the cart where she clutched the handle as everything before her eyes went black.

She heard a loud rhythmic whooshing in her ears the sound of blood rushing to her head, felt her heart pounding wildly in her chest. Her mind seemed to be spinning as she strained to regain her vision, opening her eyes wide, she looked down upon her own body, standing like a statue next to the tomatoes holding on to the cart for dear life. Linda watched herself take a few slow, shuffling steps, making her way passed the lettuce, as her view became more and more distant, moving away from herself. The blackness returned, then there was a pinpoint flash of light—an image appeared barely registering in her mind's eye, then another, and another as if she were watching a slideshow inside her brain.

Linda was compelled to focus on the images, the memories. Acrid smells, dissonant sounds, bitter tastes, and intrusive touches overran her senses. Physically she experienced panic and pain, a desire to flee but the inability to do so. She felt the flood of emotions—shame, betrayal, and fear. She was lost to her past; it was erasing any sense of her presence. The nightmare-like flashbacks continued rushing through her....

She jumped when she felt a hand on her shoulder and choked back a cry of shock—a man stood next to her "Ma'am I'm the manager. Are you alright?" He asked.

"Yes." She whispered, glancing around trying to understand where she was. Linda and her cart were in the corner of the dairy aisle. Her hands felt frozen in place, her grip had turned her knuckles white and her fingers blue. The cart held a jumble of a dozen items she didn't remember selecting. "I have to go home." She said letting go of the cart, praying that she could stand on her own. Linda slipped past the manager, moving as quickly as she could walk, got out of the store.

She made it to her car before she started to shake. Linda struggled to get her keys from her shoulder bag. Finally, after fumbling with the door lock she retreated inside her car. Her heart still pummeling inside her chest, she experienced a wave of nausea and threw the door open just in time to get her head out. She threw up bilious coffee and dry heaved a few times before the vomiting shudders stopped. Sweat ran into her eyes as she slammed the car door shut for the second time. She looked at the clock on the dash…it was three o'clock; she had gone into the store at noon, *three hours had disappeared.* Tears sprung from her eyes, a loud sob burst from her throat. Linda wiped her eyes with the back of her hands, gripped the steering wheel. Linda pushed the keys into the ignition and started the Subaru putting the car in gear. She took a deep sucking breath as she backed out of the parking lot.

Thanking God silently for the fragments of herself that had spontaneously come together, she looked up the hill seeing her home only a couple of blocks away. Her next thought was what to do when she got there—everything in her life had changed. She had always known deep down that something was very wrong, this was beyond her grasp…she knew to the bone all that had happened. How could she ever get over the horror of it…how could she continue to live?

Book I

"For we know in part and we prophesy in part. When that which is perfect is come then that, which is in part shall be done away. When I was a child I spoke as a child, I understood as a child, I thought as a child, but when I became grown, I put away childish things. For now, we see through a glass darkly, but then face to face. Now I know in part; but then I shall know even as I am also known."
First Corinthians 13: 9-12

1

"Mining is like a search and destroy mission."
Stewart L. Udall, Arizona Congressman, 1954-1960 Secretary of the Interior, 1961-1969

In 1910, Ajo, Arizona had barely fifty people, desert dwellers scabbing for copper ore hauled up in rawhide bags from a 60-foot shaft mine called "Old Bat Hole." In the next forty years, Ajo survived Indian raids, and eastern con men selling worthless mine claims to dupes from the Midwest. There were even a couple of failed pit mines attempted—by mining businesses that lacked the expertise or capital to make a serious go of it. In the 1920s, water was found in an underground aquifer, a team of men hand-shoveled a 645-foot deep well below the desert surface, and the New Cordelia Copper Mine, forty-three miles north of the Mexican border, became a reality.

Ajo in the early 1950s was the archetype of a company-owned copper mining town. The town itself rose from the mine pit, a terraced wound on the

Sonoran Desert floor, that was nearly a mile wide and hundreds of feet deep. In addition to the gaping pit, coal-fired smelters expelled pollution into the desert air, and the concentrator facility created tons of waste called "slag," which was piled into four-story high, miles long mounds on the desert floor. Seven days a week a thousand men worked the pit to bring out the copper in 100 degree plus heat, using steam shovels with tires as big as a pick-up truck. Every day the gray slag piles continued to mount up, hills that were like noxious ramparts that surrounded the town.

Phelps Dodge Mining Corporation owned the mine and the town itself. Phelps Dodge had created everything necessary to support the mine and the unearthing of its copper. Ajo had a company-owned Mercantile in the downtown square that sold everything from food and clothes to hardware.

The Michael Curley School was built by Phelps Dodge and named after the mine's general manager. The company hired and paid the teachers that taught the town's children from Kindergarten through to High School. The Curley campus included an auditorium, industrial shop, cafeteria, gym, tennis courts, playgrounds, baseball field, and the pride of the community, a football field equipped with lights for the popular Friday night competitions.

The company also had built a public swimming pool that was available to all residents—with a few restrictions—Mondays and Tuesdays were designated for the Mexicans, Wednesdays and Thursdays for the Indians, and then on Thursday night, the pool would be drained and refilled for Friday, Saturday, and Sunday's white swimmers.

A few miles northeast of downtown the Ajo Country Club with its own clubhouse, pool, and six-hole golf course served the recreational interests of its 235 white-only membership.

The company also built and ran Ajo General Hospital, a facility with forty-five beds, three doctors, and eleven registered nurses. The employees of the mine and their families, for a flat fee payroll deduction, had unlimited access to healthcare. It was a non-profit hospital, residents of town not covered could secure healthcare at a very reasonable cost.

Ajo also boasted a fully stocked public library of over 12,000 books with a library staff that ensured access for the town's residents. In the center of downtown was a large grassy, palm-lined plaza surrounded on two sides by local restaurants, the company Mercantile, a movie theatre, and local small businesses. On the plaza, the company had built a spacious air-conditioned social club used by the residents. The company had built the plaza in white stucco Spanish Colonial Revival style complete with ornate Moorish arches, colorful tile work, and red clay tile roofs.

At the west end of the plaza was the rail station for the Ajo-Gila Bend rail line also owned by the company, it had one passenger car, but was primarily for the purpose of transporting coal to fuel the mining operations, and shipping refined copper ore to the closest hub of the Southern Pacific Railroad about fifty miles away.

The east end of the town plaza had two churches, Immaculate Conception Catholic Church, and the Federated Methodist Church. Both churches filled every Sunday and on religious holidays. In Indian Village, Mexican families and Indian families who had converted to Christianity attended Saint Catherine's Mission.

The Phelps Dodge Company had built and owned the vast majority of housing in Ajo. Larger single-family white stucco homes built in the nearby eastern foothills of the Little Ajo Mountains; housed mine management surrounded by walls with private courtyards. Comfortable clapboard ranch-style homes with picket fences and well-tended lawns were built for administrative employees.

Sixteen miles northwest of town was a small enclave of eight homes built for the employees who either maintained the well, which was the single source of water for the mine and town, or were shift foremen in the mine, smelter, or concentrator facility. The homes at The Well enjoyed a lushness of vegetation that the desert didn't naturally sustain. A grove of cottonwood trees loomed over the homes due to well runoff and most of the homes had flourishing garden filled yards.

Back in town, the company had built apartment projects for the miners and their families. Closest to downtown were the projects with parking lots and front patio stoops for the white employees. To the south was Mexican Town where the company had also built housing projects for the Mexican employees. To the southwest, closest to the grating grinding noise of the mine pit, and caustic Sulphur stench belched from the smelter, were Indian Village and the company owned projects for the Indian employees. By the 1950s, everyone had electricity and indoor plumbing.

Ajo was indeed a model community; it was also a perfect model for the segregation of the early 1950s. The population was 6,600 people; sixty-five percent were white twenty-two percent were Mexican and thirteen percent were Indian. There were approximately 1,700 households in Ajo and nearly every household depended on the Phelps Dodge Company for its well-being and economic security. People worked together, went to school together, but for the rest of the time lived mostly segregated lives.

Civic organizations like the Chamber of Commerce and The Rotary Club kept the town informed of the mine and business economic climate. The Elks Club, American Legion, and V.F.W had avid memberships doing charitable works in town.

No matter how much money and thought the company had put into creating the model copper mining town filled with plenty of diversions—one of the most interesting traits of a small company owned town like Ajo, was that everyone knew a lot about everyone else's business. Secrets required great effort to keep—speculation about who was doing what with who was a big part of the town's pastime. The small town's people fueled their leisure time with partying, gossip mongering, and scandals.

On Saturday mornings, many folks loaded up their station wagons with the neighborhood kids and drove an hour to Sonoita, Mexico, just across the border, to buy one bottle of whiskey, rum, or tequila for every person in the car regardless of age. They then returned to the town social hall or the fraternal orders lodges for BYOB potluck dinner dances almost every Saturday night.

For the population of 3,500 adults there wasn't much that went on in town that someone hadn't voiced an opinion about, tattled a juicy story, or embellished a bit of rumor and there was plenty of alcohol to loosen tongues, and cliques that picked sides about the latest dirt-dishing or disreputable carryings-on.

2

"From childhood's hour I haven't done as others do—I have not seen as others see.
Edgar Allan Poe

Dorothy Louise Majors was born January 3, 1932 in Hamilton, Ohio during the depths of the Great Depression. She was a stunningly beautiful baby born, during a difficult time, in a town known for its gambling houses and brothels, and in a home with less than adequate conditions. She had an older sister Marie born eighteen months earlier. Marie and Dorothy's mother suffered from severe post-partum depression after both births. Without access to adequate medical care, the mental and emotional depression went on without relief. Marie, the toddler and Dorothy, the baby were barely taken care of, let alone nurtured. Another pregnancy followed, a brother James was born in less than eighteen months. This third child had the additional burden of being born with a misshapen foot "a club foot," for which he received no medical treatment.

Ω

By the time, Dorothy was eight years old in 1940; she was one of seven children in the Majors family. Their father, Virgil Majors had eked out the barest of livings as an unskilled laborer during the Great Depression. Their mother, Francis Majors had suffered the entirety of the hard times though a nearly constant state of pregnancy, and an emotionally crippling depression of her own. The main source of income for the family was a result of the Social Security Act of 1935, which provided a monthly stipend for the aid of dependent children of poverty-stricken families. However, Virgil Majors had taken to drinking far more than laboring, a good part of the Social Security safety net never made it to care for his wife or children.

Marie as the oldest child had taken on responsibilities far beyond her years; at the age of ten, she held the tenuous family together. Marie and her younger sister Dorothy were inseparable and although their clothes were tattered and ill fitting, they were both lovely little girls. Marie had light brown hair and hazel eyes like her mother, while Dorothy had the wavy dark brunette hair and deep brown eyes from her father.

The two girls didn't often make it to the full week of school due to the demands on them at home, although they were both good readers, which would later serve them well. At least three days during the school week they stayed home, to care for their, most often, bedridden mother. In 1940 their five younger siblings, ranged in age from seven to less than a year old. Their father was absent for days at a time, and when he came home it was to drink alone and abuse his oldest daughter. Since he could no longer demand the personal attentions of his wife Frances, he decided to use Marie to meet his "manly" needs. He called it the "hat trick." Virgil would insist his daughter sit next to him while he placed his hat on his lap. He would then force Marie's little hand under that hat to satisfy his sexual release. Afterwards he would leave their tenement apartment and not be seen until the Aid to Children checks showed up again.

By the winter of 1942, many of the effects of the Great Depression were waning because of the Second World War. The Majors family remained in a crisis moving every several months from tenement to tenement in order to slink out of a month's past due rent.

Marie was twelve and Dorothy was ten-and-a-half, their mother had recovered somewhat because she hadn't had another child in the last three years, and was at least able to look after her youngest children. Virgil Majors was gone lost to drinking and his own demons.

Marie and Dorothy had come up with their own method to help their gravely needy family. It all began when one day the two of them had used their own nickels to go to the movie theatre for the first time together. Marie had been the week before on her own, and she urged Dorothy to accompany her, promising that after the movie they would each buy a pair of shiny black patent Mary Jane style shoes on the way home.

As the two sisters sat in the darkened theatre, waiting for the movie to begin a man in a hat came and tapped Marie on the shoulder. She told Dorothy to wait for her to return. Marie went and sat with the man several rows back. She did return ten minutes later and she had a surprise for Dorothy—a shiny quarter. Dorothy sat alone in the movie house barely able to watch the movie because she was trying to keep track of where Marie was, sitting with a different man in a hat every time.

When the movie ended, Marie returned with a big handful of quarters more money than Dorothy had ever seen, her sister explained in hushed tones how she got the coins from each of the men. After the movie, Marie made good on her promise, the girls stopped at the Salvation Army Thrift store, and each found a pair of second-hand shoes that still had enough patent leather shine to delight them.

In the following weeks, Marie and Dorothy made weekly outings to the movie theatre and both of the girls left with a handful of quarters. The "hat trick" was helping to feed and clothe their younger siblings. They told their mother that they were doing odd jobs around the neighborhood to explain where the money was coming from. Frances never asked too many questions when it came to money so there was no problem.

No problem until one of the theatre employees began to notice that the two girls always came during the weekdays when they should be in school. On their last visit to the theatre as Marie and Dorothy left with their pockets full of quarters, two truant officers were waiting for them in the lobby with the theatre manager. The officers took the girls into custody, and were trying to decide whether to take them home or to detention when they discovered the pockets full of quarters. The officers asked Marie and Dorothy how they had come into the money, out of shame, both girls refused to answer. Marie tried to take a haughty attitude about it that only made matters worse. When asked how to contact their parents Marie admitted that they didn't have a telephone. When the officer in charge inquired as to her father's employment, Marie lied and said her father was dead.

Dorothy stood by Marie in terrified silence looking down at her black patent leather shoes. When the officers turned their attention on her, she burst into wailing tears. The scene in the theatre lobby was drawing a crowd so the officers felt they had no choice but to pack the two girls into the truancy patrol car. They drove them to the youth detention center at the edge of town. Having taken the girls into custody was one thing, what to do with them was another question. Most of the truants and delinquents in detention were boys. They couldn't put these two young girls in with the regulars. Marie and Dorothy spent the rest of the afternoon and evening in an office with a couple of cots pulled in for them to sleep. They were fed a modest dinner of soup and bread.

That night the two girls agreed that they wouldn't give their address up when questioned, they didn't have any idea about what would happen to them, but they both agreed that their frail mother and younger siblings couldn't have to account for what they had done. Marie and Dorothy even shared a little chuckle because while they had been forced to hand over the quarters in their pockets, they both had hidden four quarters in each of their shoes. No matter what happened, they each had two dollars apiece as long as they kept their shoes on.

After two long boring days in the office "cell," a woman came to see them. She was dressed in a long black dress with matching head covering. She said, "I am Sister Agnes with the Sisters of Mercy. Since it has been determined that you girls are without adult supervision you will come with me to the Ohio Children's Home in Springfield."

Marie reached out grabbed Dorothy's hand answering for both of them "Thank you Ma'am we would be grateful for your help."

Ω

In the early summer of 1943, Marie Jacqueline Majors turned thirteen, and Dorothy Louise Majors age eleven, had found their way out of the tenements of Hamilton, Ohio into the care of one of the most highly reputed Children's Homes in Ohio. Run by a fraternal order for over one hundred years it had saved many an orphan from lives of destitution. The Sisters of Mercy operated a hospital in Cincinnati and ran the healthcare facilities at the Children's Home.

From lives that were leading down the depraved road to Hamilton's many brothels, Marie and Dorothy found salvation from their fates. At the orphanage, the girls went to school and both quickly caught up to their grade level. They were clothed, clean, well cared for, and their physical beauty shined brightly. They did their schoolwork and chores with a happy carefree attitude, Marie and Dorothy both excelled in their own ways.

Marie became enamored with the nuns and volunteered to help in the healthcare clinic; she also studied the bible and catechism with the promise of the chance for her confirmation to the church.

Dorothy's precocious nature flourished, her long dark naturally wavy hair, deep dark eyes, and ivory pale complexion got her plenty of attention from teachers and staff who were delighted to see her doing so well and maturing into such a charming young woman.

In 1944, the news came that the Children's Home was, after its long history, going to close. The new Ohio Department of Children's Services favored foster care over orphanages. Marie who was fourteen took the news in stride; she had already decided to become a nun and would go to the Sisters of Mercy convent in Cincinnati where she would be accepted as a novice, committing to a two-year novitiate period while she would train to become a nurse.

Dorothy at twelve-and-a-half was very concerned about her prospects; however, a member of the fraternal order who did volunteer work occasionally at the Children's Home, had taken notice of the pretty Dorothy passing in the halls in her crisp white blouse and red plaid skirt. Raymond Cordy and his wife Daisy had only been able to have one child, a son James who was eleven years old. Earlier in their lives, they had considered adopting another child, just never found the right time. Now the possibility of fostering Dorothy seemed like a good idea. Raymond brought his wife and son to meet Dorothy, she of course, charmed them. By the time Dorothy turned thirteen on January 3, 1945, she was living with the Cordy family. She called them Mom and Pop Cordy in the manner she had learned at the Children's Home, when addressing the Home matron and superintendent. Dorothy loved having a little brother named Jimmy it reminded her of her younger brother James. Since Jimmy didn't have a "club foot," she decided she loved him more.

Dorothy and Marie exchanged a few letters after leaving the orphanage, as Marie became more involved in her religious vocation, she urged Dorothy to confess her past sins as she had done. Dorothy had never been much for religion although she did go to the local Methodist Church on Sunday with the Cordy family. As far as she knew, the Methodists didn't have confession and she didn't really believe she had anything to confess. The letters became rarer until finally Marie and Dorothy just lost touch.

Daisy Cordy had been ailing for the past few years with adult-onset asthma; she spent a month in the hospital in the summer of 1945. The doctors told her and Mr. Cordy that the only thing that would help would be to move to a drier climate. Raymond Cordy was a steam engineer and had heard about a copper mining boom in Arizona. After two more months in the hospital for Daisy Cordy in the fall, Raymond decided to move his family to the Southwest—he had made inquiries discovering that a position would be available to him in Ajo, Arizona at the New Cordelia copper mine owned by one of the biggest mining corporations in the world, Phelps Dodge. The plan was set for January of 1946, Raymond Cordy himself arranged with the Department of Children's Services for Dorothy to move with them to Arizona. He had grown much attached to Dorothy; she was a beautiful fourteen-year-old young woman. Raymond Cordy had a sickly wife, and was a man with a hat.

Ω

The Cordy family sold their modest home in Springfield, Ohio and made the move to Arizona by the end of January. They bought one of the few non-company owned homes in the downtown area of Ajo, a three-bedroom colonial style home with a nice porch and yard. It cost all of the $3,000 they made from the sale in Ohio. Raymond Cordy started work the very week they arrived.

Daisy was pleased with the house and felt superior to be one of the very few homeowners in the town. Her health began to improve almost immediately, as the dry desert air was a distinct change from the moist, moldy, asthma-inducing atmosphere of the midwest.

Dorothy and Jimmy enrolled in classes at The Curley School a few blocks from their new home. Dorothy Cordy enrolled with her new name in her second semester as a high school freshman. Jimmy went to seventh grade. Both of them adjusted to the new school and town. Within the first month, Jimmy was hanging out with a couple of pals in the neighborhood. Dorothy had made friends with an attractive longhaired blond girl named Pippen Burkhead, who lived with her family who owned a small horse ranch on the north edge of town.

Dorothy and Pippen were the two prettiest girls in school, and the contrast between them had everyone taking notice. They became inseparable, sat together in classes, at lunch, went to the plaza every day after school, and window-shopped at the company mercantile store. Pippen convinced Dorothy that they should both try-out for the high school majorette team in the spring, and they each bought shiny silver batons and started baton-twirling in the plaza, until Pippen's father came in his pick-up truck to take her home to the ranch. Dorothy then walked the couple of blocks home, practicing tossing, and catching the baton while marching—dreaming about how special she would look in the red satin majorette uniform with "Red Raiders" emblazoned on the front.

The dream reminded her of something she had in her book bag. A block from home she stopped marching slung her bag from her shoulder and began digging around in the bottom under her books. Finally, she felt the slender metal tube and pulled it out. It was a lipstick, one of Revlon's newest colors, "Love that Red." She said it aloud as she took off the cap and swiveled the lipstick up from its case. She couldn't dare to put it on her lips; Mom Cordy would have a fit. She pretended, holding her lips in a little pout. She turned the lipstick back down recapped the tube and pushed it back into the bottom of her bag. She decided for sure she had to be a majorette—the lipstick would be the perfect shade to match the short red dress the majorettes wore. She'd have to save it until then, which didn't bother her much since she had snitched it from the Mercantile store's make up display.

Ω

Dorothy and Pippen did try out for the majorettes in the spring just before the school year ended and they both made the team. There were practices scheduled every week during the summer, and the girls both became experts at twirling and tossing their batons. Dorothy had to ask Mom Cordy to sew her two uniforms, or else pay to have a woman in Mexican Town make them. At first Daisy said it was an imposition, then Dorothy told her about having to go to Mexican Town several times for fittings. Daisy relented and agreed to make the uniforms. She complained when she saw the pattern. "The dress is too short...it'll make you look like a hussy."

Pop Cordy weighed in telling her that it was an honor for Dorothy to be on the team. "Stop giving the girl a hard time I think she'll do great and we'll all be proud."

Dorothy gave Mom Cordy a quick hug. "Your sewing is amazing, I will have the best dresses of anyone." She gave Pop Cordy a kiss on the forehead, said "Thanks," and ran out of the house to go to practice.

Daisy Cordy, the truth be told, was more than a little jealous of her foster daughter. Daisy was a petite redhead; she was used to being the apple of her husband's eye. Daisy saw the way he sometimes looked at Dorothy and did not like feeling upstaged one bit. When school started up again in the fall Daisy's feelings didn't get any warmer toward Dorothy, she was one of, if not the most popular girls in school. Every Friday night Raymond Cordy insisted that the whole family go and sit on the hard high school bleachers to watch the weekly football game. Daisy had to see Dorothy in her white cowgirl boots, shiny red satin short dress, and bright red lipstick march around the field. The school band played while she and her little coterie of majorettes did tricks with their batons. Daisy Cordy hated how Raymond cheered, clapped, and whistled during the whole halftime performance, waving his hat in the air as if a bunch of high school kids were putting on the greatest show on earth.

 She thought about telling him what a fool he was making of himself over Dorothy but that would only serve to validate her jealousy and that, she was unwilling to admit. Daisy just stewed in her own bitter juices wishing she'd never heard of a girl named Dorothy.

$$\Omega$$

In 1948, when Dorothy turned sixteen Pop Cordy bought her a used Chevy for $50 which he had bargained away from a friend at the mine. Dorothy was over the moon excited even though the paint job wasn't good and it was missing a couple of hubcaps, she still had her own car. Daisy had never learned to drive and Raymond had his pick-up that he took to work.

He told Daisy "Look it was a good deal and Dorothy can drive for errands and take Jimmy to his horseback riding lessons at the Burkhead ranch."

"You spoil that girl something awful. What sixteen-year-old needs to own a car? There's nowhere in this town to go except looking for trouble…."

"C'mon Daisy she's a good girl, gets good grades, and helps you plenty around the house. Don't give me a hard time—I did it and it's done." He gave his little wife a big man bear hug. "Hey, I need a beer and you could use a glass of your good sherry that you like. Wha'dya say let's sit out here on the porch and have a few drinks."

Daisy did like her good sherry; she drank more of it than Raymond ever guessed. She relented and went inside while Raymond walked out to the car. Dorothy and Jimmy were sitting in the front seat talking about where they could go now that "they" had wheels. Dorothy looked up "Is she very mad?"

"No she just doesn't want to spoil you or have you get into trouble."

"I promise Pop I'll be good, careful too." She reached up and tugged at his hat. "I love you Pop."

"I know."

$$\Omega$$

In the summer of 1949, Dorothy was dating a handsome college-bound young man, Gilbert Brooks. His father Chester Brooks was the general manager of the Phelps Dodge Mercantile store. The family lived in one of the company owned houses at the bottom of the foothills where the administrative employees had very nice houses in a nice northeast neighborhood. Daisy was pleased with the arrangement; it gave her special attention when she went shopping in town from the store employees that knew that her Dorothy was dating the boss's son. Gilbert was going away to the University of Arizona in Tucson in the fall and Dorothy would be starting her senior year of high school. The two of them made a dashing couple around town and some of Daisy's jealousy abated now that someone other than Raymond had Dorothy's attention.

    The summer passed quickly for Dorothy and Gilbert, in a blur of drive-in movies with lots of necking and swim dates on the weekends at the Country Club pool, where Chester Brooks was a member. A few times Gilbert invited Daisy and Jimmy to join them. Daisy felt like she was living the good life drinking sherry in the shade with the Country Club set.

    Before Dorothy knew it, she and Gilbert were having their last date of the summer. He was leaving for U of A the next day. They had dinner with his parents—Chester and Lenore Brooks grew fond of Dorothy and knew they too, would miss her company. On the other hand, they were both too young to get serious about their relationship. Gilbert had four years of engineering to work on, and he didn't need the complications of a long-distance relationship. The dinner was perfect and all went well. Chester even allowed Gilbert and Dorothy to have some wine. The two were getting ready to go out for one last drive around, which Gilbert's parents knew was an excuse to go park at the edge of town. They said good night,

Lenore told Dorothy she was welcome to come by any time.

True to form, they went out into the desert and necked for an hour but Dorothy still had a curfew, Gilbert had her home by midnight. He left at six o'clock the next morning without looking back, a young man on his way to making a life on his own with no obligations or regrets.

Ω

Dorothy went home a cried a few tears but she was always realistic. She had her senior year starting in a few days and she was head majorette this year. Her grades were good and if she continued to work hard, she thought she could go to college too, maybe to be a nurse like her sister Marie, not the nun part for sure, but a nurse would be a good profession to pursue. She fell asleep and didn't wake up until the sun began to shine through her window.

She got up as she did every morning to make coffee for Pop, he was an early riser, and Mom liked to sleep in. Dorothy enjoyed having a little time alone with him before he went to work. She headed downstairs quietly not to wake Mom or Jimmy, and saw the back of Pop's head above the back of his favorite chair. She went into the kitchen to start the coffee pot on the stove, then headed back to the living room for her morning chat with Pop Cordy.

She said his name as she entered the room. "Pop are you awake?" He was dressed for work, he didn't answer, and he didn't move a muscle. She looked at him from across the room suddenly knowing that something was very wrong. She rushed to him and touched his balding forehead and it was cold.

"Oh no, oh no, not you, you can't be dead." She whispered. Dorothy knelt down and laid her head in his lap. She grabbed his hat from the arm of the chair where he always laid it, clutching it to her chest she started to cry.

The coffee was boiling over on the stove when Daisy came downstairs into the kitchen. She heard sobbing coming from the living room, quickly took the coffee pot off the burner, before she went to see what was wrong. She found Dorothy in her pajamas with her head in Raymond's lap. Her tears had soaked his pants. Daisy felt the blood rise in her face. "What are you doing?" She screamed at Dorothy.

Dorothy raised her head Pop's hat still clasped to her chest. "Mom, he's dead. I found him like this."

"Don't you call me Mom—I am not your mother and he is not your father. Get away from him. What you did to his pants, you should be ashamed." Daisy was hysterical.

Dorothy didn't understand until she looked down at the tear-stained spot on the lap of Pop's pants. "I was just crying."

"You know what I think, I think you're a dirty little whore who crept her way into my home, and you've killed my husband." She rushed toward Dorothy and grabbed the hat from her hands. "You think I never knew what you did under this hat? I did know, trust me, you'll go back to the dirty streets of Hamilton where you came from."

Dorothy couldn't take any more abuse she jumped up, ran upstairs to her room, and slammed the door. She threw herself on the bed but couldn't cry another tear. She was angry, scared, and ashamed at the same time. Could Daisy really mean to send her back to Ohio? Dorothy couldn't bear the thought. What was she going to do?

She heard the wail from Jimmy as he made his way downstairs to find his father had passed away. Daisy was on the phone yelling for the doctor to come to the house right away. Dorothy couldn't stand being in the house for another minute. She got dressed, brushed her hair, and pulled it back into a ponytail. She put on her shoes, ran down the back stairs, and left the house from the service porch. She got into her car, leaving with a screech of tires.

It was seven-thirty in the morning; she didn't know where to go. She drove for a while and then found herself in front of Gilbert's house. He was gone she knew, but his parents had been kind to her last night. Dorothy parked the car went up and knocked on the door. Chester Brooks already dressed for work in a button down shirt and striped tie answered the door immediately. Dorothy started to cry again not knowing what she was going to say.

"Dorothy are you alright? Gilbert already left for Tucson."

"Pop Cordy is dead. He died early this morning, maybe his heart." Dorothy choked back more tears. "Daisy blames me and threw me out of the house—she said that I have to go back to Ohio."

"I'm sorry, come in child." Chester moved aside to let her enter.

Lenore entered the living room still wearing her robe. "Did I hear you say you're your father died?"

"Yes it was terrible I got up to make coffee for him like I always do, he was dead in his chair." Dorothy could barely get the words out for her crying.

Lenore put her arm around Dorothy's shoulders and led her to a seat on the sofa. "Let me get you some water and tissues." Lenore went to the kitchen.

"Dorothy I know you're upset. Why would your mother say you had to go back to Ohio?" Chester asked.

"I'm not their real daughter, they were my foster parents. Pop Cordy took me out of an orphanage back there almost five years ago."

"I didn't realize." Chester was at a loss.

Lenore returned giving Dorothy a glass of water and put a box of tissues next to her. "Mrs. Cordy must be in shock—surely what she said was a result of terrible grief."

"I don't think so; she blamed me for Pop dying." Dorothy put her head in her hands and started sobbing again. "I loved Pop. I wouldn't have hurt him for the world."

"Of course you did dear." Lenore said.

Chester spoke up again "I think I need to look into this Ohio situation, the last thing that should happen is that Dorothy be sent away to who knows where."

Lenore shook her head in agreement. "Dorothy you will stay here with us, we'll get this figured out. You'll start school on Tuesday if you're up to it."

Dorothy leaned into Lenore's arms again. "Thank you, you're both very kind."

"I've got to get on to work. I will make some phone calls. I'll get word to Mrs. Cordy that you're staying with us and make arrangements to pick up some of your things." He slipped on his suit jacket, leaned over, gave his wife a peck on her cheek, and gave Dorothy a kindly pat on the head. "I'll see you both this evening, and Dorothy I want you to get some rest." With that he left.

Lenore went and got a pillow for Dorothy to lie down on the sofa then went into the kitchen to make some toast for them. By the time she returned with a plate of toast, Dorothy was asleep. She thought of what a shock the girl had been through and tears sprung to her eyes. She could not imagine how Daisy Cordy could blame a child for what was her husband's premature death. Lenore hadn't really known Daisy Cordy other than to say hello in passing. She thought about what must be happening in the Cordy home. Had the doctor been there by now? What about the son and the loss of his father, it must be a horrible thing to endure. Lenore had finished her toast, she left the remaining two pieces on the plate on the coffee table in case Dorothy was to wake, and she went to get dressed. In her room without thinking, she laid out a black dress and her black prosthetic bra then realized that the town would be in mourning. Mr. Cordy was well known and well liked, as far a she knew.

    Chester Brooks drove to work slowly thinking over the events of the morning. He'd been up early to see Gilbert off to Tucson. Gilbert would be arriving at the university 130 miles away right about now. He had promised to call his parents that evening once he settled in. The news about Dorothy would cause his son great concern. Chester was determined not to allow anything or anyone to distract from Gilbert's educational pursuits. However, everything he knew about Dorothy led him to believe that she was a well-mannered, popular girl who, according to his son, got good grades and had her own plans for the future. He couldn't fathom Daisy Cordy's reaction. Shock and grief was one thing, to threaten to disown a child was unconscionable. He didn't know Daisy well; she had a reputation for being pushy and for putting on airs. Raymond Cordy was the exact opposite an easy-going, hard-working, hail-fellow well met.

    As Chester Brooks parked his car in front of the Mercantile he knew today would be full of news about Raymond Cordy's demise. The town rumor mill would go into full grind. Even though he didn't know Dorothy that well Chester Brooks felt a sense of protection and defense well up inside on her behalf. He'd do his best to make sure she was able to stay in school in Ajo if that's what she wanted.

$$\Omega$$

    By noon that day, most people in town had heard about the death of Raymond Cordy. The doctor had determined a massive heart attack had killed him almost instantly. The mine manager after hearing of the news arranged with the local mortuary to help the family take care of the funeral plans. They transferred the body to the funeral home. The mine would take care of the expense. He ordered appropriate flowers sent to the home.

Chester Brooks would be responsible for delivering a care package of food, and other necessities to the new widow and her son. He decided to go that afternoon to let Daisy Cordy know that Dorothy was staying with him and his wife for the time being. He hoped to be able to get a few of the girl's clothes and such without creating an annoyance. He arrived at the Cordy home about three o'clock and knocked at the door on which a black band of mourning cloth had been secured. Jimmy Cordy answered the door, Chester Brooks stood awkwardly for a moment with his large box of provisions. "May I come in?"

Jimmy looked uncertain but stepped aside. Chester entered turning toward the kitchen to place the box on the table. Daisy Cordy came down to the bottom of the stairway, she had been crying most of the day and she had a glass of sherry in her shaking hand. "What are you doing here?" She hissed.

"Mrs. Cordy I've brought your family some food to ease your troubles, no need to come to the store, we will drop packages by for the next couple of weeks. I am sorry for your loss."

"Her clothes and everything she has are already packed up on the service porch, you're free to take them with you when you go." With that, Daisy turned and walked unsteadily back upstairs slamming the bedroom door.

Chester looked at Jimmy who stood with his head down a few steps away. "Can you help me with Dorothy's things?"

Jimmy nodded and led Chester to the back porch. There were two small suitcases and a couple of medium boxes piled with clothes in disarray. Chester picked up one of the boxes, grabbed a suitcase, Jimmy followed suit and they went down the back steps through the yard to where Chester parked on the street. Silently they put Dorothy's belongings in the back seat.

"I'm sorry about your dad."

"Yeh, thanks he was only forty-five." Jimmy said.

Chester felt bad for the boy and reached out to shake his hand. "Let me know if there's anything I can do."

"Tell Dorothy I'm sorry."

"I will." Chester said as he got into the car.

Chester went back to the store and asked one of the women who worked in the clothing department to pick out a simple black dress about a size ten, something appropriate for a teen-age girl. He then went into his office to call the funeral home to find out what the schedule was for viewing and the funeral itself. The funeral would be on Saturday, the viewing on Friday afternoon and evening. Chester knew the funeral director and asked if he could bring Dorothy by on

Friday morning for a private viewing. He agreed and Chester thanked him for his understanding.

It was obvious to him that Daisy Cordy's animosity toward Dorothy had already made its way around town. He didn't understand it, didn't care to. The widow had the right to grieve, but to be angry and vengeful toward a young girl who had lost the man she thought of as her father was outrageous; there was no excuse for it. A knock at his office door interrupted his thoughts—it was his employee with a black dress for Dorothy. Chester asked her to box it up and told her he would be leaving early. He wanted to get home to Lenore and Dorothy and see how they had faired on this difficult day.

The next morning Chester and Lenore took Dorothy to the funeral home to say goodbye to the man she called Pop Cordy. Dorothy looked frail and pale in her black dress with her dark hair curling down her back. She had tears welling in her eyes. Chester saw how hard she was trying not to cry. The casket was open and she went up to it alone and gave Pop a chaste kiss on his forehead, patting his crossed hands. She turned away giving Lenore a look that said she was ready to leave. In the car on the way back to the Brooks' house Dorothy made a strangely poignant comment. "Daisy didn't let him have his hat—she should have let him leave with his hat."

3

"It is not only a poverty of loneliness, but also of spirituality. There is a hunger for love, as there is a hunger for God.
Mother Teresa, A Simple Path

On Tuesday, Dorothy wore her black dress to school. Pippen held her hand most of the day until Dorothy finally said enough already. Jimmy was a sophomore and she ran into him once, he walked passed without looking at her. So much for having a brother, she thought, deciding to put all of this sadness and shame behind her. Dorothy went to her locker got her gold tube of "Love that Red," and put the lipstick on her lips. Daisy Cordy couldn't tell her what she could or could not do, not for another minute. In her next class, every head turned when she walked into the room in her black mourning dress, long hair around her shoulders, translucent skin, and deep red lips.

Ω

When she got to the Brooks house after school, she was surprised that Chester was home from work.

He and Lenore were waiting for her. Chester had some news. "I called the state agency for Foster Children in Ohio today, if you are okay with this plan they've agreed that Lenore and I can apply right away to adopt you."

"Adopt me? You mean I could be your actual daughter?"

"Yes it'll take some time and lots of paperwork back and forth but it seems pretty certain to go through."

"Is there anything Daisy can do to stop it?"

"No, I explained that she had abandoned you. She has no say in the matter." Chester said with emphasis.

Dorothy turned to Lenore, "Are you alright with this? I mean you barely know me."

"Of course dear we'd love to have you in our family."

Chester's voice took on a serious tone. "Now Dorothy you must understand, this means that you and Gilbert will be brother and sister. I hope there is no problem with that for you."

"No sir, I understand no problem what-so-ever."

"Then what do you say to a small celebration dinner in Mexican Town."

"Yes I've never been allowed to go there."

"Well, we are in for a treat." Lenore said.

Ω

It was two weeks before Dorothy understood that Lenore had no breasts. She had a nightmare and cried out in her sleep. Lenore came into her bedroom to check on her. Dorothy was moaning and tossing about,

Lenore sat down on the bed, put her arms around her to give comfort and gently to wake her up. Dorothy slowly came out of her bad dream hugging Lenore snugly to her. As she woke up further she realized that Lenore's bust line under her nightgown was completely flat, which was very confusing. Lenore realized right at that moment that Dorothy was shocked about how different her body felt. She stroked Dorothy's hair, "Don't be upset I had breast cancer a couple of years ago and had to have both of my breasts removed. I'm okay, I wear a bra with foam pads during the day."

Dorothy blurted out "Do you have scars?"

"Yes, but they continue to fade and they don't hurt."

"Are you still sick with the cancer?"

"No, I go to Phoenix every few months for check-ups. You don't have anything to worry about regarding my health. I'm just sorry to have surprised you when I was trying to comfort you. What were you dreaming about?"

"I don't even remember now."

"Do you think you can go back to sleep?"

"Will you lay down with me for a minute?"

"Of course sweetie." Lenore lay down next to Dorothy and waited for her to doze back to sleep before she went back to her own bedroom. She crawled quietly into her twin bed not wanting to wake Chester in his bed a couple of feet away. Lenore thought about what had just happened. She never talked to anyone in town about her surgery. As far as she knew, no one in Ajo had any idea that she'd had a double mastectomy or cancer. It just was something that she had wanted to keep quiet. She felt sure that Dorothy would keep her secret.

The adoption of Dorothy Louise Majors did go through. She legally changed her name to Brooks even at school, which made it official in the minds of the town. During her senior year, she kept her mind on the books and performed as lead majorette with her head held high. She turned eighteen on January 3, 1950, graduating with honors in May. Chester and Lenore sat in the front row for Dorothy's graduation; they were very proud parents at the reception held afterwards at the downtown social club for the graduates and their families. Gilbert had come home to attend the festivities as well. He and Dorothy were brother and sister in their minds and hearts, the town people seemed to forget about their previous summer's romance. When they arrived home, Dorothy was astonished to find a car in the drive with a red ribbon on it. Chester had gone to Phoenix a couple of weeks earlier bought the slightly used car arranging for its delivery on graduation evening. Dorothy was grateful and she gave hugs and kisses all around. She started crying when Chester suggested that he pass her previous car on to Jimmy Cordy. It was a perfect evening, one of the best of Dorothy's life.

Ω

Dorothy had been thinking about what she would do after high school and had decided that she did indeed want to become a nurse. She had done some research and discovered that with her grade point average she could qualify for a scholarship. The nursing school at Good Samaritan Hospital in Phoenix would be where she'd have to go. She told Gilbert about it in private, nervous about mentioning the idea of going away to school to Chester and Lenore who loved having her at home as their daughter. While Gilbert was home, Dorothy asked him to help her broach the subject over Sunday dinner. When he told them about Dorothy's idea, Lenore voiced her concern that Dorothy was too young to be away in Phoenix. Gilbert reminded her that he had been going to school in Tucson at the same age as Dorothy. Gilbert pointed out there were plenty of young women at the university, some that he knew were even from out of state.

Chester tried to suggest that Dorothy work for him in the company store for a year before going to school. She said that she might not be able to get the scholarship if she didn't enroll in the fall semester. Dorothy proposed a compromise, and suggested that she work at the store during the summer earning some money for any expenses that were not paid by her scholarship. After a long discussion, Chester and Lenore started to come around to the idea. Lenore even told Dorothy that nursing was a noble profession. Dorothy jumped up from the table and gave Lenore a hug.

With a smile she added, "It's also a profession with really cute uniforms and hats."

Everyone had a good laugh and it seemed to be decided. Dorothy applied for the scholarship during the next week, sending the information in the mail to Phoenix. She also followed through on her promise and went to work at the Mercantile for the summer. Late in July, Dorothy received a letter of acceptance from Good Samaritan, notification that she had a full scholarship, including room and board. She felt as if she were starting a great adventure. That afternoon she took off early from work to go to Ajo General Hospital, just to watch the nurses in their crisp white uniforms and starched nurses' caps.

Dorothy and Pippen spent many nights that summer having sleepovers, either at the ranch or at the Brooks' house. Pippen cried often, at the thought of losing her best friend. Dorothy reassured her that she would come home regularly and they would be girlfriends forever.

Late in the summer, Dorothy packed up her belongings, Chester and Lenore took her to Phoenix to finalize her enrollment, to visit the hospital, and find her room in the campus-style dormitory where Dorothy would be living. She felt lucky to discover that her room assignment was one of the few single dorm rooms, deciding that it would be better not to have to deal with a roommate. It was her first trip to Phoenix, she was in awe of the city. Good Samaritan Hospital was a large three-story building on 12th Street and McDowell Road in the middle of downtown; while she was overwhelmed by the hustle and bustle, she was too proud of herself to let it all intimidate her.

Gilbert drove Dorothy's car to Phoenix later that day and joined them for a nice dinner in a downtown restaurant near the hospital. Chester, Lenore, and Gilbert were going to stay in a hotel for the weekend, to make sure Dorothy settled in, having a chance to get somewhat familiar with the nearby area. On Sunday evening, they all were teary-eyed as they said their goodbyes. Dorothy stood outside of her dormitory waving until the car with Chester, Lenore, and Gilbert was out of sight.

That night alone in her dorm room in the small bed, Dorothy couldn't sleep for thinking about all the twists and turns her life had taken. She was not at all used to feeling introspective, she thought about Marie for the first time in years. Marie had probably been a nurse for a long time already, and Dorothy was sure that she had become a full-fledged nun. She remembered Marie telling her she should go to confession. Dorothy wondered if she did, what she would confess. Her life had turned out better than she could have ever imagined. Ohio was a distant memory that she could barely draw to mind. She didn't remember what her father or mother looked like, other than sad and poor.

Dorothy fell asleep dreaming about marrying one of the doctors she had seen in the hospital. It was a good dream.

Ω

During Dorothy's first semester, she lost more than she gained. She lost weight, she lost her interest in nursing, lost her air of naïveté, and she lost her virginity. What she gained was information about sex. There were sexual education classes that were a part of the nurse's curriculum. However, that didn't match the tales from the other girls, who talked about their sexual exploits almost as if it were a game or a sport. She was shocked when she discovered that without ever understanding, she had been doing a sex act, "the hat trick," since she was a child—Dorothy felt humiliated to discover how gullible she had been to never have realized what was happening when she did what she did. Now she knew it was a "hand job" and knew what it had meant to the men. She understood why Marie always felt the need to confess after going to the convent. Confession still wasn't in Dorothy's mind. Neither was sexual satisfaction provided for quarters or attention. It wasn't what she thought of as a good use of her talents. She was a beautiful young woman, determined to get security and status for her sexual favors. Thanks to sex education, she was well versed in the rhythm method. She understood about condoms, diaphragms. Most importantly she knew how to tell if you were pregnant. Dorothy knew that she had much needed information that her mother had never been privy to in the midst of her own constant state of pregnancy, having had seven children in less than nine years.

Dorothy discovered that nursing was much harder work than she had ever imagined, and objectionable as well. Especially when it came to bedpans and sponge baths, which were the only tasks the new students received training to handle on the wards with patients. Nursing was hours on her feet, hours of studying, and hours spent with other students, few of whom she liked. Of course, she liked wearing a uniform even though the students wore blue dresses with white aprons, and only had a small head cap, not the nurses' hat she coveted. It didn't take long for the newness to wear off, soon she felt like a servant with schoolbooks and tests. Dorothy had her pride, she wasn't willing to give up easily, for her holiday visits home that fall and winter she put up a good front with Chester, Lenore, and Gilbert.

At Christmastime when she saw Pippen, she admitted that nursing school wasn't turning out the way she thought it would. In fact, Dorothy was honest about not liking taking care of strangers. Pippen was sympathetic, but she had exciting news to share, in the summer she was getting married to Earl Wirth her boyfriend from high school.

Ω

Dorothy had her own story to tell about her new boyfriend, a twenty-two-year-old medical student named Raymond, from Arizona State College in Tempe near Phoenix, who worked on the weekends as an orderly at the hospital. Dorothy spun a tale about how maybe she would be marrying a doctor in the future. She shocked Pippen with the truth about having had sex with her "young man." Dorothy said, "It really wasn't as bad as I thought it would be." About losing her virginity, she was surprisingly casual.

Pippen said, "I can't believe you did it, even Earl and I haven't yet."

"Well I don't mean to burst your bubble, based on my reaction versus his I'd say the guy gets the better end of the bargain, but he bought me a nice necklace afterwards and seems to want to be with me a lot now that we're doing it."

Ω

When Dorothy went back to Phoenix, she had decided to stick out the spring semester, then tell her family in the summer that nursing wasn't for her. Everything changed once Dorothy went home to Ajo for Easter, March 25, 1951.

Lenore had lost at least twenty pounds since Christmas and she looked tired and worn out. On Easter Sunday, she struggled to get dressed for the service at the Methodist church, when they returned home she went to bed immediately. Dorothy had learned enough at school and at the hospital to know that Lenore was sick again, probably with cancer. While Lenore slept, she asked Chester whether she had been to the doctor yet.

"No I've been trying to talk her into it, she isn't ready yet."

"Ready for what she's sick." Dorothy said.

"Ready to hear that she has cancer again."

Dorothy took the opportunity as it presented itself. "I'm not going back to school with her like this—I have to take care of her, she's the only real mother I've ever had."

Chester broke down, crying tears that washed down his cheeks and dripped off his chin. "Dorothy would you really come home it would mean so much to her."

"Yes, in fact. Tomorrow I'll drive back to Phoenix to let the school know about the situation. I'll get my things and come back—I love you both very much. You have to promise me something."

"Anything." Chester said.

"Don't let her give up we can't lose her. I want her to go to the doctor next week." Dorothy said.

Chester mopped his face with his handkerchief. "I promise I'll take her myself whether she's willing or not."

Dorothy made her decision and left early the next morning, she was back in Ajo before sundown. When she returned, she explained her actions to Lenore, persuading her to go see the doctor as soon as they could arrange an appointment.

Dorothy went to bed that night in her own bedroom, her belongings back in her drawers and wardrobe closet. As she fell asleep, she thought about how even though Lenore was sick again, she had never felt more secure.

Ω

For the next six months Dorothy acted in the capacity of Lenore's nurse when she was home from radiation treatments in Phoenix. Dorothy took over the running of the house as well—cleaning, cooking, and taking care of both Lenore and Chester. After Lenore had a total hysterectomy for cancer, Dorothy thought of herself as the "woman" of the house.

Lenore's recovery was slow, complicated by a serious bout with depression. She asked Dorothy to move her into Gilbert's former room ostensibly because it was closer to Dorothy's room. Her true reason for moving out of her master bedroom with Chester was that she couldn't overcome the guilt of losing both her breasts, and her reproductive organs to a cancer that seemed to be determined to take her apart piece by piece. Lenore didn't feel whole anymore. She was unwilling to try to explain her hopelessness to anyone—least of all her husband. Dorothy proved to be a tremendous asset to the troubled couple and her very presence in the home helped make it still feel like one.

Ω

After the winter holidays Lenore had improved enough that Dorothy could leave her alone part of the day, going to work part-time at the Mercantile as Chester's office assistant. Dorothy worked several mornings a week, making herself indispensable to Chester. The money Dorothy earned she spent on clothes, and soon had herself a stylish wardrobe of slim sheath skirts with matching blouses and sweaters. Her gorgeous figure was set off by the styles she chose, every shopper noticed the smartly attired new employee who worked side by side with the general manager.

Ω

Chester's bookkeeper was a woman who had worked for him for many years. Della Mae's husband Daniel was a foreman in the smelter, and they lived out at the enclave a few miles out of town called The Well. Their son was graduating from Ajo High School in the spring and was the town football hero. Dorothy didn't really know him since he was a few years younger than she was. Della Mae had told Dorothy all about her son's prospects for a football scholarship to Arizona State College. One day her son came into the store to see his mother. When he saw Dorothy, he let loose with a long low wolf whistle. Chester took it as a disrespectful act toward Dorothy, chided the boy, asking him to leave the offices. Della Mae was upset that Chester had dared to correct her son and they exchanged words about it. Dorothy said nothing—taking the suggestive compliment in stride. After all she didn't really mind a whistle or two that's why she worked hard to look as good as she did.

$$\Omega$$

Lenore started losing weight again in May of 1952. Chester got her to her doctor in Phoenix right away this time, two weeks later her diagnosis was lymphoma. The course of treatment would be three weeks in Phoenix for radiation therapy every other month for six months. The weight on Chester's shoulders was tremendous; he couldn't spend more than a couple of days away from the store while Lenore was in the hospital. Dorothy offered to stay with Lenore but that would involve the cost of a hotel room and Lenore insisted that she would rather have Dorothy taking care of things at home than be hovering over her treatment regimen. Chester decided he would deliver his wife to the hospital for three weeks at a time, bringing her back to Ajo for the five weeks she would be home. The first course of radiation therapy started on June 1, 1952, would continue every other month until the final doses in December. Chester and Dorothy both went to Phoenix for the first treatment to help get Lenore settled for her extended stay away from home. That evening after leaving the hospital Dorothy drove the two hours home, Chester rode in the passenger seat teary-eyed, while he drank the better part of a bottle of bourbon whiskey. Lenore was certainly sick and suffering, but Chester had his own burdens to accept, that night he was not up to the task.

Ω

After the initial treatment on Lenore's neck lymph nodes, she had lost her hair. Once she was home for the first five-week break, she immediately had Dorothy trim the last straggly strands to her scalp. A wig had been purchased but most of the time Lenore just covered her head with a scarf. The loss of her hair was yet another indignity that Lenore felt unable to abide. That July while she was home her condition continued to deteriorate, she spent most of the time sleeping, when she was awake she stayed isolated in her bedroom with the company of the radio. She listened, dozing to episodes of "The Guiding Light" and "As the World Turns" soap operas.

Chester's forty-first birthday was in July. Dorothy made a nice dinner and baked a pineapple-upside-down cake. Unfortunately, for Lenore, being in Chester's presence was a guilt inducing, emotionally draining effort. Chester and Dorothy celebrated his birthday while Lenore slept. Before dinner, Dorothy joined Chester for a cocktail as had become their habit. She had one rum and Coke and Chester had the first of several glasses of bourbon.

Ω

The people in Ajo knew that Lenore Brooks was battling cancer. Some believed she was contagious, some believed she was radioactive, and most thought she was at death's door.

By the time she was home in November, the truth was that Lenore was very ill; the side effects of the radiation doses only seemed to weaken her. She had endured treatments to all her major lymph node locations the neck, the pelvic region, and abdominal areas. The radiation caused skin irritation, blistering, nausea, diarrhea, and incontinence. Fatigue and weakness overwhelmed her. Dorothy did her best to make Lenore as comfortable as possible, she tried to anticipate and prevent the more embarrassing effects by scheduling frequent trips to the bathroom. She gave Lenore cooling sponge baths twice a day to keep her clean and calm. A nurse from Ajo General Hospital came to the house once a week to check on Lenore. She never failed to praise Dorothy for the care she was providing and told Lenore how lucky she was to have such a caring loving daughter.

During the long months of Lenore's illness, much had changed in the Brooks' home. Gilbert rarely came home except for holidays and he had begged off on Thanksgiving just passed, claiming up-coming finals as his excuse. Dorothy and Chester's relationship had changed as well—he depended on her to take care of his wife and himself while he sunk into a pattern of drunken isolation.

$$\Omega$$

On December 1, 1952, Chester and Dorothy took Lenore back to Phoenix for another round of treatment. It was a difficult trip, Lenore was carsick several times, they stopped by the side of the desert highway where she could vomit. By the time they reached the hospital Lenore could barely look at either one of them for her feelings of sickly humiliation. They got her settled into her room and she asked them to leave her alone. It was a sad, silent drive home for Dorothy and Chester.

Dorothy sorely missed the feeling of home and happiness she'd enjoyed when she became the daughter of Chester and Lenore. To get that feeling back she was determined to make the Christmas holiday a cheerful one, no matter what it took. It was on her mind that it might very well be Lenore's last Christmas, she was going to make certain it wasn't a sad time. The first thing she did was to call Gilbert, insisting that he come home on the up-coming weekend, to help her hang the outside Christmas lights on the house. He was surprised at her assertiveness, agreeing to the assignment. Next she pulled the Christmas decorations out of the attic while Chester was at work hiding them in her room. She could go through them to figure out what she would need to buy to make sure the Christmas tree she planned to purchase would look beautiful. All of the preparations were meant to be a surprise for Chester; she needed to pull him out of his melancholy mood.

Gilbert made good on his promise coming home for the weekend—Dorothy prepared a good meal of pork chops, home-fried potatoes, and applesauce. She and Gilbert got a smile out of Chester when they turned on the outdoor Christmas lights. They all had a couple of cocktails after dinner, spent time laughing, teasing, and no one went to bed drunk or sad.

Dorothy spent the next week busy with holiday arrangements buying gifts, food, decorations, and a nice tree at the lot in Mexican Town. Her plan was that when Chester came home from work on Friday evening she would have a perfect pre-Christmas evening planned. On Friday morning, Dorothy woke up early to make coffee and toast for the two of them, giving Chester a kiss on the cheek as he left for work. Then she set to work herself. First, she set up, decorated the perfect smallish, four-foot tree, and placed it on the table in front of the bay window; the silver tinsel glittered in the sunlight. Like a thrilled child, Dorothy could barely wait to see the tree at night with the colorful lights and glitter covered Christmas balls. She wrapped the presents she had bought, one for Chester, Lenore, and Gilbert putting them prematurely under the tree. In the afternoon Dorothy baked a pan of ginger bread from a recipe she found in Lenore's cookbook. She made the meatloaf that Lenore had taught her to make, which was one of Chester's favorites. She peeled potatoes to boil and mash, and thawed the new style frozen green peas that she had found for the first time at the Mercantile.

Dorothy had bought herself a special outfit for the occasion as well. A Kelly green and black plaid sheath skirt with a matching green sweater. She brushed her hair a hundred strokes until it was dark and shiny. She turned on the tree lights, set out the makings for the cocktails on the coffee table, on a silver tray, then waited excitedly for Chester to come home. She decided to fix herself a rum and Coke while she passed the time, as the rum warmed her insides she looked around at the scene she had created. It was home, she had made it this way, after months of worry and sickness she and Chester deserved to have a pleasant evening together. In the far recesses of her mind, Dorothy felt like the woman of the house waiting for her man to walk in from a hard day at work, grateful to come home.

Ω

Chester was a little later than usual, Dorothy had made herself a second rum and Coke to sip on while she mashed the potatoes. The oven was keeping the meatloaf warm, the house smelled wonderful when Chester walked in. He followed the smells to the kitchen where he found Dorothy putting the finishing touches on dinner.

"What have you done? This is just perfect. Is that meatloaf I smell?"

"It's your favorite isn't it?" Dorothy asked coyly. "Everything is done and warming. Let me fix you your bourbon, we can relax for a few minutes before dinner."

"Sounds like just what I need." Chester replied.

They sat on the sofa together having their cocktails; Chester loosened his tie, as a sense of homey peace he hadn't felt in a long time seemed to wash over him. "The tree is beautiful. I liked seeing it in the window when I drove up."

"That was the plan." Dorothy said

Ω

Chester and Dorothy had a quiet dinner with a couple of glasses of wine. Chester was particularly complimentary about the food telling Dorothy it was the best dinner he could remember. After having the gingerbread for dessert, Dorothy started clearing the table. Chester announced he was going to take a shower. Dorothy made herself another rum and Coke to sip on while she cleaned the kitchen. She was feeling dreamy and distracted when Chester came up behind her at the sink. He put his arms around her waist, leaned his head on her shoulder, and whispered, "Do you know how I feel about you?"

Dorothy didn't dare speak she just nodded "yes" as she turned to face him—she knew what was coming. Chester kissed her on the lips as he held her gently as if she might break in his embrace. She reached up stroking the back of his neck. Chester pulled her out of the kitchen—he was wearing his pajamas and robe. Holding Dorothy's hand, he paused at the sofa. "How about one more cocktail?"

Again, Dorothy just nodded "yes," they sat down without releasing hands. Chester poured her a strong rum and Coke and three fingers of bourbon for himself. They sat back, Dorothy nestled herself into his shoulder. They drank in silence until Dorothy decided it was time. She set down her drink stood, taking Chester by the hand "Let's go to my room."

He followed behind her.

Ω

The next morning Chester and Dorothy had coffee and toast together. Chester kissed her as he left to go buy another bottle of bourbon. When he returned they made love again before noon. They spent the rest of the weekend at home enthralled with one another.

They sipped cocktails and ate leftovers just as if they were a couple in love for the first time.

Sunday night Dorothy was in her room straightening up while Chester listened to his favorite program on the radio in the living room. As Dorothy cleared off her dresser, she dropped her calendar on the floor—she glanced at the month of December as she picked it up, grabbing it with both hands, she took in what she saw. Dorothy always marked her period on the calendar with a small "p" on the days it lasted. As she stared at the dates she came to a shocking realization, she had just had sex right in the middle of her cycle—the prime time for getting pregnant. Her hands started to shake as she flipped the page back to November the first "p" was marked on November 29. She was always regular as clockwork twenty-nine days would mean her next period should start on December 27, today was December 14, exactly fourteen days until her period should start, but she knew it would not.

Lenore would be home next weekend; Gilbert was going to Phoenix to bring her home for Christmas. Dorothy started to cry—which in moments turned into full-blown sobbing. Chester heard her, ran to her room "Dorothy what's wrong? Don't cry baby it's going to be alright." Chester wasn't surprised; he had felt tears threatening behind his eyes all evening. The knowing that what had happened between them could not continue was tearing away at his heart. Seeing Dorothy in tears led him to believe she had realized their shared fate.

Dorothy regained some of her composure as Chester sat down next to her wrapping his arm around her. "I feel sad too I'll never forget this weekend, I can see you feel the same."

She looked into his sad guilty eyes knowing what she had to say. "This can never happen again we have to go back to the way things were before."

Chester breathed a deep ragged sigh that was tinged with relief. "You know I love you, I did before, and I will love you tomorrow, just not like this ever again."

Dorothy resisted with every fiber of her being blurting out that she would probably be pregnant, instead she said, "I know everything goes back to normal as of now." She took a deep breath, ending the conversation. "Lenore and Gilbert will be home next weekend."

Chester stood walking out with stooped shoulders. Dorothy heard him close his bedroom door a few minutes later. She waited about half-an-hour before venturing out to the living room. Chester's glass and bottle of bourbon were gone. She poured herself a strong rum and Coke and sat on the sofa. The radio was still on, playing a sad love song and Dorothy thought about how lost and lonely she felt.

The next morning Chester left early before Dorothy was awake. As she drank a cup of coffee, Dorothy decided she could not spend any time wallowing—she would have to come up with a plan if she was pregnant. She thought back to her nursing training and the tales the other girls shared. A few of them had experienced narrow escapes, none of them had admitted to ever being pregnant. A story in particular she remembered, it gave Dorothy the beginning of an idea. One of the girls at school had a real pregnancy scare, she had admitted that if she was pregnant, she would have to choose one of two young men to blame…the young bartender she'd met a month ago, or the intern she'd slept with about the same time. To Dorothy the choice seemed clear, the intern of course, for the nursing student nothing ever came of the pregnancy fears, the young woman didn't have to make any life changing decisions.

Dorothy hoped against hope that she wouldn't find herself in that situation. She thought about how she might prepare to keep her options open.

Lenore came home with Gilbert on December 21, with some promising news. According to Gilbert who had met with her doctor when he picked her up, the most recent tests looked as if Lenore was going into remission from her lymphoma. The results wouldn't be completed until after the first of the New Year, the possibility though gave the family something to hope for in the coming days.

Dorothy was determined to make Christmas the best family event the Brooks had ever had, she began baking and cooking a full three days ahead of Christmas. She was roasting a turkey with all the trimmings, had made three kinds of pie, mince, pumpkin, and apple. She needed to make one last trip to the Mercantile on Christmas Eve, before they closed for the holiday to get the makings for eggnog, including a bottle of rum and one of Chester's favorite bourbon.

Lenore was still feeling weak and tired even though her mood was buoyed by the news of a possible remission. Since Gilbert was home for the entire week, she asked Dorothy to help move her back into the master bedroom with Chester so that Gilbert could have his room. Dorothy did it gladly; it served as one more step back to the normalcy of her family relationships. She and Chester were both determined to insure there were no signs of strain between them. He hovered over Lenore doing everything he could do to make her happy to be home. When Dorothy was ready to leave for the store the two of them were listening to the radio—Lenore's favorite soap operas were on and they sat on the sofa holding hands while listening.

Ω

While at the Mercantile Dorothy recognized Lofty Moore roaming aimlessly around the store, she decided to "accidently" run into him. He spoke to her first, she believed that her maneuver had worked. They chatted briefly; she was deliberately short with him at one point and liked seeing him squirm a bit. He mentioned Pippen's party as if she hadn't already been invited. Evidently he didn't realize they'd been best friends for years. She left him guessing as to whether she would attend. Then did her best "watch me walk away" move as she left him staring at her from behind....

4

"Such people often tend to be highly manipulative and without a shred of remorse for their actions; even if their actions have harmed others who are close to them, or their own family members."
Understanding the Sociopath, Cause, Motivation, and Relationship, Psychologytoday.com

Lofton Dell was born on May 13, 1934, in Silver Springs, New Mexico during one of the most severe of the Great Dust Bowl storms on record. His difficult birth was at home on the small Benson family farm. His grandparents Dell and Frances Benson and father Daniel Moore did their best to protect his mother Della Mae, from the ravaging dust that blew through every crack and crevice into the three-room wood frame farmhouse. It was Mothers' Day, but nothing about that day was deemed special except for the birth of a healthy son, who soon after arriving into the world was covered with the dust of it. He spent his first weeks on a pillow in a dresser drawer most often covered with a woven serape to help keep the normal levels of dust at bay. He grew and thrived in spite of his harrowing start, as soon as he could walk he had the run of the farm.

The farm was a barely subsistent operation, Daniel worked alongside his father-in-law moving half-dozen cattle from one desert grazing area to the next. Frances and Della Mae milked the one dairy cow, fed the chickens, gathered eggs, and when there was enough water in the well, they watered the small quarter-acre orchard of plum and peach trees. They churned butter and made a little cheese. Eggs and fruit preserves, that they sold to people in town paid for flour, salt, sugar, coffee, and masa. Frances made tortillas once a week outside on a wood-fired grill.

The depression had made everything hard; they could feed themselves, owned their home and farm. Lofty chased the chickens and the dog, never knowing he was poor. When he was six, going on seven years old, Grandma Frances taught Lofty to read, write, and do his numbers, since the school in town was too far to take him every day.

Ω

In 1942, Daniel heard about a copper mining operation in Ajo, Arizona that was a boomtown because of the war. He decided to pack his wife and son up in an old Ford pick-up and move to the Sonoran Desert. Laborer jobs were always available, he was willing to work in the smelter, a place hotter than Hades, in a town that was already too hot for most. The family moved into the miner projects in town. Della Mae got a job at the Company Mercantile. Lofty was finally enrolled in school for the first time when he was eight years old, he tested well enough to go into third grade with the other children his age. After school Lofty would play with the other kids with two working parents, mostly from Mexican Town, in the central plaza until his mother got off work.

In three years, Daniel had worked his way up to a smelter foreman position achieving an opportunity to move his family out of the projects into a two-bedroom house at The Well. It meant they would be living sixteen miles out of town but would have a large yard and privacy. The Moores made the move and finally had a home they could think of as their own, even though Phelps Dodge held the deed.

In 1944, Lofty was ten years old. He played on The Curley School intramural football squad. He could run and catch the football, his favorite position was half-back. Early on he proved to have a remarkable talent for the game and both of the in-school teams always wanted him on their side. He was growing up to be a good-looking boy dark wavy hair, dark eyes, and olive skin.

Most of his friends were the Mexican Town kids, they played sports, had BB guns, and even a couple of 22 rifles amongst them. Now that Lofty was older, he and his friends ventured out into the desert areas outside of town. They went to Indian Village at the edge of the mine area and shot "stray" dogs and cats for fun. Out in the desert they pretty much shot at anything that moved, from lizards to coyotes. If Lofty didn't kill an animal straight away, he started a small fire and tossed the wounded, still living animal into the flames. More than once the fires got out of control especially when they were hanging around Indian Village. Some of the residents had to put the fires out with water buckets, running the boys off with threats of bodily harm.

Lofty was, in his mother's eyes, capable of doing no wrong. Whenever she got complaints of his appalling or dangerous behavior, she would take it personally. An Indian Town resident confronted Della Mae at work about the fire setting and her response was, "Next time I hope he burns the whole place to the ground. Now get out of here, keep your bad-mouthing of my boy to yourself."

Chester Brooks, Della Mae's boss, overheard the encounter and reprimanded her—she refused to back down. "They think they can come in here spreading lies about Lofty, well I won't sit still for it." Chester backed off deciding to pick his battles when it came to Della Mae Moore and her son.

The relationship between Daniel and Lofty was very different. Daniel believed that sparing the rod spoiled the child, while he didn't use a stick Lofty was more than familiar with the buckle end of a leather belt. In spite of Della Mae's efforts to protect her son, Daniel routinely took Lofty to task for minor infractions leaving him with bruises and bloody welts on his legs and backside. As for Lofty's reaction to the beatings, he refused to shed a tear or beg Daniel to stop—in fact, over time he became immune to his own pain, just as he was immune to the pain of others. This imperviousness only served to make him stronger-willed, more competitive, and more insensitive.

Once when Lofty was eleven years old he climbed the nearby cottonwood tree and was stung on the arm by a bark scorpion. He rushed home to tell his mother. She called the doctor to determine what should be done. While she was talking to the doctor, Lofty started running as fast as his legs could run around the perimeter of the large yard. It was early fall, still very warm in the midday desert, but Lofty ran, ran, and ran. The doctor, after he heard what was happening, advised that he be allowed to run the scorpion venom out of his system. Lofty ran for something over an hour before he collapsed in the yard. Della Mae carried his sweat-soaked limp body into the house, filled the tub full of cold water, placing him in it—Lofty soon revived, very thirsty, apparently no worse for the wear. His stamina was to become part of his football personae; those he played against and outran, called him The Scorpion.

By the time Lofty was in his early teens he had a gang of friends from both school sports teams, and the Mexican Town buddies that he spent most of his time in town with. Some of the Mexican Town boys were older, some younger, but they had one thing in common they weren't concerned about getting into trouble, they were up for anything. For some of the younger members of the gang sexual assault by the older boys was the price of admission. Lofty played the role of dominator, during the sodomy of several young Mexican boys, who were eager to join the gang. Lofty himself never had to submit to that aspect of initiation. The gang had its own plans for young Lofty.

One of the older boys drove an old beat up pick-up truck that he "found" broken down on the side of the road. He hot-wired it and drove it home. No questions ever asked. It simply became his truck.

Lofty was mouthing off one day about some girl, and his friend challenged him "I bet you haven't ever even had a girl."

Lofty responded that he hadn't found the one he wanted yet. Therefore, a trip to Sonoita just across the border became the gang's plan. They drove Lofty to the whorehouse and let him pick out the one he wanted. Lofty took them up on the dare and when he was thirteen, he lost his virginity to a two-bit Mexican whore. He bragged about the conquest all summer long.

Ω

When Lofty started high school, he was the first freshman ever to make the varsity football team, he was first-string half back of the Ajo Red Raiders in the fall of 1948. This first, got him a write up in the local newspaper, The Copper Times News. A picture of him posing with football in hand soon made him identifiable to most of the town. Lofty was now five feet ten inches tall and his dark good looks got plenty of attention from the girls. He also had a reputation that was considered wild, not many parents were enthusiastic about their daughters having a crush on the young football star.

During the football season the Ajo Red Raiders played teams from as far away as Tucson, Yuma, and Morenci, Arizona. The season schedule was ten games. The team traveled to away games, and played at home in stadiums full of Friday night fans. The rumor circulated that in Lofty's freshman year he was already being scouted by Arizona's several colleges. That first season was a winning one for the Red Raiders, Lofty took lots of the credit.

Lofty didn't care about much else than football. He was innately intelligent, studying the bare minimum, still getting good grades. Most of his time in town was spent practicing and hanging with his fellow teammates, many of whom were part of his Mexican Town gang. When he did date a girl, it was to go to the drive-in with some older kids doing his level best to get lucky—he developed the character of being rough, insistent, and not taking "no" very well. His justification was that at least the few girls who succumbed to his "charms" could say they'd been with a football star.

Ω

Dorothy Cordy was a junior that year and was dating Gilbert Brooks, a senior. She knew of Lofty mostly because Jimmy Cordy was a freshman as well. Dorothy thought of the people who lived at The Well as somehow lower class than the "townies." She took little notice of the football team star except when she was on the field in her capacity as majorette cheering on the home team.

Ω

In the next four years, Lofty's star continued to rise and by the time of his senior year, the Ajo Red Raiders had made it to two double AA conference championships. By the end of his last season playing half back, Arizona State College in Tempe, Arizona had scouted him hard. The ASC Sun Devils were a top team in the Border Conference, and their coach Clyde Smith himself, had come to Ajo to see Lofty play in the final championship game. In January of 1952, Loften "Lofty" Dell Moore garnered a full scholarship to Arizona State College to play football in the fall 1952 season. Lofty's star had risen to its zenith the whole town took notice. His parents Daniel and Della Mae became minor stars themselves, they were always welcome at any social event or club in town. Della Mae was the proudest mother in Ajo; she didn't let anyone forget it.

As for Lofty, he continued to run wild with his fellow championship teammates and his old Mexican Town buddies. In the spring of 1952, Lofty and his gang nearly got caught setting a fire that threatened the Indian Village projects; the town elders saw to it that the Pima County Sheriff never got involved. Lofty graduated with honors in May of 1952, with the unassailable prestige of a college-bound football scholarship hero.

Lofty left for the big city of Phoenix and its suburb Tempe, where the ASC campus was located in early July, for the beginning of six weeks of football training camp before the school semester and football season officially began. Because of his scholarship status, he was also required to enlist in the campus-based Reserve Officers Training Corps. Since the country was involved in the Korean War as a student with a scholarship deferment, R.O.T.C. was mandatory. Not only did Lofty get to wear a maroon and gold Sun Devils football uniform, he also got to strut about in his starched khaki military uniform complete with an officer style cap with a black leather front brim. He loved the role of big man on campus from the moment he arrived. Even though he was a freshman, again he had been tagged for a starting spot on the varsity squad.

Lofty discovered a campus restaurant called, "The Library," where students drank, ate, and socialized. The new crop of female college freshmen girls were quite taken by his dark "movie star" good looks, and his dual standing in both football and R.O.T.C. He was never without a young beauty on his arm hanging on his every word.

Ω

The fall 1952, semester went by in a blur of winning football games and winning hearts. Lofty and the Sun Devil team won The Border Conference Championship in his first year playing; he had lots of field time with plenty of touchdown scores to show for it. His R.O.T.C. drill duties took up another slot of his first semester. He was majoring in business administration and at the end of the semester had a "B" average for grades. When he went back home for the winter break he was greeted by all as the golden boy returning.

Ω

His first night home on December 20, 1952, his parents had planned a huge welcome home party at the plaza social club. The potluck included every casserole and Jell-O mold imaginable plus fresh handmade tortillas, and all the favorite Mexican food dishes. The beer was in kegs, the wine in jugs, and the other alcoholic choices were varied and vast. Lofty wore his

R.O.T.C. uniform, was greeted when he entered the social hall with applause and cheers. Della Mae was in her tipsy glory, Daniel was well on his way to drunk. Pippen and her new husband Earl Wirth were at the party, during the evening they invited Lofty to the New Years' Eve bash they were having at the ranch. Lofty said he'd be glad to come, asking if it would be all right to come "stag." Pippen just laughed, "Well if after a few days in town you're still coming stag I promise you won't stay that way at one of our parties for long."

"Sounds like I shouldn't miss it." Lofty said with a movie star smile and a tip of his military hat.

One of Lofty's new friends Kay Kelly from ASC was also enlisted in R.O.T.C., was in uniform, and had accompanied Lofty to the party. The two of them allowed anyone and everyone to make sure they always had a drink in hand. At the Mexican food buffet table both Lofty and Kay did a few shots of tequila to go along with spicy homemade tamales.

$$\Omega$$

It wasn't until Christmas Eve that Lofty ran into Dorothy Brooks at the Mercantile when he had gone to pick up his mother Della Mae from work. He was more casually attired in jeans and his varsity athlete's sweater, he managed to get Dorothy's attention for a few moments of conversation. "Hey I thought you went to Phoenix for nursing school." Lofty said.

"I did. Lenore is very sick, after a year away I came back to take care of her." Dorothy answered.

"Your last name is Brooks now?"

"Yes they adopted me not that it is any of your business."

Lofty stepped back. "I wasn't trying to butt in, just wondered about your name. I remember you as Dorothy Cordy." He wasn't used to a girl as pretty as Dorothy using a sharp tone with him.

"Sorry, I've got a lot on my mind, Lenore just came home from the hospital a couple of days ago." Dorothy smiled in apology. "I've got to run hope you have a good holiday."

"Hey" Lofty called as he watched her walk away. "Any chance you'll make it to Pippen and Earl's New Years' Eve party?"

"I might." Dorothy called out over her shoulder as she strolled away in her slim red sheath skirt and Christmas green sweater. "I just might."

As Lofty turned around to go find his mother he thought just how much he hoped to see that woman at the party, in fact he damn well hoped to see her again.

5

"We mute the realization of malevolence—which is too threatening to bear—by turning offenders into victims themselves and by describing their behavior as the result of forces beyond their control."
Predators, Pedophiles, Rapists, and Other Sex Offenders,
Anna C. Salter

The mine was closed during the week between Christmas and the New Year—a town-wide vacation except for those employees tasked with annual equipment maintenance duties. As for most of the residents of Ajo, they would have quiet family-oriented Christmas celebrations, including for most a church service or midnight mass.

New Year's Eve fell on Wednesday night, the town went all out to welcome in the New Year. The social club downtown was booked for a large dinner dance. All the benevolent societies had parties planned for the evening. Most of the residents would make it to two or three parties—for the most part the whole town would be considerably less than sober. Many would gather in the town plaza a midnight to countdown the last minutes of the old year and cheer in the new one.

The big house party for the younger crowd was at the ranch that Pippen had inherited, that she and Earl Wirth operated. They made a good living boarding horses, giving riding lessons, and providing guided horseback tours through the desert in the winter months to a few tourists. They also sponsored the local Ajo Rodeo each year drawing amateur and professional rodeo riders from all across the state.

Daisy Cordy had remarried was now the wife of William Ross a member of the Ajo County Club. She begrudgingly accepted the friendship between Dorothy and Jimmy Cordy. In fact, the two of them had agreed to drive to the ranch party together. Dorothy picked Jimmy up in her car. Gilbert Brooks was also going to the party—his college girlfriend Collette had arrived from Tucson early in the afternoon and would be sharing Dorothy's room for the night or whenever they all got back home.

Lofty Moore and Kay Kelly were going to the party stag as promised, Lofty had warned his friend of his intentions toward Dorothy Brooks that evening. "Hey I've decided I could use a hometown girlfriend and the prettiest girl in town is my choice."

Kay said, "You've never had a problem at school finding a date."

"Yeh, it's too easy for those girls to get clingy, if I have a girl back at home I have an excuse for not letting a little fun get too serious." Lofty answered.

"If you didn't make it your goal to bed every skirt you meet you wouldn't have that problem." Kay claimed with a smirk.

"What's the point if you don't score, as coach would say?" Lofty laughed.

Ω

By nine o'clock people started showing up to the ranch in droves, there had to be almost a hundred guests ranging from age seventeen to twenty-two, it was turning into a multi-year Ajo High School reunion.

Dorothy arrived with Jimmy Cordy, they split up almost immediately, no one would mistake them as each other's date. Dorothy wore her best black crepe sheath skirt. Lenore had lent her an ivory lace blouse that was a bit see-through and a pair of real pearl clip-on earrings. She wore nude seamed stockings and black patent heels. She definitely turned heads when she walked up to the makeshift bar asking Earl to make her a strong rum and Coke. Pippen in a red poodle skirt and embroidered satin cowgirl shirt came rushing up to hug her telling her how beautiful she looked. "You look great hon…the good news about Lenore has done wonders for you. The last time I saw you I was worried about how you were holding up—you have got the shine on tonight…Happy New Year.

"Same to you Pippi. My God I didn't know you had this many friends." Dorothy said

"Hey a good party brings 'em out of the woodwork. Gotta go mingle." Pippen dashed off.

Dorothy left the kitchen herself to circulate in the crowd, she saw Lofty Moore and Kay Kelly come in and head straight for the bar. Making sure Lofty wouldn't see her yet, she went outside to the ranch house's wrap around porch, finding Gilbert and Collette relaxing on a porch swing. Gilbert offered Dorothy his seat she said she'd stand. "Quite a crowd."

Collette answered, "You'd never know that Ajo was such a small town."

"I don't think I know half of the people here," added Gilbert.

"You've been away for almost four years, no wonder" Dorothy giggled, "You're one of the old-timers Gil."

Dorothy heard a loud voice at the other side of the porch and she knew Lofty had found her. "Dorothy Brooks you made it after all." Lofty boomed.

Dorothy looked in his direction, then turned back to Gilbert and Collette. That didn't stop Lofty, within seconds, he was at her side with his hand on her elbow starting to steer her away. "Lofty you haven't met my brother Gil Brooks and his girlfriend Collette they're here from Tucson."

Gilbert held out his hand and Lofty took a second too long before he reached out to shake it. "You've got a good-looking sister here Gil even though you're not blood related I bet you're proud."

"Yes, proud," Gilbert said, "Dorothy are you okay?"

"Yes, sure." Dorothy said

Lofty interrupted. "You look like you could use another drink c'mom Kay and me are headed back to the bar." He took her elbow again and this time Dorothy allowed him to steer her away.

Ω

After that, Lofty stayed glued to Dorothy's side and close to the bar for the next couple of hours. He and his friend Kay were downing tequila shots. Dorothy had lost count of how many they'd had. She kept nursing her rum and Cokes but at Lofty's insistence kept getting a fresh one before her last one was finished. As they stood and drank Dorothy had made a fateful decision—she knew the direction the evening was heading and was willing to let it play out. Her period was a week late, she knew for sure she was pregnant; tonight she was going to find a father for her baby. Lofty with his college future and good looks was the best option she could think of, she knew he was more than eager to do his part.

Ω

An hour later Dorothy and Lofty made their way to the stable room out near the barn. It was set up like a guesthouse for occasional overnight visitors to the ranch. Dorothy felt like she had the situation well in her control. Lofty was drunk. Once they were away from the party crowd, he seemed to get short-tempered. She didn't worry at first when he kissed her hard and bit her lip she pushed him away. "Not so rough!" she said.

"Don't tell me how I like it, rough and tumble is what gets me going." Lofty growled.

Dorothy had a brief thought of running then decided she could handle whatever Lofty could do in his drunken state. She kicked off her heels right at him "Is that what you like?"

Lofty reached out, giving her the back of his hand across her mouth, her lip that was already cut from the bite gave way, and blood sprayed on her ivory lace blouse. Her pearl earrings flew across the room. "No that's what I like." Lofty whispered as he grabbed her blouse and ripped it open in front.

He pushed her down hard onto to the double bed and was on her before Dorothy could even think. This was worse than she expected, she decided just to be still now that she knew what he was capable of doing.

About ten minutes later Lofty staggered around the room gathering his shirt and belt stumbling out of the bunkhouse looking for another drink. Dorothy waited until she was sure he was gone before she got up from the bed to survey the damage. Her lip was bloody and swollen, the left side of her face was red and puffy. Lenore's blouse was bloody, in shreds, Dorothy's skirt was rumpled, and the zipper was broken. She could only find one of her shoes until she looked under the bed and found the other. The pearl earrings were gone. All she wanted was to find Jimmy Cordy and have him drive the car home. She left the guesthouse avoiding going back inside to what was left of the party. It was after midnight, she went straight to her car, nearly fainting with relief when she found Jimmy passed out in the passenger seat. "Jimmy" she shook him gently "wake up I need you to drive me home."

Jimmy sat up startled and looked at Dorothy's battered face by the light of the moon. "What happened to you, did you fall?"

"No don't ask any questions—take me home right now." Dorothy was close to tears.

Jimmy got out of the car, Dorothy slid into the passenger seat. Her whole body was sore as she moved. Jimmy started the car, began the long drive home. As they pulled on to the main road he asked again, "Dorothy what happened?"

She yelled this time. "Just shut up and drive."

Not another word passed between them, in front of the Brooks' house, Dorothy got out silently. Jimmy wanted to ask about her car but he decided better to keep his mouth shut, he'd worry about getting the car back to her tomorrow.

Ω

Dorothy was relieved to find that Chester and Lenore were already asleep but she had forgotten about Gilbert and Collette. When Dorothy went into her dark room, Collette turned on the bedside lamp and stifled a scream when she saw Dorothy's condition. Gilbert came from his room next door urging Dorothy to sit on the edge of the bed.

Dorothy couldn't hold back any longer, tears sprung from her eyes. The salt from her tears made her busted lip sting. She just shook her head indicating that she couldn't speak. Gilbert did the talking for her. "Lofty Moore did this didn't he?"

Dorothy nodded "yes," hanging her head into her hands.

Collette got up, quietly went into the bathroom to get a wet washcloth for Dorothy's face. When she returned Gilbert was examining the hand print bruises that were coming up on both of Dorothy's arms. "That son-of-a-bitch I'll kill him."

Collette shushed him "Be quiet you'll wake up your parents. I'm sure Dorothy doesn't want that right now." Collette gently dabbed at Dorothy's wounded lip, putting the cool cloth on her swollen cheek. "You go back to your room, let me get her to bed. She needs to lie down, maybe get some sleep."

Gilbert relented, whispering to Dorothy gently, "This will be taken care of I promise you." Gilbert left closing his bedroom door behind him.

Collette understood that Dorothy was in no shape to make any explanations; she helped her undress and put on a cozy nightgown. Collette noticed that Dorothy's bra and panties were torn and bloody, of course, Lenore's blouse and Dorothy's skirt were ruined. She took the whole mess, slipped it into the back corner of the wardrobe closet. She got Dorothy tucked under the sheets watching as she fell asleep almost immediately, as if she were succumbing to shock and exhaustion. Collette finally fell asleep herself in the armchair next to the nightstand. They would all need sleep to deal with what the New Year was about to bring.

$$\Omega$$

Gilbert barely slept at all; his outrage over what had happened to Dorothy kept him tossing the rest of the night. He got up at five o'clock deciding to attempt to wake his father without disturbing his mother. He crept into their bedroom and found his father already awake, signaling him to come quietly he eased out of the room. In the kitchen Gilbert began making coffee while in whispered tones told his father everything he knew about the party and Dorothy's condition. He said, "I don't want you to be shocked when you see her, based on how she looked last night she's going to be in worse shape this morning."

Chester came right out with the question "Was she raped?"

Gilbert hung his head and said, "I think so she couldn't even speak last night."

"Lofty Moore did this?" Chester said.

"Yes, Dorothy did admit to that."

"Was Dorothy drunk?"

"I don't know how much she drank. Lofty was way off the deep end, drinking shots of tequila. Everyone at the party will agree that he was past drunk."

"Who knows about this?" Chester asked.

"Jimmy Cordy drove her home—we need to get her car back today. I don't think anyone else saw her after the beating except Jimmy. I don't believe he will say anything to anyone. Lofty was at the party with Kay Kelly. I doubt if he knows much. He was nearly as plastered as Lofty." Gilbert picked up his coffee cup, refilled it, and offered his father another cup.

"Does Dorothy need to see a doctor?" Chester grimaced as he asked.

"I thought about that—what about seeing if the nurse that came here to check on Mom could take a look at her. I think seeing a doctor would upset Dorothy more."

"That's a good idea son. I've got the phone number at her home, I'll call once we get more of this figured out." Chester rubbed his face with his hands. "I'd love to see Lofty Moore in jail, we have to think about Dorothy's reputation in all of this."

Neither one of the men had noticed Collette standing in the kitchen doorway until she spoke. "Yes Dorothy's reputation should be the priority in any decisions about what is to be done, she has suffered enough."

Gilbert offered Collette his seat at the kitchen table and went to get her a cup of coffee.

Collette continued in a quiet voice. "I heard you mention a nurse Chester—I think that would be a good start. Dorothy's not in good shape, I helped her into bed after Gilbert left the room last night and she is going to have bruises all over. I doubt if she'll be out of bed today maybe not even tomorrow."

Chester hung his head "My God, how could I let this happen."

"You didn't let it happen neither did Dorothy. She was brutalized by an out of control drunkard." Collette was angry even though she kept her voice low.

It was six o'clock; the three of them were lost in their own thoughts. Not wanting to say any more of what was going through their minds.

Collette got up from the table. "I'm going to check on Dorothy I don't want her to wake up alone."

Chester said, "Lenore took a sleeping pill last night she should sleep for a couple more hours. At eight o'clock I'll call the nurse see if she can come around ten." He sighed, "That will give me some time to explain this to Lenore." Chester wiped a couple of tears from his eyes. "This will upset her more than any of us."

"I'm going to walk over to Jimmy's house and get Dorothy's car I could use the air and some exercise." Gilbert went to get dressed.

Ω

Chester sat alone at the kitchen table fighting the urge to break into sobs. Dorothy had been through so much in her young life how she would manage to get through another trauma like this was beyond him. He loved her more than anyone knew, he wanted nothing other than revenge, but knew he'd have to settle for much less. It occurred to him that Dorothy's 21st birthday was the day after tomorrow. With that thought he broke down put his head in his arms crying silently.

Collette came into the kitchen; put her hand on Chester's shoulder. He sat up with a start. Collette whispered, "Dorothy's awake she'd like to talk to you alone."

Chester went to the sink splashed cold water on his face and wiped it with the kitchen towel. "How is she?" He asked.

Collette shrugged "As good as could be expected, go talk to her."

Chester went to Dorothy's door tapped lightly before opening it. She was sitting up in bed in her nightgown. The left side of her face was a red and purple swath of a bruise and her left eye was turning black and blue. Her lower lip was split and still bloody. Her upper arms were covered in bruises in the shape of obvious handprints. He closed the door rushed into the room sitting down in the armchair that Collette had pulled up close to the bed. "Oh my God Dorothy." He choked on the words.

"It looks worse than it is." Dorothy said slurring her words a bit because of the size of her lips.

"It looks like you're damn lucky to be alive—I can't stand to think of what you went through." Chester was tearing up again.

"Please just listen to me without crying. I have to explain something before you or Gilbert goes off half-cocked." Dorothy took a deep breath. "I'm pregnant."

Chester interrupted "You can't possibly know that, what happened last night doesn't mean you're pregnant."

"I mean that I know that I'm pregnant—I've known for over a week." She stopped talking letting her words make their way into Chester's distraught consciousness.

He finally got what she was saying slumped back into the depths of the armchair. "You mean from before."

"Yes, from last month." She whispered

"Are you sure, I mean really certain."

"Yes, that's why I went with Lofty Moore last night. I didn't expect all of this," she waved toward her face, "I decided I had to do something to save us both from a disaster that we—I mean our family couldn't recover from. I love you, Lenore, and Gilbert. I love being your daughter. I couldn't, I wouldn't risk losing that."

"So what is going to happen? We can't just let this go he beat you and he hurt you." In spite of himself, tears came again to his eyes.

Dorothy reached out taking his hand. "In a couple of weeks I'll go and have a pregnancy test done and when it comes back positive Loften Dell Moore will be forced to marry me at your and Lenore's insistence. If everything works as planned we'll get married by January 31st."

"How can you consider marrying a man that would do this to you?"

"Lofty was drunk—I wouldn't be surprised if he barely remembers what happened. All the people at the party last night saw us together and my ruined clothes are in the wardrobe." She paused as she thought about Lenore's blouse and lost earrings. "I don't want him to get away with beating me either, when you confront his mother and father you need to have the whole story, the long-term goal, in your mind. Lenore doesn't need to know anything that would hurt her. I will be married to a college boy with a future. Brooks will be my maiden name. Trust me somehow this will all work out for the best. Just remember I love our family."

Chester shook his head "yes," as he took it all in. Dorothy had been thinking about what to do for longer than he had. He couldn't argue with the pure logic of her plan even if the morality was challenging, he had as much of a stake in it working as she did. He heard Gilbert pull up in her car in the front drive, decided to finish the conversation quickly. "I love you Dorothy that's the only reason I'm going to go along with this. I'm calling in the nurse that came to see Lenore here at home, you need to be checked out, make sure you will heal up, you might need a stitch or two in your lip." He paused "Lenore will be up soon she's going to be upset I'll explain what happened with Lofty, the two of us should decide how to handle things with the Moores. My first impulse was to fire Della Mae immediately and to make sure that Daniel loses his job at the smelter. I'll save those threats for later if it becomes necessary. You're sure about this, because today is going to change all of our options."

"You know we don't have any options Chester. Just do what has to be done to get me married by the end of the month."

$$\Omega$$

Lenore was just waking up when Chester came out of Dorothy's room and Gilbert came back home. She knew something wasn't right and demanded an immediate explanation. This time Collette started to explain figuring the two men had just about reached their limits of talking coherently. After hearing that Dorothy had been hurt Lenore insisted on seeing her even if she was sleeping. She rushed into the bedroom, burst into tears when she saw Dorothy's face. Lenore closed the door sat on the bed pulling Dorothy into her arms. She rocked her while the two of them cried together for a few minutes before Lenore got her wits back. She asked Dorothy to pull down the blankets and take off her nightgown. Then she could see the full extent of her injuries. When Lenore saw the bite marks on Dorothy's breasts, bruises on her hips and thighs, there was no doubt as to what had happened. She whispered the words "Lofty Moore raped you."

Dorothy hung her head "Yes. I'm sorry I let this happen."

"Don't ever say that you're sorry again—this isn't your fault I promise you that your father and I will take care of this." Lenore stood up filled with resolve calling out to Chester "Call the nurse Dorothy needs stitches and some care."

Ω

When Alicia the nurse arrived, she came equipped with a camera to take pictures of Dorothy's injuries. She did a complete examination took detailed notes of the extent of the damage the assault had caused. After all the documentation was complete she put a small stitch in Dorothy's lip and administered a prescription sedative that she kept under her own name just for such an emergency situation. Dorothy was again exhausted from the ordeal and fell into a deep sleep about fifteen minutes after taking the two pills.

Alicia gave the documentation to Chester and Lenore promising that her husband would develop the pictures himself providing them with the prints and negatives within twenty-four hours. Alicia delivered the pictures as promised, by noon on Dorothy's 21st birthday, Chester and Lenore were on their way to The Well to meet with Daniel and Della Mae Moore. They were arriving unannounced and didn't know whether Lofty would be at the Moore home or not.

Lenore was still in a weakened state. Her angry determination to defend Dorothy's honor had filled her with an emotional and physical energy that she hadn't felt in months. In the car Lenore held the file folder with the medical report and photos, in a brown bag she had brought the bloody blouse that had been ripped off Dorothy. She felt she was more than prepared for whatever was about to happen.

The Moores didn't seem surprised to see the Brooks when they opened the door to the bungalow. The first thing Della Mae said was "Lofty's gone back to school he had R.O.T.C. training starting this weekend." It was clear that they had some idea of why Chester and Lenore were there at their doorstep.

Chester asked, "Can we come in? We have a matter of importance to discuss."

They were all seated in the living room when Lenore began to speak. "On New Year's Eve your son assaulted our daughter Dorothy. I assume since you're not surprised to see us you have some impression about what happened."

Della Mae tried to take the offensive. "It was a big party everyone was drunk—I don't believe that Lofty did anything to Dorothy that she wasn't asking for."

Chester leaned forward and took the folder from Lenore. "These are photos and a medical report of Dorothy's injuries. She was beaten nearly beyond recognition, required stitches, and sedation for her wounds and suffering." Chester opened the folder fanning out the photos on the nearby coffee table.

Daniel made a choking, coughing sound looked away from the pictures his face reddened with humiliation. He said nothing.

Della Mae took another run at defending her son her response considering the evidence before her seemed unhinged. "Dorothy was dressed like a hussy she could have been hurt in a drunken fall—I don't give a damn about your pictures and reports. Lofty has gone back to school that's where he's going to stay."

Lenore couldn't stand anymore, as she watched Della Mae rant, she noticed something important. Lenore stood walking toward Della Mae; reached out, and grabbed at the earrings she was wearing one with each hand. "These pearl clip-on earrings are mine. I lent them to Dorothy to wear to the party. Your son slapped them off of her when he viciously attacked her." Lenore reached for the brown paper bag and pulled out the lace blouse. "I also lent this blouse for Dorothy to wear as you can see it is in bloody shreds from when your son ripped it off of her. My daughter didn't ask for any of this and she didn't deserve an attack by an animal like your son. You have the gall to try to blame her while you sit here wearing my earrings"

Della Mae was shamed and embarrassed into silence. Chester finished the meeting with a warning "If

Dorothy suffers any other consequences to her person or her reputation as a result of your family's action this will become a legal matter. Anything short of Dorothy's complete recovery will be dealt with as harshly as the Moore family could imagine."

Daniel had no doubt that crossing the General Manager of the Company Mercantile could cost them their jobs and home. He shook his head "yes" in meek acquiescence. The meeting was over.

On the way home from The Well Lenore was still outraged "To think that brute son of theirs took the earrings as some sort of trophy and gave them to his crazy mother is truly sick."

When Chester and Lenore arrived home Gilbert and Collette had Dorothy settled into the sofa with pillows, and a blanket. Collette had made a birthday cake for Dorothy. The five of them had cake, coffee, and a quiet celebration.

Dorothy stayed inside for the next two weeks to prevent anyone from seeing her injuries and bruises, she healed well, the stitch in her lip prevented a scar from forming. Jimmy Cordy came by to see her. He swore that he hadn't and would never tell anyone what had happened.

On Monday, January 19, Dorothy called Alicia the nurse for further private care. Alicia came by the house took a blood and urine sample from Dorothy promising her results in three days. By Thursday morning, Dorothy had the positive results of her pregnancy test. That weekend Chester and Lenore returned to the Moore home to break the news of

Dorothy's pregnancy to Daniel and Della Mae. They explained that Lofty would be expected to do the right thing by Dorothy. Chester insisted that Lofty come home from school the following weekend to marry Dorothy in a small family only church ceremony. Chester had bought a set of wedding rings for the ceremony and already arranged for a wedding announcement to appear in the newspaper.

    Daniel Moore promised that Lofty would do the right thing. Della Mae cried at the prospect of losing her only son to a "shotgun" marriage. They both understood that their whole way of life was at stake. Daniel drove to Tempe to bring Lofty the news of his impending marriage and fatherhood. Lofty was initially obstinate, when Daniel told him that both his and Lofty's mother's jobs were on the line, that without their jobs they would lose the house. Lofty realized he had been painted into a corner that he couldn't escape. Lofty agreed to the marriage saying he planned to return to school immediately after the ceremony. Lofty's terms were more than acceptable to Dorothy, Chester, and Lenore. The wedding was held in Federated Methodist Church the guests included only both sets of parents. Eighteen-year-old Loften Dell Moore and twenty-one-year-old Dorothy Louise Brooks were declared man and wife on Saturday, January 31, 1953. A brief reception was held at the Brooks home for wedding cake pictures. Lofty true to his word left within an hour of the ceremony to return to the College.

    Dorothy slept in her own bed that night content that her problems were solved. She was married, once again, all was right in her world. However, the marriage between a beguilingly deceptive narcissist and a predatory sadistic sociopath would not turn out to be a match made in heaven. It would turn into something that came up from a deep pit, deeper than the Ajo copper mine itself.

6

"Sometimes the narcissist mother simply uses the child to keep a sick marriage intact, because the alternative is being divorced or having to go to work. The child is sexually molested but the mother never notices, or worse calls the child a liar when she tells the mother about the molestation."
The Narcissist Mother, Light's House.org

For the four months of the remaining college semester, nothing changed in Lofty's life. He continued to behave in Tempe as if he were the single big man on campus and continued to earn his R.O.T.C. commission. No one at the school other than Kay Kelly knew that Lofty was married or that a child was on the way. Lofty still dated socially as he had before his life's path had changed.

Dorothy also lived the same life as before. She, of course, was still the daughter of Chester and Lenore Brooks. She worked mornings at the Mercantile and in the afternoons helped Lenore with the house and dinner preparations. Dorothy watched her weight very carefully. In fact, during the first three months of her pregnancy, she actually lost a few pounds. By the beginning of May, she was starting to show a bit and had to change from wearing her slimmest skirts to shirtwaist dresses that were more disguising.

According to the Moore family Lofty was planning on going to summer school then continuing to football camp in mid-July. There were no plans between the two families to have the pair come together as a married couple. All that changed a week before the semester at ASC ended. Somehow the school found out that Lofty was married, based on the terms of his football scholarship this was a disqualifying event, the school declined to extend his scholarship past the end of the current semester. Shortly after this bad news came, he lost his R.O.T.C. commission because he was no longer a registered student, the enlistment college deferment no longer applied to him.

This news was a terrible blow to the Moore family Lofty was livid, convinced that Kay Kelly had decided to let his secret out. Lofty believed it had happened over a girl that he was dating. Kay Kelly had a crush on her, resented that Lofty, a married man, was deceiving the girl. Before Lofty left to go home to Ajo, he filled Kelly's car gas tank full of sugar ruining the engine. At least he had some revenge to brag about when he returned home.

Ω

The change in Lofty's college status was a real blow to Daniel and Della Mae, try as they might they couldn't find a way to come up with the money for

Lofty to re-enroll in the fall semester. When Lofty came back to Ajo, he had no other choice, than going to work as a laborer in the mine.

The whole town already knew that Lofty and Dorothy were married, when Lofty came home went to work in Ajo, people started gossiping about their separate living arrangements. Dorothy was well past being able to disguise her pregnancy rather than causing more reason for chin-wagging around town, Dorothy called Lofty asking him to meet her at a restaurant in Mexican Town. She told him not to mention anything to his parents indicating that she would do the same. The secrecy of the meeting intrigued him, he agreed.

Dorothy dressed in her best black linen shirtwaist that was the only dress she could still reasonably fit into without looking too pregnant. They each drove their own cars to the restaurant, met at six o'clock for dinner. Dorothy did her best to be open and nice, for once Lofty was a gentleman pulling out her chair for her, as they sat down at the table. Dorothy ordered beers for the both of them. "Dinner and drinks are on me."

Lofty was surprised but just nodded, "Thanks."

"I heard you're at the mine you must not be happy." Dorothy said.

"That's an understatement—I lost my scholarship because we got married."

"We got married because I'm pregnant. Difficult situation for us both."

"We wouldn't be here if you didn't have something in mind right?" Lofty said.

"Let's move in together, we can get an apartment in the projects. I'll make it a nice home."

"That works for you what's in it for me?" Lofty took a long swig of beer.

"You promise *never* to hit me again"

"I was drunk I wouldn't have done any of that if I hadn't been so plastered"

"Why should I believe you?" Dorothy asked

"Because I assume you still have the pictures you showed my parents." Lofty said

"Look we're married, we have a baby coming in a few months, it just seems to me it is time to make the best of it." Dorothy sipped at her beer. "You have to hate all the gossip as much as I do."

"I hate this town, let alone the gossip." Lofty said.

"Okay we both work to get out of here, to get you back to the College and both of us back to the city." Dorothy smiled her sweetest smile. "What if we agree that we just got off on the wrong foot, try to start over. I do think you're the best looking man I've ever met."

"You're not too bad yourself except for that baby belly you got going there."

"It's your baby too."

"Okay it's a deal, in two years I want to be out of here." Lofty insisted.

"Two years it is." Dorothy agreed.

Lofty and Dorothy had a conciliatory dinner and actually kissed each other good-bye.

Ω

Lofty told Daniel and Della Mae that evening when he came home after dinner. His parents' relief was palpable. They promised to help the couple save money for his return to school in two years' time. The threat of losing their own jobs and home had been hanging over them for months and finally Della Mae could relax.

Ω

The next day Mrs. Loften Dell Moore rented an end unit apartment in the projects; began moving in her clothes and some small furnishings.

That night she told Chester and Lenore that she and Lofty had agreed to move in together to live as husband and wife. They were both skeptical, but knew that something like this had to happen sooner rather than later. Chester agreed as a wedding present to buy them the furniture they would need to start a household. Lenore promised to sew draperies for the windows. When Dorothy got up, hugged her, Lenore added, "I also better get busy making you some maternity clothes you're about to bust out of that dress."

Dorothy and the Brooks family were all relieved that life would be getting back as it should be. Dorothy was due to have the baby in late October; it was good having reached this final resolution.

Mr. and Mrs. Loften Moore were married; they had reconciled five months after the ceremony. It wasn't a good start, but it was the start of something.

Ω

By mid-September, Dorothy was starting to spot slightly and have mild painless contractions. She put herself to bed claiming that she was suffering from back pain and exhaustion. She didn't tell anyone that she feared she was close to going into labor early that the date of conception could be questioned. For three weeks she ate only clear broth and Jell-O claiming that she was nauseous as well. Her efforts were to keep the weight of the baby in check so that when she did go into labor the baby would be small

On October 7, 1953, Dorothy went into labor and she delivered a 6-pound 9-ounce baby girl. She was named Linda Dell Moore. Lofty and Daniel were working in the mine when the birth occurred. Chester, Lenore, and Della Mae were at the hospital to welcome the child, congratulate the mother. Baby Linda was perfect and healthy; the doctor declared that even though she was at least two weeks early she would have no ill effects from being born slightly premature.

Dorothy and baby Linda spent a week at the hospital then went home to the project apartment. As Chester and Lenore had promised, over the months before Linda's birth, they had helped Dorothy and Lofty furnish their apartment creating a comfortable home. Linda's first place was a bassinette, a full size crib was also ready for her when she was a few months older. The four grandparents were thrilled that the baby was healthy, and that Lofty and Dorothy were apparently working together to make a go of the marriage.

Lofty was relieved to discover that being married, having a baby was an automatic draft deferment. He wouldn't have to worry about going to war in Korea. However, Lofty hated working in the mine although he did receive some special consideration because of his father's position he was working as a backhoe operator, instead of a general laborer, he still had plenty of complaints. He was literally counting the days of the two years he had to go until he returned to the College.

Lofty wasn't much interested in being a father and almost every day after work he went to Mexican Town to have a few beers with his old gang of friends. He also spent a late afternoon or two a week with the younger sister of one of his buddies. Dorothy, of course, didn't know about the sister, she wouldn't have really cared if she did. As long as Lofty brought home a paycheck or most of one, didn't ever raise a hand or his voice to her, she happily allowed out of sight to be out of mind.

Dorothy and Linda spent a lot of time with Chester and Lenore they were truly doting grandparents. Lenore was in remission feeling nearly as well as before she got sick. Lenore volunteered to take care of Linda for a few hours in the mornings, then spent the afternoons sewing baby clothes insuring that Linda was dressed like a little princess.

Dorothy lost what little weight she had gained during her pregnancy almost immediately. She looked beautiful, if not more than before. Having her mornings free meant that Dorothy could go back to work in the Company Store. The extra money went toward clothes, food, and a little she socked away for the two-year move back to the city. It also gave Dorothy and Chester time together. Time that meant more to both of them than either was willing to admit.

Linda was a calm and easy to care for baby. She took to the formula well since Dorothy decided she didn't want to affect her figure negatively with the nuisance of breast-feeding. By three months old, Dorothy was feeding Linda Gerber rice cereal and applesauce or bananas to supplement her formula feedings, the baby was thriving on the regimen. When Linda went to the hospital for her checkups, everything was normal, she was growing and developing as would be expected. Linda had a healthy headful of light brown wavy hair and dark brown eyes. Dorothy loved taking her into town in her stroller to show Linda off to everyone she knew.

As the holidays came, Linda had her first Christmas and Easter with Dorothy, Lofty, and all her grandparents around. From an uncertain beginning Linda seemed to bring the two families together in the way only a child could do.

When the summer came around Lofty's work in the mine and his mood suffered from the heat. He asked to change to the second shift, which started at three o'clock in the afternoon, he worked until eleven at night. The work was the same, but done with floodlights, cooler temperatures. Lofty still went for a couple of beers, still had his other diversions several nights a week after getting off his shift.

It was a hot morning in July when the incident happened. Linda was almost ten months old and had just started walking using furniture to make her way around a room. She could take three or four steps on her own. Lofty was sleeping in as usual. Dorothy was up and getting herself and Linda ready to leave when Lenore called to say that maybe Linda shouldn't come over because she had awakened with a bad summer cold. Lenore didn't want the baby exposed to her germs. Dorothy agreed with the decision, called the Mercantile to let Chester know she wouldn't be in to work. Dorothy settled down to have another cup of coffee letting Linda play on the living room floor. At ten o'clock Della Mae called from the store to let Dorothy know that the new clothes she had ordered from Phoenix had arrived. Dorothy said she would come in later to pick them up.

By eleven-thirty, Dorothy had already fed Linda her lunch. She was ready to put her in her crib for a nap. Linda usually slept for almost two hours. Lofty was still sleeping. Dorothy wanted to go pick up her clothes from the store, she decided to take a chance, dash out for just a little while to be back before Linda, or Lofty awoke.

Chester was at the store and was surprised to see her, he followed her into the back stock room, came up behind her, and put his arms around her waist. "Dorothy I was missing you this morning." He kissed her on the back of her neck.

"I can't stay I just stopped by to pick up my clothes."

"Stay for just a few minutes." Chester pleaded.

"Della Mae could come back here any time." Dorothy warned.

"No she went to lunch in Mexican Town. We have time."

Dorothy knew what he wanted; Chester had his own version of the "hat trick" only he used his handkerchief while she used her hand. The whole thing took only a few minutes. Then he kissed her as he always did. Dorothy pulled away "I do have to run, Lofty and Linda are both home sleeping I want to be back before either one of them wake up."

"Give the baby a kiss from me." Chester called out after her as she headed out the door.

Once in the car, Dorothy took a second to fix her lipstick then drove the five minutes home. When she arrived she was very quiet at the door hoping not to wake any one. She walked in on a scene that forced a scream from her throat. Lofty was sitting in the wooden rocker in his briefs and sleeveless undershirt eyes closed. Linda was naked on his lap with her face pressed into his chest her legs splayed out around his hips. Dorothy knew immediately what he was doing. Dorothy's scream made Lofty jump up from the chair Linda came sliding off his lap. Her feet were caught in the side arm supports of the rocking chair. Lofty nearly stepped on her chest as he leapt over her dangling body. Linda started screaming as her legs twisted awkwardly while her feet were stuck. Dorothy ran over grabbing her up, she and Lofty both heard the little popping noises from Linda's legs as her feet finally came free from the rocking chair arms.

Dorothy shrieked at Lofty as she watched the spreading stain on the front of his underwear. "I can't believe you'd use a baby like this!"

"I didn't mean to it just happened I couldn't figure out how to get a diaper back on her."

"That's bullshit she was fully dressed, you managed to get her naked. You are sick. Get dressed and get out right now."

Lofty ran to the bedroom and emerged seconds later with his work pants on and a shirt in his hand. He hurried to the door leaving without another word. All the while Linda was crying in pain as Dorothy stood frozen holding her in the middle of the living room. Dorothy's mind was racing. What should she do? Linda's legs were hanging limp from her body. She took her carefully laid her on her back in her crib. Linda was still crying as Dorothy put a fresh diaper on her. Once she lay still for a moment Linda's cries seemed to subside. Dorothy went to the kitchen to fix her a bottle and thought of the paregoric that was in the cabinet. The doctor had given the prescription when Linda was teething, the instructions were to use half-a-dropper to rub on her gums. Dorothy returned to the crib tried to give Linda the bottle; she wouldn't take it, starting to cry again. Next, she tried the paregoric, put a blanket over Linda's legs, they didn't look right even though Linda was moving her arms and crying she wasn't moving her legs at all. It took about ten minutes for the opium-laced paregoric to work. Linda's cries changed to occasional whimpers as she fell asleep. Dorothy left the room long enough to make herself a strong rum and Coke then returned to check on Linda. She was sleeping, breathing normally when Dorothy returned. She downed her rum and Coke in a couple of gulps then felt calmer. She tried to think of what to do.

What she had found Lofty doing was disgustingly perverted—she had left him alone with Linda while she met with Chester. If she called someone, right now a doctor or a nurse, Chester would know that whatever was wrong with Linda's legs had happened when she was with him. She couldn't bear the thought of taking any of the blame for Lofty's loathsome actions. No matter how she tried to think of explaining, it all came down to her being gone when it happened. She couldn't stand the idea of people thinking she was a negligent mother.

Dorothy assumed that Lofty had gone to work his regular three to eleven shift. She was sure that he wouldn't come home tonight. That would mean that tomorrow she could call Della Mae telling her that Linda had somehow gotten her legs tangled in the crib railings. Dorothy was sure that the popping sound she'd heard was the sound of Linda's hip joints dislocating. If she could keep Linda sedated until tomorrow it might just work out. Dorothy went to fix another rum and Coke so she could keep working on the plan. She checked on Linda again—the baby seemed to be sleeping without any pain.

Dorothy decided that when Lofty didn't come home by morning she would call his mother Della Mae asking her if she knew where Lofty was. She could then explain Linda's injuries as a crib accident. Her plans were interrupted by a loud wail from the bedroom. Dorothy ran to check on Linda. She had a wet diaper and it had soaked through the sheets since Dorothy didn't dare to try to put on elastic plastic pants over the diaper.

Dorothy picked Linda up as carefully as she could, the baby squealed in pain, she laid her on the bed quickly changed the crib sheets while Linda wailed. Dorothy remembered that she had one pair of snap on plastic pants and searched through the dresser until she found them. She then got a fresh diaper and carefully as possible maneuvered Linda into a dry diaper with the plastic pants. Dorothy then put a rubber waterproof cover in the crib gingerly lifted her daughter back into place on her back. Another dose of paregoric soon Linda was sleeping again. It was five o'clock Dorothy had a long night ahead of her, at least it was cocktail hour.

Dorothy slept that night on the twin bed in Linda's room. She continued to wake up every three hours throughout the night. Dorothy tried to give Linda a bottle several times; she wouldn't take it. Whenever Linda's crying became constant, Dorothy gave her another half-a-dropper of paregoric. Finally, at eight o'clock in the morning she called Della Mae looking for Lofty. When he wasn't there she explained that she found Linda stuck in the crib railing a couple of hours ago. Della Mae insisted on coming to the apartment. Dorothy quickly straightened up the room washed her rum and Coke glass and was taking Linda's temperature when Della Mae arrived.

"She's running a fever seems dehydrated." Della said. "When did you find her like this?"

"Just before I called you I woke up Lofty wasn't here. Linda was crying I came in here to find her legs were stuck in the bars." Dorothy claimed, "I changed her diaper she screamed bloody murder. I knew something was wrong."

"Well we're taking her to the hospital right now." Della gently picked Linda up from the crib setting off a fresh crying fit. "Why didn't Lofty come home last night?"

"I think he has a girlfriend in Mexican Town."

"What makes you think that?" Della asked

"I've heard rumors—look none of this matters let's get Linda to the hospital."

Della Mae finally got her mind back on the urgency of Linda's condition and told Dorothy "Get the door, you drive I'll hold Linda."

Once they got to the hospital, Linda was barely whimpering, the baby was exhausted. A doctor was called to examine her right away. His diagnosis didn't take long; both of Linda's hips had been dislocated. He questioned Dorothy about how and when the injuries had occurred. Dorothy again told the same story she had concocted about finding Linda that morning with her legs twisted in the bars of the crib. She did admit to giving Linda paregoric when she was crying, insisting she only gave her one dose.

The doctor was suspicious but was more concerned with taking care of his patient than quizzing Dorothy any further. The doctor instructed the nurse to begin an intravenous saline drip because the baby was dehydrated. Linda barely cried when the nurse stuck her arm. When the doctor returned he told Della Mae and Dorothy to stand on each side of the examination table holding Linda's shoulders down firmly. The baby was terrified, began tearlessly screaming. During one of the screams the doctor grabbed Linda's right leg twisted and pushed her hip joint back into place. Before another scream could commence he did the same procedure with her left leg. He frowned when her left leg didn't pop back into place. He had to twist and push her leg again. Linda had stopped screaming because she had lost consciousness from the pain. The nurse checked her vital signs, heartbeat, breathing, and blood pressure, and relayed to the doctor that the child was all right. The doctor then told the nurse to get him a fine gauge surgical wire. He explained to Dorothy, "Because she is dehydrated your daughter's tear ducts have closed up or become blocked, she could get a serious eye infection if I don't do a procedure to open them up with a small surgical probe. Hopefully, she will be still; I need you to hold her head firmly."

The nurse returned with a sterile pack surgical wire, the doctor proceeded to ream out both tear ducts the procedure took about ten minutes, and Linda remained unconscious. The doctor ordered a second intravenous saline drip for the baby then turned his attention to Della Mae and Dorothy. "She will require a brace for her left leg. I'll take some measurements, it will take a week to have the custom brace made. You will have to hold her or have her in a stroller at all times when she isn't sleeping; she can't put any weight on her leg."

Dorothy nodded her understanding. "What about her eyes?"

"We are giving her saline for the next couple of hours. She is severely dehydrated. Her eyes will be fine once she has had some fluids."

The doctor took measurements of Linda's left foot, leg, hips, and waist. Before he turned to leave, he listened to the baby's heart and chest with his stethoscope "I'd suggest you get a different crib—the one you have nearly crippled you daughter." He walked out.

Dorothy knew the doctor didn't believe her story, as she looked at Della's face she saw a look of fear that she couldn't resist capitalizing on. Dorothy said, "I don't want to see Lofty for a while—you should let him know I'm taking Linda, we're going to Chester and Lenore's for a couple of weeks."

Della Mae was thinking the worst of her son at that moment—imagining that he was the cause of Linda's injury that was why he had run off. Della just nodded "yes," she said, "I'm going to the phone and try to find Lofty—please don't tell anyone that you blame him for this."

Dorothy responded, "The doctor said we need a better crib—maybe you should try to find one of those too." Linda started to regain consciousness and let out a weak cry. Dorothy told Della "You should go, take my car back to the apartment. I'll stay with Linda and call

Chester to come get us when the doctor says we can go."

Ω

Dorothy and Linda were at Chester and Lenore's home about three hours later. Dorothy retold the crib story saying that Lofty was off with a girlfriend when it happened. She explained as the doctor had that Linda would need a leg brace on her left leg for possibly as long as a year.

For a week, whenever Linda was awake, she was carried or in a stroller, at the end of the week her leg brace was fitted. It was made of leather straps and metal splints that went from the bottom of her foot to being strapped around her leg and waist to secure the stability of her hip joint. Chester had special ordered a pair of corrective baby shoes to give a stable base for the brace. Within another week of getting used to the leg brace Linda started walking with a shuffling gait, she was up and moving under her own power.

During the separation, Lofty called every day. He wanted to make certain that Dorothy continued to cover for him. He had no idea that she was covering for herself and Chester as well. Dorothy moved back to the apartment in less than a month. Lofty seemed to be chastened by what Dorothy had to hold over him. He still went out for a couple of beers after work, he stopped seeing his girlfriend in Mexican Town. He couldn't hide his resentment toward Linda beginning to call her "gimp," as a joke when she was walking around the apartment. Luckily Linda's exposure to Lofty's derision was limited to the weekends. Dorothy took

Linda to Lenore every morning before she went to work at the Mercantile. She didn't return home with her until Lofty had left for his swing work shift in the afternoon.

Dorothy and Lofty were living as roommates in a two-bedroom apartment. Dorothy was sleeping in Linda's room, still fostering resentment of her husband for cheating on her with some Mexican girl. However, he remained her best chance of getting out of Ajo, the goal Dorothy wanted more than anything. She knew the longer she kept him at arm's length the more she risked her escape to the city and a different life.

By the time Linda's first birthday came in October, Dorothy instigated a thaw in family relations by inviting both pairs of "grandparents" to a birthday party at the apartment.

Lenore had made Linda several pairs of baby blue jeans to hide her leg brace for her birthday had sewn a blue satin embroidered cowgirl shirt to wear with her jeans at the party. Lofty was on his best behavior for a couple of hours refraining from calling Linda "gimp," actually playing the role of doting father in front of the families.

Later that night Dorothy rewarded Lofty's "good" behavior by not sleeping in Linda's bedroom. In three short months, she reconciled with Linda's abuser.

Ω

At Christmas in front of the family, Dorothy presented her own bank account book indicating a savings balance of five hundred dollars, which was at least a third of what they would need for Lofty, Dorothy, and Linda to move to Tempe and get Lofty re-enrolled for a semester at the College. Her revelation served to further shore up her commitment to Lofty's college aspirations, to put her in Daniel and Della Mae's good graces. They promised by summer to match whatever amount Lofty and Dorothy had managed to save. In private they extracted a promise from Dorothy, no more babies until Lofty had graduated from college. Della Mae insisted that they would withhold any financial support if Dorothy became pregnant again anytime soon. Dorothy easily agreed she had not intended to have another child for several years at least. She told the Moores that they had nothing to worry about from her. Later alone with Della Mae, Dorothy couldn't resist giving Lofty's mother something else to worry about. "I've promised not to have another child; maybe you better have this conversation with Lofty about his girl in Mexican Town.

Della Mae said, "He's done with that. He told me."

"You know better than anyone that Lofty tells you what you want to hear I'm just warning you, if you don't take my advice that's your problem." Dorothy walked away leaving Della with a frown and a wrinkled brow.

Linda's second Christmas was more of an event because she was old enough to be excited by the decorations and gifts. Chester and Lenore were more reticent about the young family's prospects. They showered Linda with Santa surprises including a small rocking horse that Linda could ride even with her leg brace.

Dorothy had her twenty-third birthday on January 3, 1955. Lofty had arranged for a dinner party in a Mexican Town restaurant for Dorothy and a number of their friends. Della Mae had agreed to care for Linda for the weekend of the party. Dorothy made Lofty swear he would only drink beer abstaining from tequila shots and he reluctantly complied. He was being much more agreeable since he realized Dorothy was as serious as he was about leaving Ajo within his two-year limit.

Dorothy's party went off without a hitch. Pippen and Earl Wirth, and Ben and Marlene McGrady, made it a Mexican fiesta for six. Dorothy wore a royal blue sheath dress and was the best-dressed woman in all of Ajo that evening. For once Lofty truly appreciated his wife's stunning beauty. As he watched her during dinner, he thought about how she had covered for him for months. It made him wonder if their mutual motivations weren't more in line than he had imagined. For the first time since their marriage he felt a surge of trust and maybe love for Dorothy. He liked that she was his.

The rest of the winter and spring went by without incident. Lofty remained distant from Linda but didn't do anything to harm her except ignore her. Lofty and Dorothy were on track to have one thousand dollars by mid-summer and Daniel and Della were prepared to match it. Lofty could move his family, pay for school, and get a place to live. Even though he and Dorothy would both have to work. At least Lofty would be back to pursuing his business degree. He still resented having lost his football scholarship, but completing his degree would put him on track for success. After working in the mine for a year and a half Lofty figured any night shift job he could get in Tempe while going to school would be better than going into the pit.

Dorothy with her year of nursing training was planning to start a small nursery school for pre-school age children. Her idea was that it would provide income, friends for Linda, and allow her to work from home.

Pippen and Earl planned a 4th of July going away party for Dorothy and Lofty at the ranch. There were kegs of beer with food cooked on a wood-fired grill. Linda was twenty-two months old and Dorothy dressed her in a red, white, and blue gingham dress without making her wear her leg brace. As the party went on into the afternoon Lofty had drank plenty of beer and went outside to get some air. Linda followed him into the barnyard area where chickens wandered freely pecking the ground for seeds. Lofty found a spot just inside the barn door from where he watched Linda chase the chickens. Without her brace she had a slight limp. Her hip joint had been deemed healed at her last doctor's visit.

From the corner of the barnyard, a large Tom turkey caught sight of Linda playing amongst the chickens—the turkey spread its tail and began to move menacingly toward Linda. Lofty watched from the shadows as the scene played out quickly. The three-foot tall bird charged Linda knocking her to the ground, it started clawing, pecking at her. Linda screamed. Earl who was manning the grill heard her frightened squeals ran across the barnyard chasing the big turkey away. Lofty came walking out of the barn acting as if he'd seen nothing of the attack. Earl yelled for him to come. Linda's legs and arms were covered with bloody scratches, deep peck bites that would turn into bruises. Lofty jerked Linda up by one arm, while dragging her he called out to Dorothy. "Your little gimp cupie doll is a mess—she smells like chicken shit—it's time to go home."

Earl watched in disbelief as Lofty roughly off-loaded Linda into Dorothy's arms. Dorothy was yelling, "What happened? What did you do?"

"I didn't do a damn thing. She was gimping around in the muck and a turkey took a dislike to her. C'mon I said we're going home."

Pippen came running with a wet towel to help Dorothy clean the dirt and debris from Linda's wounds. Linda had gone quiet not making a sound while Dorothy swabbed the scratches, bites, and wiped the filth from her little body. Linda's dress was torn to ruins. Dorothy took it off as Pippen handed her a small blanket to wrap up Linda.

"I said we're leaving, the brat is fine." Lofty said.

"You were supposed to be watching her." Dorothy hissed.

"I was watching" Lofty admitted—"that turkey must really have hated her."

Dorothy didn't say a word on the drive home, Linda seemed to be in some sort of shock, not a cry or a whimper. When they got home Dorothy took Linda in for a cool bath, while Lofty grabbed another couple of beers from the refrigerator, going to sit out on the front stoop. Unfortunately, for Lofty, Chester and Lenore picked that exact time to stop by for a visit, while they went into the house, Lofty jumped in his truck heading for Mexican Town.

When Linda's grandparents saw her condition, they both demanded an explanation from Dorothy. She explained about the turkey attack, leaving out the part about Lofty's disregard for Linda, as the cause. Both Chester and Lenore tried to insist that they take Linda to the hospital. Dorothy convinced them that her nurse's training enabled her adequately to care for the injuries Linda had sustained. She said, "It looks a lot worse than it is Linda barely cried at all. I have some ointment the doctor gave me for skinned knees and such."

Chester had gone out to the front door to talk with Lofty, finding that he had left, it made him suspicious he returned to question Dorothy. "Are you sure Lofty didn't have anything to do with this he's left to go who knows where."

"He was meeting a few friends from work to say goodbye—he'll be back later." Dorothy lied. "Let me get Linda to bed she's had a long day."

Lenore took the hint "Chester let's go home let Dorothy take care of Linda without us hanging over her shoulder."

Dorothy rewarded Lenore with a smile, "I'll call you in the morning and let you know how she is. I'm sure she'll be fine."

After Chester and Lenore left Dorothy gave Linda a dropper full of paregoric put her to bed. Linda fell asleep without ever making a sound. Dorothy made herself a strong rum and Coke then fell asleep on the sofa. When she woke up the next morning Lofty still hadn't returned home from Mexican Town.

The 4th of July was over for the Moore family and again Linda had suffered the worst of it, while Lofty had watched and savored the child's fear and pain. Lofty returned late in the morning with a small trailer hitched to the back of his truck—he told Dorothy to start packing up the apartment, which they were leaving as soon as possible for Tempe. Dorothy complied without question; Lofty was not in the mood for talking. He loaded up the furniture into the back of his truck and trailer, putting the bags and boxes Dorothy had packed into her car. Lofty, Dorothy, and Linda left Ajo by late afternoon on July 5, 1955.

7

"Home of the Arizona State Sun Devils."

    Lofty, Dorothy, and Linda slept in a cheap motel room their first night in Tempe. The next day they found, rented, and moved into a small house that was on the wrong side of the tracks from ASC campus. It cost sixty dollars a month including electric and water. The 450 square foot two-bedroom house had an old refrigerator, stove, an evaporative cooler, and ancient hand operated wringer washer out on the back porch. It was what they could afford close enough to the college for Lofty to make it to classes on time. The house had a small fenced yard, a clothesline, and a swing set that Dorothy thought was perfect for her nursery school. She made a sign hung it on the fence within a month was taking care of four children at five dollars a week for each. Lofty found a night shift job at a gas station and mechanic shop a few minutes drive from home. He made one dollar an hour working from three o'clock until eleven o'clock, five shifts a week. He was happy;

across the street from work was a strip bar called "Guys and Dolls" where he spent a couple of bucks a week on beers and strip shows.

When Lofty enrolled at ASC again he decided to start fresh by using his middle name "Dell." He wanted to leave his football and ROTC experience behind. Anyone he knew was two years ahead of him or in the case of Kay Kelly had been married and dropped out, so there wasn't going to be any long-standing grudges or former relationships to deal with. Dell Moore was enrolled as a sophomore majoring in business administration. His semester tuition was $125 and his book fees were another thirty dollars.

Considering that they had left Ajo with a little over $2,000, by the end of July they had only spent about $400 including the purchase of a black and white television set they got at a floor model sale for eighty bucks. Dell and Dorothy both had jobs making $240 each month had money in savings. Dell started school in September right after Labor Day, it seemed that all was well with the young family and their fresh start.

Ω

In October, both sets of grandparents came to Tempe to celebrate Linda's second birthday. Dorothy planned a party with lunch, cake, and decorations. She made sure to have plenty of beer for Dell and his parents, she bought a bottle of bourbon for Chester, and she and Lenore were both happy with rum and Coke. Linda got plenty of presents including several new dresses that Lenore had sewn for her and a baby doll with a stroller from Della Mae. It was a good day they all enjoyed the afternoon watching the new television set. Both Daniel and Chester decided to get themselves one of the newest forms of entertainment. Dell took them to the appliance store where he had bought his set. Both men came back to the house with televisions in the trunks of their cars to take back to Ajo.

Della Mae had an issue with Dell about his name change. He insisted that she go along with his wishes she agreed, although after a few beers she had to be reminded when she called him Lofty.

The grandparents left to go back home to Ajo around four o'clock in order to make the two hour drive before it got dark. Dorothy was delighted with how well the day had gone. She felt for the first time that she was really part of an extended family. That night Linda went to sleep early from all the excitement. Dell and Dorothy had a romantic evening together. Dorothy went to sleep that night thinking that she hadn't done badly after all.

Most of 1955 and 1956 were uneventful for the Moore family. They celebrated Thanksgiving and Christmas in Ajo, with family and friends. Dell paid for his second semester at college with money from savings. Dorothy had five children in her nursery school and made twenty-five dollars a week, more than enough for groceries, clothing, and the occasional drive-in movie night. Dorothy was twenty-four and looked as beautiful as she had ever looked. During the days while taking care of Linda and the other children she wore slim black capri pants with light cotton tunic tops. Her hair was still long; she wore lipstick, eye makeup, and did her hair every day. Dell came home most nights after work without going to the strip club because his own wife was better looking than any of the dancers. Dell and Dorothy had a good sex life with Dorothy being in charge about when it was safe to engage without worrying about getting pregnant. The straight mission-style sex was a little tame for Dell's wilder side, he had decided to only cheat to get his more unorthodox needs met.

Linda was thriving in the nursery school setting; she had playmates that showed up every day like clockwork. Dorothy fed the children all the same meals each day one-half of a peanut butter grape jelly sandwich or the same with mustard and bologna, and a glass of milk with two vanilla wafer cookies. Every afternoon the children took naptime for an hour while Dorothy watched her favorite soap opera "Guiding Light" on the television. The kids all played outside in the yard on the swing set while Dorothy did laundry on the back porch and hung the clean clothes on the line.

Dell left for school at eight-thirty for his first class at nine o'clock went to classes until two, then ate a late lunch, buying an extra sandwich at the college cafeteria to take to work before going to the gas station at three. His life was routine, mundane, and he sometimes felt trapped. Getting his degree was his goal, he resigned himself to having to work through lots of boring routine days to get there.

Just before the end of the spring semester Dell met a girl on campus and struck up a friendship with her she was a freshman and going to be a teacher majoring in physical education. The young woman's name was Sandia Sanchez and they started meeting for lunch every day. Sandia had dark hair and eyes but was more naïve than Dorothy was so Dell felt much more in charge of the possible relationship. Not to say that he liked them young and stupid, but actually Dell did. One day he asked her if he could meet her after class, she agreed. Dell called work saying he was going to be a couple of hours late and had his buddy at work Kenny cover for him. Dell and Sandia drove to her apartment had an afternoon of sex. Sandia turned out not to be a naïve as Dell had imagined, she liked it rough and really got him going. The affair started that day. Dorothy was busy in her own world, so when Dell announced he was going to take a summer school class, she didn't give it a second thought.

$$\Omega$$

After a couple of months of afternoon trysts at Sandia's apartment, she began to pressure Dell for more time and attention. He continued to provide excuses including his dorm roommate who was always in the room studying and his night shift job at the gas station. Sandia was starting to get needy, demanding, and wanting to go out on actual dates, to get to know Dell's friends. She suggested that they meet after he got off work at eleven o'clock they could go out for a few drinks, do some dancing—the clubs were open until one o'clock, some even had BYOB afterhours. Dell insisted that after work he was exhausted that he got up early to study. He was successful at putting Sandia off for a couple of more weeks, then she started to get impatiently suspicious.

Ω

One day after Dell left her apartment; she snuck out into the parking lot planning to follow him to make sure he was going straight to work. Dell, certain that he had everything in control, never considered his lies were about to be revealed. He headed home as usual to change into his work clothes, grab a bite to eat, and the late night snack that Dorothy always had packed for him. Dell never noticed Sandia's car following him; she pulled over when he turned down a residential street just past the railroad tracks. From inside her car she watched him park on the street in front of a small house. As Dell got out of the truck, Linda ran out of the front screen door with two of the nursery school kids right behind her. Dorothy stepped out on the porch to call the kids back inside as Linda ran into the yard calling "Daddy," just as Sandia pulled her car up across the street.

Sandia quickly took in the scene and started screaming curses at Dell in Spanish. The other two kids ran back into the house, Linda stood frozen in the yard a few feet from Dell. Next door, the neighbors, Dwight and Viola Harkins, were gardening in their yard they followed the screaming to see what was going on next door. After a few more Spanish epithets, Sandia put her car in gear screeching away down the street.

Dell was humiliated, furious that his secret was out, realizing that Linda having called him "Daddy" left no room for any possible excuses. He strode toward

Linda while taking off his belt, when he reached his three-year-old daughter he struck her across the chest and belly with his heavy leather strap. Linda dropped to the ground and curled up while Dell continued to deliver whipping lashes to her back and legs He didn't say a word as he hit Linda a half a dozen times, not caring where the stinging leather landed.

Viola and Dwight ran out of their yard yelling at Dell to stop—Dorothy finally came off the porch when she saw the two neighbors intervening. Dell had his arm raised to strike another blow when Dorothy screamed "Dell stop right now, that's enough."

Dell looked up, his face contorted into a rage; he saw Dwight and Viola running toward him. Viola reached Linda first, scooping her up from the ground.

Dwight said, "Man what are you thinking, you can't do that to a little girl."

Dell still in a rage stepped threateningly toward Dwight and said, "Mind your own god damn business." He turned away walked to the house bushing roughly passed Dorothy as she went to take Linda from Viola.

Viola said, "Why don't I take her to my house for a while, you have the other kids in the house, they shouldn't be in there alone with him."

"You're right the parents will be coming soon to pick them up. Thanks I'll come get Linda after Dell leaves for work."

Viola added, "I speak Spanish I can tell you what she was screaming about when you come to get Linda."

Linda hadn't made a sound during the whole ordeal she clung to Viola for dear life as they walked across the yard going into the Harkins' house.

By the time Dorothy was back inside Dell had changed his clothes was grabbing his packed dinner. "Don't say a word." Dell hissed he walked out slamming the door as he left.

Dorothy turned her attention to the three children that were cowering in the corner of the dining room. "How about some ice cream cones for everyone?" Dorothy herded the kids into the kitchen and quickly got ice cream cones in their hands.

"Was Linda a bad girl?" Asked the oldest of the three preschoolers

"Yes she was going to run into the street. Now eat your treat before your Moms come to pick you up."

Within the next hour, all three children were picked up. Dorothy could only imagine the stories they were telling their parents about Linda's belt beating. She'd be lucky if any of the kids came back tomorrow.

Dorothy poured herself a double rum and Coke drank it while she refreshed her make-up—only then did she make her way next door to check on Linda and get the low-down on the Spanish tirade that was undoubtedly a bad break-up between Dell's Mexican girl who had followed him home.

$$\Omega$$

Viola took Linda into the bathroom ran warm water into the tub. She took off her little sundress trying not to irritate the red, raised welts on her body. Linda was muddy because she had wet herself while curled up in the dusty yard. Once Linda climbed into the tub, Viola gently washed her with a soft washcloth. One of the worst of the lashings was across Linda's chest, stomach, and her back and legs hadn't fared much better. Through it all Linda had not made a sound she seemed to Viola to be in a trance or in shock. She was compliant but unresponsive—Linda was there but she was not there.

Viola dabbed Linda dry and put a clean T-shirt of her five-year-old son's on her, it would cover her angry red and swelling welts. She took Linda to the living room and gave her a glass of apple juice that Linda sipped on in silence.

Dorothy arrived a few minutes later briefly checked on Linda who was watching cartoons with Viola's son Danny. "Viola tell me what was going on—I barely saw the whole scene since I was inside the other kids."

"Linda hasn't made a sound not even a whimper since I brought her here. I think you should take her home put her to bed. Dell beat her badly, she's in shock."

"Yes of course, you said you understood Spanish, tell me what that crazy girl was saying." Dorothy was insistent.

"She called Dell a cheating son-of-a-bitch and told him to kiss her ass goodbye." Viola added, "I'd say whatever was going on between them didn't include her knowing he was married or had a family."

Dorothy claimed, "I've known that something was going on but didn't have any proof."

"Dorothy let this go, focus on Linda she needs your attention—she is hurting, I am sure that belt did a lot of damage. Take her home, give her some baby aspirin, and put her to bed."

"You're right thanks for taking her—the last thing I needed was for the parents of the other kids to catch wind of this—I need to keep the nursery school going."

Viola was stunned by Dorothy's lack of concern for Linda. "Stop worrying about everyone else, take care of your daughter." Viola's voice was sharp and adamant. She went to get Linda, carried her to Dorothy, then led them to the door. "Make sure you give her plenty of fluids and baby aspirin every four hours—she isn't reacting. I promise you she is hurting. She needs to sleep."

Dorothy was fighting back the impulse to take offense with Viola's tone of voice insinuating that she didn't know how to care for Linda. They said short brittle goodbyes. Dorothy carried her daughter across the yards into the house. She told Linda to go in to potty while Dorothy went to get some pajamas and baby aspirin. In the bathroom she removed the T-shirt, for the first time saw Linda's injuries. Dorothy was scared, what if Viola called someone to report this beating—Linda's condition was clearly wrong for a three-year-old child, the welts looked horrible, the worst of them were already turning into purple blue bruises.

Dorothy gave Linda the aspirin, a glass of apple juice laced with a dropper full of paregoric, and coaxed her into bed. She kissed her forehead telling her to go to sleep. Linda closed her tired eyes seeming almost to pass out.

Dorothy left the room closing the door behind her. She hoped that Linda was asleep until morning. She also hoped Dell wouldn't come home tonight. She didn't care if he went to try to patch things up with his Mexican girlfriend. At this point, all Dorothy cared about was having a couple of cigarettes, with a strong rum and Coke or two. Dorothy drank until she fell asleep on the sofa in front of the television she woke up at four o'clock in the morning when Dell came sneaking into the house, she pretended to stay asleep.

Dell took a shower and was dressed for classes sneaking out as he had come in. He went to the college coffee shop to get some breakfast, to nurse his hangover. After work he'd spent several hours at "Guys and Dolls" strip club drank a lot of beer. While he slurped his coffee Dell considered how he'd have to make sure to avoid Sandia for the time being—that meant either going home as soon as he finished with classes or finding somewhere to spend early afternoons where she would be unlikely to run into him. He decided that he'd never seen her in the library studying, that's where he'd hide out. As Dell mulled his situation, he blamed Linda for running out into the yard. If she hadn't called him "Daddy" he could have talked his way out of the confrontation. As he thought about it, he decided that Linda did deserve the beating; after all, he had been beat with his father's belt for years for causing fewer problems than Linda had created for him.

Ω

Linda woke up the next morning but lay in bed afraid to get up—her bedroom door was closed in her child's mind, she felt like she was locked out of the house. She heard the other kids show up, heard Dorothy talking to their parents as they dropped off the children. Linda had been awake for almost an hour before Dorothy came into her room with some more juice and baby aspirin. Linda drank the juice took the aspirin without a word. Dorothy raised the bedroom window shade then she pulled out some long pants with a long sleeved t-shirt for Linda to wear, then helped her get dressed.

Dorothy noted that the belt marks had turned into deep bruises overnight and cursed Dell under her breath "Damn him."

Linda went out of the room, going into the kitchen to have a bowl of cereal with her nursery school friends. She ate quietly, when they had all finished their breakfast, they went into the living room to watch morning cartoon shows, while Dorothy did her household chores. Dorothy had decided that since Linda wasn't talking she'd leave the incident alone. She never said anything to Linda about being beaten. When Dell came home at two o'clock to change for work both of them acted as if nothing had happened the day before. Linda hid in her room while Dell was home—closing her own door. She could feel safe isolating herself, she wouldn't be a "bad" girl again when her Daddy was home.

Linda became an extremely introverted child—she listened to everything from an ever-growing instinct of hypervigilance, rarely spoke unless she had to respond to meet her basic needs. For the rest of the summer into the fall even Dorothy believed that Linda was a star example of a well-behaved child.

Ω

As was typical of Dell and Dorothy's relationship they made a tacit deal in their own best interests—the girlfriend was never mentioned—Dorothy never felt any jealousy unless her sense of material security was threatened. With her silence about the beating hanging over Dell's head, she had him caught in a trap once again.

Ω

Linda turned four years old in October. She was a beautiful, quiet, obedient child. She had her nursery school playmates except for Georgie who had started Kindergarten. A birthday party in Ajo with both sets of doting grandparents seemed to draw her out of her shell for the day she was delighted to sit on all four grandparents laps opening her presents. It was a good day for Linda she didn't have very many to remember.

One of Linda's presents was a bright red princess-style dress that Lenore had made for her. Dorothy had purchased an Olan Mills photography package from a door-to-door salesman. She promised Lenore that she would have photos taken of Linda in her new dress.

Two weeks later back in Tempe, Dorothy fixed Linda's long hair in a curled ponytail even put a little make-up on her daughter. She dressed Linda in the red dress with a black patent belt, white lace socks, with shiny patent Mary Jane shoes. They headed to the photography studio in downtown Tempe. Of course Dorothy also dressed herself in a favorite photogenic outfit—a low-cut red sweater, black sheath skirt, and patent high heels. She did her own hair and make-up to perfection, she looked like a model when the two of them walked into the studio.

The photographic portraits turned out beautifully—although in spite of the photographer's urging, none of the photos were of Dorothy and Linda together as mother and daughter. Linda was posed precociously at Dorothy's insistence and photographed alone. Dorothy requested sexy glamour shots for herself.

The pictures were ready in three weeks, when Dorothy went to pick them up, she was surprised to find a large picture of Linda posted in the store. She was incensed that her own photographs had not also been chosen to advertise the Olan Mills outlet. Dorothy hid her frustration. The studio manager explained that the promotional package that Dorothy had purchased specifically allowed for commercial use of photos deemed as appropriate quality for display purposes. Dorothy left with the photos but in the car she angrily rescinded her promise to take Linda for ice cream. For Linda the best part of the day was seeing her picture in nearly life-size posted on the wall of the studio.

Dorothy went home promptly sent all but one 5x7 print of Linda, to Chester and Lenore, and to Daniel and Della Mae in Ajo. She had already purchased two frames for her own 8x10 portraits, she sent one to

Chester at the Mercantile Store, hung the other one in the dining room alongside a football photo of Dell.

Dorothy not only didn't get Linda any ice cream she gave her a glass of milk with a dropper full of paregoric then put her to bed without any dinner. Dorothy sat at the dining room table with her rum and Coke drinking and gazing at the pictures of herself and Dell hanging side-by-side. Dorothy poured herself another drink and uncharacteristically pondered why she was angry with Linda. She resented the attention her picture had received at Olan Mills, but was that it—no she couldn't imagine that she could be that petty. It was because of Linda that she was married to such a cheater like Dell. Yes, that was it—her unsatisfactory marriage was Linda's fault.

Dell and Dorothy could agree on two things— they were both willing to be disloyal to each other and they were both willing to cast four-year-old Linda as their mutual scapegoat.

$$\Omega$$

By Christmas 1957, Dell had one more semester before graduation. Dorothy had decided to get pregnant again. She of course had the timing down to the best day in her cycle. When she had sex with Dell on Christmas Eve, she had nearly guaranteed she would be announcing a pregnancy on their anniversary, the last day of January. Dell had no idea of his upcoming New Year's surprise.

When Dell and Dorothy got married Della Mae had made Dorothy promise not to get pregnant again for at least five years. Considering that the baby would be due around Linda's fifth birthday Dorothy figured she was meeting her promise. She also didn't want Dell getting any ideas of leaving her once he had graduated. The new pregnancy was her way of securing the relationship. She also believed that if they had a son, she would bond the marriage permanently. Dorothy did not care about the fidelity of the marriage from either Dell or herself. Appearances—material security meant everything to her.

On January 31, Dell and Dorothy's fifth anniversary, she announced to the family in a gathering in Ajo that she was expecting. The response was mixed—Dorothy had not even given Dell a heads up privately, the grandparents seemed happy but personally concerned. Dorothy managed to force a public kiss and hug from Dell in front of everyone, in her estimation the announcement was a success.

Privately Dorothy was relieved to be pregnant because she would curtail any sexual relationship with Dell—he still had a bad habit of trying to force his rough, and in her mind perverted, preferences on Dorothy. Pregnancy was as good an excuse as any just to say "no." Dell took the announcement in stride; he knew he would still have plenty of opportunity for casual sexual encounters with a couple of the dancers at "Guys and Dolls."

Graduation in May stalled because Dell was missing one credit hour in a required course for his B.A. in Business Administration, during the summer he would have to take a three-credit course in business law in order to graduate. Instead of getting in on the May and June job hunt, he had to work another summer at the gas station. Most nights after working Dell went across the street with his workmate Kenny to have a few beers and ogle the girls. Dell often made a private visit to the parking lot with one of his favorites.

Dorothy at home with Linda, often as not was asleep for at least four to five hours before Dell arrived home, sneaking into the house. Dorothy had discontinued the nursery school as her pregnancy progressed, finding herself more easily exhausted than during her first pregnancy.

Dorothy was in her seventh month when Linda came down with the German measles. Linda had to be quarantined from her mother. The neighbor, Viola Harkins took Linda during the day to keep the sick child away from her mother. Dorothy's doctor had insisted that Linda had to be kept away from her mother, because German measles posed a significant threat to the pregnancy and the baby.

At night, Linda slept upstairs in the small attic space on a padded cot while she was ill. It was as far from Dorothy as they could figure out in the small two-bedroom house. On the fourth day Linda's rash was beginning to fade, her temperature was normal, she was starting to feel better. When Viola brought Linda home at six o'clock she asked Dorothy if Linda still needed to be in the attic—Dorothy who had isolated herself in her bedroom told Viola that Linda should still sleep upstairs for a couple of more nights just to make sure she wasn't contagious anymore. Viola got Linda settled in the attic with her dinner then put her to bed. Linda had been sleeping a lot, by the time Viola left at seven o'clock she was sound asleep on her cot.

That night Dell and Kenny spent a couple of hours at "Guys and Dolls." Dell missed his usual parking lot connection. He drove home drunk after sharing tequila shots and beers with Kenny. It was one o'clock in the morning when Dell arrived home. When he came into the house he was greeted by Dorothy's loud snoring, as well as Linda's plaintive crying from upstairs. He quietly closed the door to the bedroom where Dorothy's bulging pregnant body lay snoring away—with his drunken sexual frustrations he walked toward the kitchen up the attic stairway.

Linda's whining was turning to wails as she heard the attic stairs creak. "Mommy. Mommy" Linda called out.

"Your Mommy isn't coming and I want you to shut up and go back to sleep." Dell hissed at Linda.

His tone terrified Linda, she couldn't help herself "I want my mommy" she sobbed.

"I'll give you something to cry about if you don't stop right now." Dell noticed that the streetlight was shining through the small attic window as he was making the fateful decision, thinking drunkenly about what he wanted to do. He slowly staggered to the window pulled down the rolling shade. The attic became as dark as a moonless night.

Linda was quiet as a silent terror overtook her four-year-old mind and body. She couldn't see Dell, though sensed that he was getting closer. The floor at the end of the cot squeaked as Dell came upon her. He undid his belt and pants, then grabbed Linda like a rag doll flopping her onto her stomach on the cot. As he pulled off her pajama bottoms, Linda's mind took her up away to the highest corner of the attic ceiling—she floated above the dark scene below dreaming she was holding a flying stuffed toy rabbit that she slept with. She was away from her body as she watched Dell move toward her from behind. She watched him move against her, grunting like an animal, then she heard him moan as he raised himself off the cot. Dell pulled up Linda's pajamas turned her limp body on to her back. He cursed her as he noticed she had wet and soiled the sheets on the cot.

A minute later from her mind's perch on high she heard the attic stairs creak. Linda suddenly felt herself falling, falling, and falling. When she stopped falling she was back in her urine soaked, soiled bed. Her bottom and her belly felt on fire. She was awake—she didn't dare make a sound. She clutched her stuffed rabbit, closed her eyes tight. Her small body began to shake as her little heart pounded in her chest. She was terrified, though still wouldn't allow herself to cry out. Linda was breathing in fast shallow breaths after a couple of minutes of hyperventilating; Linda fainted from panic, pain, and shock.

The next morning Viola called Dorothy to say she would be a little late to get Linda—Dorothy finally decided that Linda was not a threat to her or the baby, she told Viola that she'd take care of Linda. About half an hour later Dorothy made her way up the attic stairs, she planned to get Linda back into her bedroom, so that she wouldn't have to negotiate the stairs again with her belly making the passage on the narrow stairway so arduous.

When Dorothy reached the attic, she smelled the soiled sheets. She went across the room to raise the shade in order to see what kind of mess Linda had made. As light entered the room, Dorothy saw Linda curled in a fetal position at the top of the cot. The bottom half was a mess of urine, feces, and blood. Linda's pajama bottoms were also stained and Linda was glassy eyed and trembling.

Dorothy rushed to the cot asking Linda "What happened?"

Linda closed her eyes said one word. "Daddy"

Dorothy started gathering the soiled and bloody sheets—when she started to take off Linda's pajamas, she shrieked in pain.

Dorothy told Linda "Be quiet. I need to get these messy clothes off of you."

Linda fell silent with fear in her eyes.

Dorothy then had her daughter follow her down the attic stairs to the bathroom. Dorothy began running warm water into the tub as she helped Linda into the bath, she could see that Linda was freshly bleeding again from her bottom.

Dorothy turned off the water with about four inches in the tub told Linda to sit still, she handed her a washcloth saying, "Get clean I'll be right back."

Dorothy made her way back upstairs gathered all the soiled sheets and clothes, took them downstairs out on to the back porch where she stuffed everything into the wringer washer. She added soap with bleach, filled the washer from the hose, started it up.

The whole time she was cleaning up the mess Dorothy was thinking about two things, the one time that Dell had tried to force himself on her from behind—and Linda's only spoken word "Daddy"

Dorothy went back into the bathroom began washing Linda's back with the washcloth. "You must have had a bad dream last night since you've been sick."

Linda looked at her mother with blank eyes.

Dorothy said, "You'll be back in your room tonight, if you have any more bad dreams I'll come and make them go away."

Linda sat perfectly still in the blood-streaked tub water feeling the softness of the wet cloth on her back. She said, "I'm sleepy."

Dorothy said, "Okay let's get you into some clean pajamas, back into your real bed."

Linda stood as still as a statue as Dorothy dried her with a bath towel—the bleeding seemed to have stopped. Dorothy was relieved; she couldn't imagine having to explain this to a doctor.

Dorothy got Linda settled into her downstairs bedroom gave her two baby aspirin and a glass of milk laced heavily with paregoric. Linda was compliantly silent falling asleep with her rabbit almost immediately.

It was ten o'clock when Dorothy went out to check on the washer. She drained the soapy water rinsed the clothes with the hose then filled the washer for the final rinse. As she turned to go back into the house, she saw Linda's soiled and bloody underwear on the floor under a kitchen chair. She picked them up started back out to the porch to put them in the washer. After a couple of steps she stopped to think—the underwear proved what Dell had done to Linda maybe she should keep them hidden, kept somewhere safe. Dorothy never knew when she might need something to use against him. Dorothy put the underwear in a small brown paper bag then walked to the corner of the dining room. She used a butter knife to raise a small piece of the wooden floor. Inside she had an envelope of money that she'd been hiding away she added the paper bag. She put the floorboard back in place deciding it was time for a rum and Coke and a cigarette—it was almost time for one of her soap operas to come on the television.

    Dorothy drank her rum and Coke slowly since she was pregnant she'd cut back on smoking but still had a few drinks every day, a couple during her shows and a few in the evenings before bed. She thought about what to do about Linda, so far she seemed to be scared into silence. How long would that last? Dorothy would have to cut back on the time that Linda spent with Viola, which would be a real inconvenience. At least for a few weeks she would have to keep Linda under close watch to make sure she wasn't going to blurt out what had happened in the attic.

    When Dell got home after class at two o'clock in the afternoon Dorothy was already on her third rum and Coke. She had decided to tell Dell about the mess she found with Linda in the attic, not what she knew was the cause. Let him worry about whether he had dodged a bullet or not. Making him sweat for a few days was the least she could do for Linda's pain and suffering. Dorothy had also decided as she drank away the afternoon that she needed to cut off Linda's waist length dark brown hair. Dorothy had concluded that between the photographic incident and the latest issue with Dell that maybe Linda was just too pretty for her own good. Cutting off all her hair would change Linda's appearance a great deal; it would be easier to take care of when Linda went to school in the fall. Yes, cutting off Linda's hair would be a step in the right direction—a correction for an unspeakable problem. Dorothy felt she had solved the dilemma before Dell left to go to work at the gas station.

Dorothy got up from her chair it was seven o'clock—she staggered a bit, blamed it on the imbalance of her big belly—she was going to have one more rum and Coke and another cigarette before going to bed. She first went to check on Linda and found her curled up tightly around her rabbit and pillow, all three a little pile under the sheets. She would sleep through the night that's why paregoric was worth having.

Dorothy returned to the task of pouring her last rum and Coke….

8

"...I the Lord your God am a jealous God visiting the iniquity of the fathers on the children...."
Exodus, 20:5

Linda started school in September 1958. She began Kindergarten at age four but would turn five in October. Dorothy was eight-months pregnant, spent most of her time in bed—not for any reason other than she was tired of being pregnant. Martin Dean Moore, a healthy son, was born on October 1, 1958 and he weighed in at 7-pounds 9-ounces a full pound more than Linda had weighed at birth. Dorothy was fully sedated during her labor, which was typical of giving birth at that time. Dorothy awoke to Dell's beaming smile as he declared that he had a son.

The relationship between Dell and Dorothy had taken another important step forward; Dell graduated from college and was out job hunting. His first job out of school was for Electrolux Vacuum Cleaners, he sold them door to door. He worked commission only during the days, still working at the gas station at night. Dell got smarter at cheating. He figured out how to make his sales commissions pay-off big. Three out of four of his vacuum sales that summer included long afternoons with the housewives to whom he had sold his charms as well as his product. Unfortunately, Dell didn't like cold calling door to door even with the added benefits of bedding some of his customers.

Dorothy wanted to believe that the birth of a son would change Dell's philandering habits. She thought that he didn't have the temptation of college coeds around all the time that he would settle down—all she hoped for was that he could quit the gas station and not work across the street from a strip club.

Dell had also applied for a position with Allstate Insurance Company. The hiring process was arduous including multiple meetings, along with the requirement that he go to school on the weekends to get his insurance sales credentials before he could be considered. Dell had done his research, selling a product like insurance, which in the case of auto insurance was mandated by law and homeowner's insurance that was the responsibility of every homeowner, made perfect sense to him. Selling a product that the law forced people to purchase was the kind of product he was sure he could be successful selling.

During the time after her brother's birth Linda experienced a difficult period coming to terms with another child in the house. She shared her room with her new baby brother as well as sharing her mother. Because of the stress, Linda wasn't sleeping well she was plagued by nightmares that resulted in her waking up in urine soaked sheets. Dorothy, of course, was tired so she, more often than not, took her frustration out on Linda, especially with the bed-wetting. Linda was becoming very insecure yet she had no one to turn to—her mother was very absorbed with Martin so except for being chastised each morning Linda got little attention.

In school Linda was having a hard time staying awake; in early November she drew a depiction of her frequent nightmares. Her nightmares were of the attack by Dell during the summer. Linda did her best to draw with stick figures what had occurred—using many black and red crayons, she illustrated the attack while up on the ceiling a wild-eyed fearful face watched what was happening below.

Linda's teacher already concerned with her student falling asleep in class, with the dark circles under her eyes, took the picture to the school psychologist. After seeing the drawing, the woman counselor decided to talk to Linda about the picture. During her attempted conversation with Linda, she found out that Linda was not only exhausted; she was also quite scared of her parents. The counselor decided to contact Linda's parents to see if they knew of their daughter's distress. A meeting was arranged for the next week.

Dorothy was nervous and Dell was agitated claiming he didn't have time for a meeting about Kindergarten. Dell's concerns of course went deeper—he was afraid that Linda had said something that made someone at the school suspicious about him. He knew she hadn't been right since the night he had come home drunk. He had been trying to believe that she didn't remember that the shock had driven the "incident" from her mind. Linda had a blank empty look anytime she was around Dell, which with him working day and night wasn't often. Since Dorothy had chopped off all of her long hair Linda looked like a scared little boy—Dell hated her, deep inside, he also feared her.

The meeting at Linda's school proved to be a fateful day for her. Dorothy whined about all the work of having a new baby to care for, insisting that Linda's biggest problem sleeping was a result of reverting to wetting the bed. Dell was both aggressive and dismissive, "It's ridiculous for me to take time off from work for a child's awful picture, the most I can tell from looking at it is she has no artistic talent—I resent your insinuating yourself into our family's business."

The counselor tried to overcome his attitude by suggesting that if Linda was having problems with sleeping and bed-wetting that she should possibly see a doctor.

Dell had enough "I think the best thing for Linda is to take her out of school, she is obviously not ready for the stress of a day in the classroom. By law she doesn't have to attend Kindergarten." He grabbed Dorothy's hand and pulled her up from her chair. "Please bring Linda along—we will be taking her home."

The counselor saw the look of angry determination on Dell's face. She decided it would be useless to argue with such a bully who was used to getting his way. She said, "I think it is an over-reaction on your part to take Linda out of school, it is your choice as ill-considered as it may be."

Dell turned to Dorothy "You can get Linda, take her home, and I'm going back to work." With that he walked out of the office leaving Dorothy and the counselor with no option other than to pull Linda out of school.

On the way home Dorothy told Linda that she wasn't going to go to school until next year. Linda sobbed, cried, and begged to be allowed to stay in school. Dorothy said, "If you hadn't drawn that horrible picture, weren't wetting your bed all the time this wouldn't have happened, it's your own fault, stop whining and crying. Maybe you'll understand only big girls who don't wet their beds get to go to school."

Dorothy's cruelty drove the tears from Linda's eyes she became like a little statue sitting in the front seat of the car. Dorothy said, "I have to go in and get Martin from Viola you better not be crying again when I get back."

$$\Omega$$

By December 1, Allstate Insurance Company had hired Dell. The family moved from the little house on the wrong side of the tracks to a red brick three-bedroom rental house in Southeast Phoenix, on the corner of 40th Street and Van Buren.

Martin was two months old he still was waking up at night. Linda had her own room; she slept with the door closed by her own choice. Now that someone wasn't coming into her room at night, she was sleeping through until morning. She had stopped wetting the bed. She still had occasional nightmares but had a night-light in her room, which gave her the necessary comfort to fall back to sleep.

For Linda the worst thing was that she couldn't go to school. She had learned her alphabet and a couple of months of phonics. One day alone in her room she discovered that she could figure out how to read a couple of books that she had gotten as gifts for her birthday. Linda was in the living room with her books and Martin was in his baby swing. Linda began to read the storybooks aloud to her baby brother. Dorothy came into the room behind Linda, stood listening to her as she read the story of Snow White— Linda was reading word for word, struggling occasionally, but she read very well.

Dorothy said sharply, "What are you doing?"

Linda jumped, startled by her mother's voice. "I'm reading to baby Martin."

"How did you learn to read?" Dorothy questioned.

"From school and my books." Linda started to get nervous as if she had done something wrong.

"Don't you dare let your daddy hear you reading." Dorothy scolded, "He'll be mad."

Linda slammed the book closed ran into her room closing the door behind her. She hid her two books under the bed, then she laid down falling into a deep immediate sleep.

Dorothy checked on Linda before dinnertime found her sound asleep in her clothes—she closed the door. Linda went without dinner that night, Dorothy had another rum and Coke before Dell came home.

Ω

Dell's job at Allstate, began at Sears and Roebucks, in a small sales booth in the middle of the Sears store at Papago Plaza Mall, in Scottsdale; a fast growing suburb of Phoenix. He worked the booth from nine to five making appointments with potential clients at their homes in the evenings. Dorothy had to have dinner ready at six o'clock in order for Dell to eat before leaving for scheduled appointments by seven. At least three or four nights per week, Dell didn't return home until ten or ten-thirty. His efforts were paying off. The majority of the clients he met with in their homes succumbed not only to Dell's sales skills with auto and homeowners' insurance; but he would manage to sell many of them life insurance as well. Dell's commission on life insurance was the highest of all. Dell was doing fine and making good money—sales were his definite forte, he had found his career niche.

Dorothy was home alone, it didn't bother her much—she always put the kids to bed early and drank enough rum and Coke to be asleep before Dell came home.

Ω

Christmas 1958, was spent in Ajo with Daniel and Della Mae. Dorothy took Linda into town to see Santa in the central plaza then the two of them went to visit with Chester and Lenore. Dorothy was shocked to see how thin and wan Lenore was. Chester took Dorothy aside and explained that Lenore was sick again, this time it was bone cancer. The prognosis wasn't good. The doctors had said that Lenore maybe had a year to live. The doctors were treating her pain. She had refused to have radiation treatments again. When Lenore and Linda came in from outside, Lenore knew that Chester had told Dorothy how sick she was. They embraced and Lenore made Dorothy promise to bring Linda to Ajo as often as she could. Dorothy was teary-eyed as she left with Linda to go back to Daniel and Della Mae's house. She knew it wasn't likely that she'd see Lenore alive again.

Ω

In February, Linda got a bad sore throat and stopped eating, only willing to drink milk and cold juice—she was running a fever. Dorothy began plying her with baby aspirin and paregoric. After three weeks, Linda was not getting any better and was losing weight. At the end of February, Dorothy took Linda to the doctor that she knew Dell had gone to when he was in college, Dr. William Payne. When Dorothy told Linda that she was going to see Dr. Payne Linda ran to her room slamming the door. Dorothy had to drag Linda kicking and fighting to go to the doctor. Their neighbor Kay Harmon was taking care of Martin she saw the whole ugly scene of getting Linda into the car. Linda cried all the way to the office of Dr. Payne. Linda was terrified of going to the doctor. She was feeling quite awful, and was going to see someone named "pain." Linda thought for sure she was being punished. The doctor's visit was a nightmare for Linda. The diagnosis was upsetting for Dorothy—Linda had severe tonsillitis, would need a shot of penicillin, as well as a prescription to take for two weeks.

Dr. Payne told Dorothy that once the acute infection was cleared up that he wanted to do a tonsillectomy. He would schedule it for next month. Linda heard all the words spoken between her mother and the doctor; she of course, didn't understand at all what was in her future. All she knew was that a nurse came in to give her a big shot in the bottom. Linda could not cry out because her throat hurt and her voice was nearly gone.

Dorothy took Linda home to put her to bed, Martin was sleeping already and Kay Harmon left to go home. Dorothy headed straight for the rum and Coke she'd been craving all morning. She was worried about the surgery because Linda was only five years old. Even though a tonsillectomy was common, it was not usual for such a young child. As she sipped her drink, she felt a pang of guilt for waiting so long to take Linda to the doctor. Fortunately, for Dorothy by the time she had finished her second drink the guilt had dissipated, she was thinking about how lucky they were to have such good insurance.

$$\Omega$$

On March 27, Dorothy got Linda up early in the morning dressed her in clean pajamas, told her she was going to a place called Good Samaritan for her tonsillectomy. Linda still had no idea what was going to happen. She didn't expect that it had anything to do with Dr. Payne since she no longer felt sick. Linda had the surgery at ten o'clock and was in recovery by eleven-thirty, the surgery went as expected Dr. Payne removed Linda's tonsils and adenoids, she was going to be sent home late in the afternoon.

Dorothy took Linda home to bed; she was still very groggy from the anesthetic. Kay Harmon had again stayed with Martin for the day. She helped Dorothy get both children settled in for the night. Kay and Dorothy both had a drink together at five o'clock, Kay left to go home shortly after. Dorothy expecting Dell home at any time had made a quick casserole for dinner. At six-thirty the phone rang and it was Dell calling to say he had appointments scheduled and wouldn't be home until late. Dorothy was relieved, it had been a long day, she planned to be asleep before Dell got home. Dell didn't ask about Linda's surgery and Dorothy didn't mention it. By nine o'clock Dorothy had several drinks with just a few bites of the casserole. She checked in on Linda who was still sleeping, changed Martin's diaper giving him a bottle to make sure he would sleep through the rest of the night. Dorothy then lay down on the sofa to watch television. She was soon passed out, snoring away.

Dell had lied to Dorothy; he had sold auto insurance to his friend and former workmate at the gas station Kenny. The two of them had agreed to a reunion evening at the "Guys and Dolls" club. Kenny was still working at the gas station. He closed up early, he and Dell met at the club at eight o'clock. They started drinking beer, tequila shots, and danced with the girls they knew there. At one point they both went out into the parking lot to their cars to get "lucky" with a couple of the strippers. Dell and Kenny parted company at midnight and Dell drove home slowly because he was very drunk from all the tequila shots he'd had.

When Dell finally arrived home, he entered the house as quietly as he could manage in his condition. Dorothy was still fast asleep on the sofa. Dell looked down the hallway hearing Linda whining and moaning from her room. He didn't want her to wake up Dorothy, he went to her room hissing at her, "Shut up."

Linda was scared when she saw her daddy standing in the doorway, in spite of herself, she let out a weak squeaky cry. In three steps Dell was at the bed grabbed Linda around the throat, "I told you to shut up. I can make you be quiet."

Suddenly from the pressure of Dell's hands on Linda's neck, blood started pouring from her mouth. She began gagging and choking on the bloody flow from broken stitches in her throat. Dell grasped her throat harder to try to stop the bloody mess. Linda's body began to shake and twist. Dell felt the sheets go wet as Linda lost control of her bladder and bowels. Dorothy woke up, ran into the room just as Dell released his grip on Linda's throat. He jumped up to avoid the mess on the bed sheets. Blood was everywhere as Linda's throat continued to bleed. Dorothy screamed, pushed Dell aside. She picked Linda up along with the messy sheets. "Go start the car we have to get her to the hospital" Dorothy shrieked.

Dell, scared sober, ran out of the room. Dorothy heard the door slam as he went out to the car. Dorothy carried Linda putting her in the backseat—still bleeding profusely. She ran back into the house grabbed Martin out of his crib. Dorothy ran back out to the car. "Go to Good Samaritan." She commanded Dell, without a word he began the race to the hospital. Linda lay in the back seat choking and coughing up blood. Dorothy held Martin on her lap; as Dell drove, he tried to cover for what had happened. "I went in to check on Linda when I got home—she was bleeding when I found her I grabbed her throat to try to stop the bleeding, she got scared and started to thrash around."

Dorothy not believing a word of what Dell said answered calmly "Okay that's how you will try to explain this whole mess when we get to the emergency room." She added, "I'm going to tell them that I was asleep so I don't have anything to add until you woke me up."

Dell looked across the car seat at Dorothy in shock, she was willing to let him hang alone on this, he couldn't believe that she wasn't going to back up his story. Stopped at a light Dell glanced into the back seat at Linda who was unconscious with blood clotting around her mouth and face. The car smelled of urine, feces, and blood. He couldn't believe this was happening to him. The trip to the hospital was a bad idea, Linda was probably dead or dying they should have just called an ambulance—had them find her at home in bed. He'd have an easier way to explain that he came home found her already gone.

Dorothy was scared for herself more than for Linda. Would the hospital believe their story? Dorothy wasn't sure of what had actually happened but she knew of Dell's rage toward Linda, this wasn't by any count the first time he had hurt her. Was this an attack trying to take advantage of her vulnerable state after surgery, or was it an accident? She knew Dell was drunk when she found him, he smelled like cheap perfume. What would she say if the doctors and nurses didn't buy the story Dell was about to put forward. Who would believe him he still smelled of tequila and beer. Dorothy wondered if Linda was going to survive as she clung even tighter to Martin who was silently awake in her arms.

At Good Samaritan Emergency Entrance Dell carried Linda into the hospital calling out, "Help I need some help." The nurses seeing the bloody child in his arms immediately responded. They took Linda from Dell getting her to a room where a doctor began to examine her. Dell and Dorothy stood outside the room, Dell started telling his story to the nurse who had taken Linda from him. "I came home late she had a tonsillectomy this morning. I went into check on her. I found her bleeding and thrashing about in her bed."

The doctor working on Linda overheard the story, told Dell and Dorothy to go to the waiting room until he had finished his examination. Dell tried to argue but the doctor ordered him out. Dell and Dorothy, still clutching Martin, went silently to the waiting room.

Dell's hands were shaking and bloody—Dorothy had blood on her clothes, even Martin had blood on his pajamas. A nurse came out of the exam room with papers to authorize Linda's return to surgery. The stitches in Linda's throat had somehow burst apart they would need to re-stitch her surgical wounds. Dorothy signed while Dell sat silent. The nurse left, the wait began. Dell did realize what a mess he was, he went to the bathroom to wash up a bit. He couldn't stop shaking; nothing was going to stop his attack of nerves until he felt as if he was in the clear.

Linda was in surgery for an hour and a half. The doctor came out telling Dell and Dorothy that Linda was sedated during surgery. The tonsillectomy had been repaired they could see her in about an hour. The doctor said, "Your daughter will be staying here for a few days to make sure there are no more problems. We need to make certain she doesn't get an infection or pneumonia." He turned to Dell questioning him "Linda has significant bruising on her throat, clear finger and hand prints. Can you explain that to me?"

Dell spoke for the first time in a couple of hours; he tried to force his voice to sound calm. He knew was failing. "When I saw the blood all I could think of was to try and stop the bleeding, I put my hands around her throat—I just wanted the bleeding to stop." He added for effect.

The doctor shook his head sternly, "Your efforts weren't at all helpful; you almost strangled your daughter." He continued, "Her voice-box and thyroid gland are badly bruised, your ill-advised impulse probably caused more of the stitches to fail, in fact, from what I could see they all seemed to fail from pressure being applied to the wounds. You're lucky that she's alive and that I'm talking to you not the police." The doctor turned to Dorothy, "Why didn't Linda spend the night in the hospital instead of going home right after surgery?"

Dorothy answered, "Dr. Payne said she was fine that I could take her home."

The doctor shook his head "It is very serious surgery for a five year old to have general anesthetic and a tonsillectomy—she should have spent a couple of days here to make sure there were no complications. I suggest you get a new doctor for Linda in the future." He turned to walk away then turned back to Dell. "Your daughter almost died tonight I believe you need to know and to think about that." The doctor left Dell and Dorothy standing speechless.

Ω

Dorothy looked Dell in the eyes as she stood holding his son. She knew deep down that he had hurt Linda on purpose—again another victim of one of his tequila-driven rages. She also knew she had yet something else to hold over him. Dorothy knew that Linda had nearly died. She didn't want to allow herself to believe that he had tried to kill her, but it was the only explanation. He looked angrily away from her gaze, she held Martin a little tighter. Dorothy knew that having a son meant a lot to Dell. She'd have to protect Martin with all her being. Dorothy might not be able to protect Linda from Dell—she knew that he hated her. Martin would not end up in the same situation; Martin would be the bond between them. Dell had a good job and Dorothy's plan for her life was becoming a reality; she was determined to see it through.

Ω

Dell never made another appearance at Good Samaritan Hospital. He told Dorothy that they would never go to that hospital again. Dell understood all too well that Dorothy had a level of power in the relationship that he could have never imagined. He had at one time dreamed of divorcing her after he had finished school, landing his job. Now she held his secrets about Linda. From the very beginning that kid had been a thorn in his side. Her existence had changed the very arc of his life—and he had a son, two kids to deal with. He didn't want to be married let alone have kids. Martin was something he could someday be proud of, at least when he stopped shitting his pants and drooling all the time. Yes, he would raise his boy but as for Linda, his hatred was too deep—it didn't matter to him that she was a child; she had ruined his dreams, he would always be her worst nightmare.

Ω

In the fall of 1959, Linda again started school again. Her hair had grown back to shoulder length, on the first day she wore a turquoise squaw dress with shiny silver zigzag trim matching a silver and turquoise Concho belt. Her grandmother Lenore had sent it to her for a special back to school present. Linda loved the dress with its full skirt and beautiful belt. Her first day of school was a wonder for Linda. Her first grade classroom at Baltz School was bright, sunny with big windows along one whole wall of the room. Her teacher Mrs. Yates was a kindly matron with a quick smile that made Linda comfortable. By the end of the first week Mrs. Yates had discovered that Linda was reading far beyond the first grade level. She moved Linda to the top of the reading program where she would be reading from chapter books while the majority of the other students learned to read from the "Fun with Dick and Jane" readers. Linda was progressing well due to her advanced reading skills she took to writing like a fish to water. Soon she was writing book reports on her own without being assigned to and was doing well in math also. Linda loved school finally she had a place where she felt safe not lonely.

At the end of September, Linda was walking the three blocks home from school as she did every day. Her path took her alongside the banks of a large usually dry canal bed. Suddenly she heard a voice calling from over the edge of the canal. "Hey you up there I need help. I've fallen, I'm stuck in some roots, I think my leg is broken."

Linda went as close to the edge as she dared. "I'm just a little girl in first grade I can't help you."

"Go home and tell your mamma that an old man is stuck in the canal, hurry run on home and tell her."

Linda started to run as fast as her legs would carry her in a few minutes, she burst through the front door of her house yelling, "Mommy an old man fell in the canal and broke his leg." Linda rushed into her mother's bedroom, found her mother hurriedly zipping her skirt while Eddie Harmon, Kay Harmon's husband, was awkwardly trying to button his shirt while pulling up his pants at the same time.

"Linda Dell how dare you run into this house screaming like a wild animal, get outside in the backyard don't come in until I say you can." Dorothy scolded.

Terrified and upset Linda ran out to the backyard, a dusty fenced-in patch of ground without a sliver of shade. Linda began pacing along the fence worrying about the old man in the canal. A garbage truck turned the corner lumbering down the alley toward the house. Linda climbed up on the fence near the gate where the trash bins were. She waved at the truck as it came to a stop. Linda began to yell out to the black man who was driving the truck. He turned off the engine to hear what the scared-looking child was upset about; Linda told the driver in her most earnest voice that a man was stuck in the canal with a broken leg, that he had told her to go get help. The man at first shook his head in disbelief, then he saw tears start to run down Linda's face—"Clem come on get on the truck we've got to go check for a man stuck in the canal. The driver's partner jumped up on the back of the truck and the driver started the engine he waved to Linda as he drove out of the alleyway heading toward the canal.

Linda was exhausted she found the only small spot of shade in the yard next to the house, curled up, fell asleep. Dorothy came looking for her about an hour later waking Linda up with a continuation of the harangue that had started when Linda came home. Linda was confused, exhausted so she simply followed her mother into the house went to her room, again falling asleep. It was another night without dinner for Linda.

School turned out to be the best aspect of Linda's life. She excelled, got perfect grades, and notes about her excellent behavior. Baby Martin was a toddler, becoming the apple of his parents' eyes. Linda's academic achievements went unnoticed Linda didn't mind, she also enjoyed the peace and quiet that anonymity provided in her family.

The holidays were spent in Ajo visiting the grandparents and friends from high school. Their grandparents doted on both of the children; however, it seemed that Linda was more attached to Chester and Lenore. Martin was clearly the favorite of Daniel and Della Mae. The time Linda spent with Lenore that holiday season would be the last time they would be together Lenore's illness only left her with weeks to live. Dorothy spent more time than usual with Lenore during Christmas that year knowing the end was coming soon.

Ω

By New Year's Eve Dell and Dorothy were back in Phoenix with plans for an Allstate company-sponsored party. Dorothy was excited to be going, she had bought beautiful black velvet deep V-neck sheath cocktail dress for the occasion. Dorothy had arranged for Patsy Gonzales a young college student originally from Ajo to babysit for the night. Dell was going to pick her up around eight o'clock. At the last minute Dell told Dorothy that he was taking Linda with him to pick up Patsy. Dorothy was surprised because Dell rarely even spoke to Linda, let alone took her with him. Since she was busy getting ready for the party, she agreed. Eddie and Kay Harmon were going with them, as guests, would be coming over early for a couple of cocktails. Dell got Linda out of her room insisting that she was going for a ride with him—Linda tried to say she wanted to stay home Dell told her to stop whimpering to head to the car. Linda in fear did as she was told.

The trip to pick up Patsy should have only taken ten minutes, once in the car Dell took a detour—earlier in the day, he had heard on the radio a warning to motorist that New Year's Eve was one of the most dangerous times to be on the road. Dell did not care about going to the Allstate party. He had his own plan for the evening. Dell drove to Van Buren and 44th Street, which was a busy intersection, he took a couple of test runs around the block and through the intersection before his plan came together. Linda was sitting in the front seat of the 1949 Plymouth sedan as Dell came to a stop at the front of the intersection at a red light. He looked both ways waiting until just the right moment when two cars were coming in opposite directions on a green light through the intersection. He allowed his car slowly to move out into traffic, as he did so he opened his driver's side door, tucked, and rolled himself out of the car toward the nearest corner. Linda was in the car alone. The two other cars, one from each side were bearing down on the Plymouth. Neither of the other vehicles could stop in time, they hit the sedan almost simultaneously from the right and the left. Linda was bounced around in the car. When all three of the vehicles came to a stop, Linda was on the floor of the passenger side of the car curled into a fetal position crying hysterically.

Dell who had rolled out of traffic was standing on the corner watching the crash as it happened. Once the vehicles came to a stop he began to yell as he ran toward the middle of the intersection. "My daughter is in the car help she must be dying." He claimed as the other drivers started looking around at the damages.

Within a minute or two, a police car arrived at the scene, the officer was met with Dell's demands to check on his daughter. The policeman rushed to the crushed Plymouth, looked inside expecting to find an injured or dead child instead he discovered Linda on the floor crying, shaking, yet unscathed. Dell watched from a short distance as the officer pulled Linda out of the car and walked toward him "Sir, you are really lucky. She doesn't have a scratch on her, angels must be watching over this little one for sure. Your car is totaled, she is just a bit shaken up."

Dell had no choice except to take Linda from the officer, he felt her body stiffen as he held her in his arms. The officer asked what happened. Dell lied "I was stopped at the intersection when my door opened I fell out of the car then the car moved into the intersection into oncoming traffic. I rolled out of the way to save myself from being run over the next thing I heard was the crash."

"Well I'd have to say the two of you are lucky tonight. I won't be giving out any citations on this one since it was clearly a freak accident." Several other police cars had arrived, the officer added "Give me a minute to let them know what's up then I'll take you and this little one home."

Dell was stunned with disappointment doing everything he could not to show it. He had taken a chance that had failed. He was lucky not to be getting a ticket. That was where his luck ended. Linda was fine, his plan had not gone as he had hoped. He thought that at least he didn't have to go to some stuffy company party; he'd be home in time to celebrate the New Year with some beer and tequila with Dorothy, Eddie, and Kay Harmon.

9

"The West's most western town"
City of Scottsdale, Chamber of Commerce

In the summer of 1960, Dell's insurance job had taken off, Dorothy was itching to have them buy a house. Homebuilders, at a pace that was staggering, were subdividing the suburb of Scottsdale. Dorothy and Linda spent many a weekday touring the model homes of a score of builder's sites. Dorothy would push Martin in his stroller as they looked at every fully decorated model. Dell had refused to be involved in the search until she had narrowed down the field of choices to her top five favorites.

The plan was that Dell would borrow the down payment from his parents then pay them back as the equity grew in the house. It was a financing plan that he had learned in college in a class that taught Dell how to avoid using his own money whenever possible.

After a long summer of home searching, Dorothy had her favorites. Her most favorite of all was a large four-bedroom, two-bath home, with a formal living room, a family room, and a large eat-in kitchen. The base price of the model was $14,000. By the time Dorothy added wall-to-wall carpets throughout the price was $14,900. She got up the courage to tell Dell that he should come see what she had narrowed the search down to; she took him to the Hallcraft development first hoping that he would like the house as much as she did.

Dell was looking to find a house he could feel proud of, growing up in company housing in Ajo had left him with a desire for something much better than his parents had. When he first drove up to the model he was pleasantly surprised, once he went inside, he was sold. He didn't even want to look at any of the other homes Dorothy had on her list. In fact, Dell insisted that they go to the sales office to sign a contract right away. The house was at the top of the price range Dell had set, he liked the big front and back yard, the large rooms inside. He even agreed with Dorothy about the carpet throughout. By the end of July 1960, the Moore family had bought a new home in Scottsdale, Arizona. They would move in before the start of the school year. Linda would be going to second grade at the newly built Hohokam Elementary School, two blocks from home.

Dorothy was gratified, her lifelong plan of having a family of her own, with a home that she could love had come together. She was full of goodwill toward Dell and his parents who lent them $3,000. With the down payment made, the financing went through quickly. Dorothy was buying new furniture at Sears and

Roebucks using Dell's Allstate employee discount, along with the store credit card they had because of Dell's job with Allstate. Dell and Dorothy both felt as if they had arrived. Dell was 26 years old and Dorothy was 28. He had a very good job and Dorothy planned to be a stay at home mother with Linda and Martin.

Dell was doing some splurging of his own as he bought a 1960, Ford Falcon Station Wagon, the perfect car for the family man and successful salesman.

The façade was complete all looked well from the outside, the Moore family life was up and coming. Old habits don't just disappear with a little success. Dorothy still drank more than half dozen rum and Cokes a day, at the time they closed on the house, Dell was having affairs with two of his married women insurance clients. Linda was still the quiet frightened child, Martin was a spoiled two year old who could do no wrong in either of his parents' eyes. A new chapter was beginning in a new home and new town. The underlying story was unfortunately on track to stay the same.

$$\Omega$$

Hohokam Elementary School was brand new; Linda was looking forward to starting school again more than anything. She was a little nervous hoping that her new teacher would be as nice as Mrs. Yates had been for first grade. Linda knew she loved school her worries were few. School started the day after Labor Day, Linda was awake at dawn; she had five new dresses from Sears and Roebucks She picked the red one with navy blue trim on a white collar. She had fresh new anklet socks and brand new Mary Jane shoes to wear.

Dorothy took Linda to school the first day to make sure she found the right classroom. The teacher assignments for all the grades had been posted on the cafeteria windows for a couple of weeks so Linda already knew her teacher's name was Mrs. Patterson in Room 14. When Linda and Dorothy made their way to the room Linda was almost buzzing with excitement as she saw the decorated classrooms, books, and maps on every wall. Linda wanted nothing more than to get into the classroom on her own, Dorothy wanted to introduce herself to Mrs. Patterson. Linda had to wait patiently holding Dorothy's hand as they both waited behind other parents with the same idea.

Mrs. Patterson was a middle age woman with light brown hair and green eyes; Linda hadn't ever seen anyone with green eyes and was amazed. Dorothy thought of her sister Marie as soon as she saw Linda's teacher. Mrs. Patterson smiled and shook Linda's hand—she had never had an adult treat her with such respect. She took an immediate liking to her teacher, she was glad when her mother left to go back home. Linda would walk home after school; she had been practicing the two-block route for the past month when she would come to the schoolyard to play on the swings.

Within the first two weeks of school Mrs. Patterson recognized Linda's reading was well above grade level and she had her placed in a third grade reading class. One of the first books that Linda found on the bookshelf in the reading room was "A Wrinkle in Time." She loved the book, read it twice before writing a book report; she turned in the book report to Mrs. Quinn her reading teacher, receiving a gold star. Linda took the papers home where she kept them in a special drawer in her vanity.

Everything went well for Linda that fall of 1960 until one day in early November her mother told her that her Grandma Lenore had died. Linda and Martin would be staying with the O'Hair family across the street overnight, while Dorothy and Dell went to Ajo for the funeral. Linda didn't know what a funeral was, she was too afraid to ask. Linda did understand that her Grandma Lenore was gone and wouldn't ever sew another beautiful dress for her.

After Linda's parents came home from Ajo, a few days later, on the weekend Dorothy settled on to the sofa next to Linda while she was watching cartoons with Martin. "I have some news to tell you, you're going to have a new brother or sister in a few months." Dorothy said in her most cheerful voice.

Linda's heart started pounding in her chest it was hard to catch her breath. She tried not to let her mother know she was in distress. Dorothy went on talking about how she would decorate the new baby's room. All Linda could think of was that something very bad had happened the last time a new baby was coming. Linda's mind flashed back to the attic, she saw the window shade come down, then everything went black. Linda fainted right where she sat on the sofa. Dorothy went on talking not even noticing that her daughter had lost consciousness. A few minutes later Linda regained consciousness. Dorothy was playing on the floor with Martin. At least Linda's heart pounding had slowed so she could breathe again.

Ω

By mid-December, Dorothy had curtailed any sexual relationship with Dell because of being pregnant. It was a good excuse Dell was having at least a couple of affairs with clients so it didn't matter to him. Around Christmas time his "lady friends" got busy with holiday preparations, they weren't available for the usual bi-weekly trysts. Dell still had client appointments most evenings by the time he got home Dorothy was asleep snoring in bed for the night. Dell would have a late snack usually peanut butter and honey on white bread sit in his recliner watching television for a couple of hours. Some nights when he hadn't closed a deal he'd get out the bottle of tequila and have a few shots with a beer or two smoking a pack of cigarettes. Those were the most dangerous nights in the Moore house. Dell would head down to the end of the hallway turn out the hall light and silently open Linda's bedroom door.

Linda had developed the habit of placing pillows all around herself tucking the sheets into the pillows so that she was encased in the bed linens. At least when she went to sleep she felt she was secured against whatever might come. It didn't always work, some nights Linda would have terrible recurring nightmares when she woke up in the morning she would discover she had wet the bed. Often there was blood on the sheets. Linda was seven years old, she knew that she was not supposed to wet the bed. She hid the dirty sheets in the bottom of her closet, put clean ones from the linen cabinet back on the bed. Later in the week, she would sneak the dirty sheets into the washing machine when her mother was having her afternoon rum and Cokes. Linda's life was complicated, the worst part was she had no idea of what was happening to her, she just knew for sure that it was bad and wrong. After a while Linda began to feel that *she* was bad and wrong, that made her feel terrified all the time like she was going to get into trouble—face a terrible punishment at any moment.

Sometimes when Dorothy was angry with Linda she would tell her that she might be sent to a "foster home," Linda didn't know what that was, whether it was the punishment she always feared or a place where she would just be all alone. The all alone idea didn't seem that bad, Linda dared not ask her mother any questions.

Ω

Except for school, Linda didn't know what was happening in her day-to-day life. She knew she loved school especially reading, even though the rest of her life was a dark blur. Dorothy was on her fourth drink by the time Linda got home at 2:45 in the afternoon. Linda would take Martin out of his crib when he woke up from his afternoon nap to play with him on the family room floor. Dorothy would often fall asleep on the sofa Linda knew to wake her up by five o'clock so that she could start fixing dinner. Dell would be home at six. Linda would eat dinner then go to her room to read. Once Dell was home, Linda had a need to be behind a closed door—she didn't know why, she just did. Reading was her escape; she always had the maximum number of five books checked out from the school library every week. Linda believed that she would be lost without her books. She finished out the school year with excellent grades. There was some talk about having her skip third grade and go right to fourth. Dell said, "No." He didn't want Linda to get a big head thinking she was smarter than other kids were. At the end of the school year, she passed to third grade in spite of her innate abilities because of Dell's inherent insecurities.

Once school was out Linda's life darkened even more, she didn't have her scholarly self to rely on and her child self was most often overwhelmed by the adult responsibilities that she had to take on, or the adult appetites that she had to endure.

Ω

Dianna Lenore Moore was born on July 26, 1961, she weighed 6-pounds and 12-ounces and was a healthy blond haired, blue-eyed baby. Considering that Dell's hair was almost black, his complexion swarthy, and he had dark eyes like coal—and Dorothy had dark hair and dark eyes Dianna or Deedee as they called her was quite a surprise. Dorothy wasn't saying anything, Dell wasn't asking, but the neighbors and friends were sure discussing the shocking lack of familial likeness.

Dorothy wasn't feeling very well after the birth she moved Deedee's bassinette into the master bedroom. Dell started sleeping on the twin bed in the baby's room. Linda learned how to lock her bedroom door, a solution that kept the nightmares away a few weeks, before Dell decided to change all the doorknobs to the children's rooms with ones that couldn't be locked from the inside, only from the outside.

For the remainder of the summer Linda lost all sense of time. During the day, she felt very small and vulnerable it was almost as if she were going back in age and maturity. She had to try very hard to make it to the bathroom and not wet her panties; sometimes she did, then had to hide them. At night when she went to bed she built her pillow fortress trying to fall asleep as soon as her head hit the pillow. She felt like she could outrace the nightmares if she could fall asleep before they came. Linda's life was full of anxiety and fear; everything had a negative consequence that she didn't understand.

$$\Omega$$

She found an old Olivetti typewriter in the outside storage room decided to bring it into the house to clean it up. She saw a typewriter in the school office she knew you could write on paper with it. Linda got the idea to write a story for Deedee her new little sister. She put the typewriter on the built-in desk in the family room, Dorothy showed her how to put in the paper. Linda practiced all afternoon copying from one of her other storybooks to learn how to work the typewriter keys.

Linda helped Dorothy make dinner as she had started to do that summer, the meal was on the table when Dell walked in from work. He noticed the typewriter first thing and began complaining about it. "What's that old piece of junk doing on my desk?"

"Linda found it in the storage room she has been playing with it all afternoon." Dorothy said, "Dinner is ready come on let's eat."

They sat down to dinner. Dell would not stop about the typewriter. "I need the space at *my* desk to make my calls. I want that piece of crap out of here."

Linda said, "I'm writing a book for baby Deedee, Daddy."

"Are you back-talking me? I said I want it gone."

Dell barely finished dinner and had to leave for his evening appointments he didn't mention the typewriter again.

Linda went to sleep that night thinking about the stories she would write. When Linda woke up the next morning, she noticed that the typewriter wasn't on the desk any more. She ducked out the front door to see if it was back in the storage room. It was not. She didn't dare ask about it when her Daddy came out for his coffee and toast. After he left for work, she started doing her chores. First thing was to take out the garbage. Linda went out to the back yard opened the gate to the alley where the trashcans were, there on the ground was the typewriter. It was smashed apart as if someone took a heavy hammer to it, the keyboard was broken the paper roller was no longer attached to the typewriter. The typing keys were bent splayed out like a broken fan. Linda started crying and her heart started pounding in her chest. She knew her Daddy had done this. Why she would never understand.

$$\Omega$$

When Linda started third grade for the first time there were several students named Linda in her class. She became Linda M. In her own way, it only made sense that her school self should have a different name since she thought and acted differently in school than at home. Linda had a level of confidence, of mastery at school that she could never bring home. In class, Linda volunteered and participated, at home she tried to be invisible. In school, Linda was considered by her teachers to be mature for her age; at home, Linda most often reverted to a scared silent child.

The day of the open house at school was coming up Linda had several of her work papers on display around the classroom. She thought up until the last minute that her mother would be coming for the evening event. Unfortunately, Deedee was running a fever Dorothy asked Dell to take a few minutes to go by the school before he went on his client appointments. Dell, of course, argued but eventually gave in considering that the argument was taking more time than stopping by the open house for a few minutes. Linda was very concerned that her father was going, she didn't know what to think about him seeing her schoolwork posted around the room. When Linda brought home her schoolwork neither her mother nor father took any notice.

Dell and Linda arrived at the school at six-thirty she led him to her classroom. Linda rushed to greet Mrs. Appleton to have her meet her father. Linda was in for a shock. When Dell saw her teacher he reached out a gave her a big hug called her by her first name,

Lois, the two of them began talking as if they had known each other for years. As it turned out Dell and Lois had dated in college before either of them had married, they began sharing memories of their times together. Linda was embarrassed, she stood some distance away from Dell and her teacher. Linda felt overwhelmed with a sense of betrayal by Mrs. Appleton. How could she have a teacher that was close with the person who terrified her?

Dell looked at his watch saying he had to run to his business appointments but promised to keep in touch now that he knew she was at Hohokam; he didn't even give Linda a second thought as he rushed out the door. A new set of parents came in and captured Mrs. Appleton's attention. Linda slipped out of the room walked the two blocks home. When she arrived, her mother was dealing with Martin's bath and Deedee's fever. Linda went to her room began making her pillow fortress so she could go to bed.

Linda thought about what to do in school knowing that her father was close friends with her teacher. Linda so far had liked Mrs. Appleton, she wasn't sure that she could still feel the same way. Did she need to be afraid of her like she was of her father? Linda's young mind did not know how to manage such an adult problem. She fell into a deep dreamless sleep luckily that night the monster didn't come.

$$\Omega$$

Linda ended up with very few memories of her early years in school; they were overshadowed by the on-going abuse she unconsciously endured. Her personality affected a split between the childish Linda at home and young Linda who worked hard to excel in school. Her memory was focused on learning, without actually knowing, she used her interest in school to block out much of the rest of her life experiences. Linda's relationship with her teacher changed somewhat, she still had reading with Mrs. Quinn so she put her best efforts into the time with her reading teacher.

Ω

Linda spent a lot of time at the doctors that Dell had insured; she had chronic bladder or kidney infections that were bad enough some times to land her in Scottsdale Memorial Hospital. The doctors always seemed to blame the problems on something innocuous like "bubble baths" which Linda never understood because she took showers, didn't even use bubble bath. There were several occasion when Linda got infections that left sores in her private parts. The doctors would give her penicillin and tell Dorothy she should get a shot as well. Linda never knew how she got sick or why it happened so often.

Ω

By the time Linda was in fifth grade Martin was in Kindergarten so she walked to school with him. Linda's fifth grade teacher was a youngish woman in her early thirties named Miss Royer she was the first unmarried teacher that Linda had and she liked her immediately. Miss Royer had a library of books in her classroom, the entire sets of Nancy Drew, Hardy Boys Mysteries, and Tom Swift the science fiction series for young readers. Linda chose a seat in the back corner by all the bookshelves. Miss Royer knowing that Linda excelled in reading allowed her free reign to read as much as she wanted to write book reports for extra credit. Linda still studied math, social studies, and science but most of her time was spent reading and writing.

It was a terrible day in November of 1963, when President John F. Kennedy was assassinated. Linda had never seen an adult cry before, as a ten-year-old seeing Miss Royer sobbing at her desk as the news was called out over the school intercom, shook Linda to the core. She began crying as well, even though see did not understand the full nature of what was happening. School was let out shortly after one o'clock that afternoon. Linda walked home from school with tears still streaming down her face. She was a half a block from home when Dell pulled up to the curb in the car. "What are you crying for?" Dell barked at Linda.

"The president is dead everyone is crying." Linda answered.

"Stop crying, in our family we aren't crying. We're glad he's gone. Now get in the car." Dell shouted.

"I don't want to I'll walk home."

"Get in the god damn car."

"No." Linda had no idea what was driving her refusal but she didn't want to get in the car with her father.

Dell screeched away from the curb swerving into the driveway at home. He stood at the doorway waiting for Linda with his belt in his hand ready to beat her for her impertinence. Linda walked up the driveway saw her father waiting for her. She decided at that moment that she wouldn't cry while he beat her. She had cried for the President like Miss Royer she wasn't going to shed one tear during the beating.

Dell began hitting Linda as soon as she stepped in the house he continued to beat her with his leather belt and the buckle as she writhed on the floor. Finally, after he caught her in the cheek with the buckle drawing blood, he stopped, walked away yelling for Dorothy to come get Linda in her room for the rest of the day.

Linda felt the blood trickling down her face; she carefully leaned over her lap so that no blood would go on the carpet. Her eyes were dry. She did not cry even when Dorothy washed her wound with stinging antiseptic on the cut. Linda went to her room; began to build her pillow fortress. She knew she wasn't going to eat dinner she was exhausted anyway. The President was dead, her beloved teacher had cried, Linda had been beaten until she bled, and The John Birch Society was meeting at her house that very night. Her father was the leader of the local chapter. She fell asleep in minutes.

$$\Omega$$

In sixth grade, Linda experienced the fright of her life when her period began. Dorothy had never mentioned anything to Linda about it she thought that the monster dreams were creeping into her daylight existence when she saw the blood on her panties in the school restroom. Luckily, it was near the end of the school day because Mrs. Gates was a cranky old teacher. Linda wouldn't have gone to her with a problem in a million years. When school was over Linda went to Miss Royer's classroom whispered to her that she was bleeding. Miss Royer suspected right away what was happening she took Linda to the nurse's office. The nurse called Linda's mother explaining that Linda had started her period. The nurse said she was sending Linda home with a book that she could read that made clear, everything a sixth grader needed to know. She also sent her with a Kotex beginners' kit and told Linda to have her mother help her with it. Linda walked home in her bloody panties stuffed with toilet tissue by the time she got home, she was scared, she was shaking—she had no idea what her mother would say.

For once Dorothy was a comfort to Linda, calmly explaining that what was happening was normal. It just meant that Linda was becoming a young woman. Dorothy showed Linda how to use the Kotex pad with the strap to keep it in place. She also told Linda that she always had to tell her mother the very day her period started so she could write it on a special calendar. Linda was relieved, Dorothy told her not to tell her father about the special secret.

Of course, Dorothy knew she would be telling Dell that very night, maybe he would decide to leave Linda alone. However, in either case she would have Linda's menstrual timing down to the day so that if Dell was still determined he could follow the rhythm method.

Ω

Many of Dell's most loyal clients were the networks of doctors and their practices that he covered with insurance. He made a lot of money helping them manage the business liabilities of the medical and dental practices his company covered. As soon as Dell discovered that Linda had started her period he talked to one of the doctors telling him that his daughter had terrible cramps and vomiting with her period. The doctor without asking any questions or asking to examine the eleven-year-old Linda put in a standing order twice a month at the local emergency room for Linda to get a Demerol shot, whenever Dell brought her in to Scottsdale Memorial Hospital. Dell's plan was to make sure that Linda would be in a drugged sleep at least twice a month during her period and shortly after her period so that he could have his way and not worry about the consequences.

Ω

Linda however still did have to deal with the consequences of frequent bladder and kidney infections that put her in the hospital for antibiotics and even more Demerol. By the time Linda was in eighth grade she was likely addicted to the powerful pain medications that she had received—in order to assure Dell that his perversion would still go undiscovered by Linda, who had no conscious memories of what he did, and go uninterrupted by Dorothy's meddlesome, ineffectual insinuations.

Ω

When Linda graduated from eighth grade, she was thirteen years old. Her mother had bought her an adult women's cocktail dress for the occasion. While Linda's schoolmates were wearing colorful, frilly full-skirted dresses Linda wore a beige empire-waist sheath dress with a lace trim on the scoop neck bodice. Linda knew she was dressed inappropriately for the occasion, she didn't say a word. By thirteen Linda was already too depressed to put up much of a fight. Graduation came just two days after Linda had been given her second monthly Demerol shot. She was barely able to be out of bed let alone enjoy her graduation. Linda did not attend any parties with friends like the other graduates. She went out to dinner with Dell, Dorothy, Martin, and Deedee. After dinner Linda went home and went to her room to build her pillow fortress she hoped the nightmares would not come that night.

Book II

"Talking won't change it but sometimes it was what she wanted most, to tell someone. Often though she just wanted to escape those horrid feelings, to escape herself so there was no pain, no fear, no ugliness."
Melissa Marr, Ink Exchange

10

"I encountered many Zuni Indians and had a war. I Coronado, killed many of them."
Expedition notes Don Coronado, 1540-1542

In the fall of 1967, Linda started as a freshman at Coronado High School in Scottsdale, Arizona. The school's sports team mascot was the image of a Spanish conquistador whose leader was referred to as The Don, so the teams were called the Coronado Dons. Instead of majorettes or pompom girls, they had cheerleaders and a dance team called the Donnettes. They wore Matador styled outfits with short shorts. They had red and blue capes that they danced with as if in a bullfight. The school colors were red and navy blue and the favorite cheer was "C C C O R O—N N N A D O—C O R O N A D O—GO CORONADO!!!" At least it proved that the majority of students at the pep rallies or sporting events could spell in unison.

Linda had two friends from grade school that made the Donnette team, Michelle and Shelley were her closest friends, considering how circumspect Linda was they weren't that close. She could never have them over because her mother was drunk; of course, there were never any sleepovers at Linda's house.

When Dorothy drank, Dell yelled, bellowing his way around the house, finding fault with everything and everyone. When Dell drank, Dorothy taunted him about his affairs, threatened him about his less than above board business dealings. Now that Linda was in high school, the scholarly aspect of her took over as much as possible, but at home, she was essentially lost to the dysfunction that held her captive.

Linda's anxiety was a real issue that she fought hard to combat. Based on the minimal sex education she had been privy to she understood that having a period meant that your body was capable of becoming pregnant. She didn't recognize why her anxiety level soared whenever she thought about that—it just did. Linda also hated getting shots at the hospital whenever it was close to her period or during. She had never been explained the reason why she had to sleep for two or three days, to miss school, other than her mother telling her it was the best thing for her.

Linda's anxiety began to affect her at school. She had English as her first period class. She loved English and her teacher Miss Kajakawa. A few weeks into the new school year, after about fifteen minutes, Linda suddenly couldn't keep her eyes open she would pass out into a deep sleep at her desk. The first couple of times that it happened; her teacher waited until class was over, gently woke Linda up, sending her on her way to second period. After several instances, Miss Kajakawa decided to speak to Mrs. Steen Linda's guidance counselor. The next time Linda passed out when her teacher woke her up, she took Linda directly to Mrs. Steen.

Linda was horribly embarrassed, assumed she was in big trouble, by the time Mrs. Steen opened her door to her office Linda was crying with tears running down her face. The counselor put her arms around Linda, drew her into the office, making clear that Linda was not in any trouble. "Miss Kajakawa is just concerned about you. You are such a good student she is worried that something is wrong to make you be so tired that you fall asleep in her class."

Linda whispered "I'm sorry I don't mean to fall asleep I just can't seem to help it. My eyes won't stay open then I just have to put my head down." Linda paused "I've even tried biting my on lip to stay awake. It didn't work."

"Have you been staying up late at night?"

"No the rule is that I have to go to bed by nine."

"Are you having bad dreams or nightmares that wake you up in the middle of the night?"

Linda's eyes started to tear up again "Yes, sometimes I have very bad dreams I can't always remember them. They seem to be the same dream over and over only sometimes it's a little different. Anyway when I wake up in the morning I don't remember which dream I had."

"Well I'd like to call your parents, tell them what's happening…" Rose Steen stopped mid-sentence as she saw the terror come over Linda's face.

"Please don't call my parents if you do they won't let me come back to school I couldn't bear that." Tears were running down Linda's face her hands were clutched in her lap as if she were holding on to herself for dear life.

"Linda I promise it will be okay. Since today is Friday how about if I wait until we can meet again next week to talk about your parents?" Rose Steen reached across to Linda's lap unclenched her hands, "Now I want you to take a couple of deep breaths with me it will help you calm down."

Linda did as her counselor instructed and it did help her settle herself a bit. "You promise you won't call them until we talk again Mrs. Steen?"

"Yes I promise."

Linda asked if she could go wash her face in the office bathroom; so that the other students wouldn't know she'd been crying Rose Steen agreed. Before Linda left the counselor took her hand again, "Next week when we meet you can call me Rose. I'd like us to be friends."

Linda smiled just a little wiped her face with her hands. "Thank you." With that, Linda headed out of the office to the private bathroom across the hallway.

Ω

Rose Steen sat and thought a long time about Linda. Why she was so terrorized at the thought of having her parents called? She wasn't in trouble in school, in fact the concern was more for her health. Passing out into a deep sleep didn't make any sense for a young girl, Rose was worried about the nightmares. She'd be sure to do some research this weekend before raising the issue with Linda again next week.

Rose Steen had a Master's Degree in Counseling and Psychology she was very concerned at Linda's reaction as well as with her sleep issues—she was wondering about some sort of neurological cause for the sleep episodes perhaps some type of seizure disorder. However, Rose had also seen the terror on Linda's face, watching the freshman in high school decompensate to a much younger version of herself right before her eyes—Linda's voice even changed to that of a much younger child, the counselor felt as if she had spoken to two different girls in her office that day.

On Monday, Linda came to school and did something that changed everything; she brought with her the bottle of phenobarbital with which her father regularly dosed her. The bottle was half-full. Linda took several of the pills in one of the girl's bathrooms. A couple of upper class girls who found her unconscious informed the office of Linda's condition. Rose Steen found the nearly empty bottle of pills with Dell Moore's name on the prescription near Linda. She was rushed to the emergency room of Scottsdale Memorial Hospital. Rose Steen took the prescription bottle with her to the hospital to meet Linda's parents there.

Linda was given medication intravenously to mitigate the effects of the sedatives that she took, by the time she made it to the hospital; it was too late to pump her stomach. Dell was pacing the floor, Dorothy sat in the waiting room when Rose Steen arrived. Mrs. Steen introduced herself to Linda's parents telling them what had happened. She showed Dell his prescription bottle asking him if he knew a reason that Linda would attempt to overdose on the pills. Dorothy choked back a sob as she listened to the counselor question Dell. Rose Steen was an imposing woman nearly six feet tall in her heels, with dark hair, and dark penetrating eyes. She had command of the situation, both Dell and Dorothy were nervously tense.

Mrs. Steen had done her homework over the weekend. She had some instructions for Linda's parents which she insisted in a no nonsense manner had to be followed through within the next few days. The counselor had already made an appointment for Linda at Barrows Neurological Institute in downtown Phoenix for a complete neurological work-up and EEG tests. She just happened to be friends with Dr. Udell, the head of the neurology department at the institute. She had told him about Linda's symptoms, had called him telling him about the overdose attempt. Mrs. Steen also told Dorothy and Dell that she strongly recommended that Linda see a child psychiatrist, Dr. David Durfee, she had already contacted him to do a consultation on Linda while she was hospitalized.

In one fell swoop, Rose Steen had taken control of the situation and wrenched it away from Dell and Dorothy Moore. Rose didn't have any illusions about how long the circumstances would be in Linda's favor, she hoped it was long enough to get some answers about what was happening in the young girl's troubled life. Dell and Dorothy were cowed for the time being. Rose Steen was determined to stay on watch to see her plan for Linda though.

Dr. David Durfee came that very evening after Dell and Dorothy had left. He briefly spoke to Linda. He determined that he would see her on a regular basis in his office if Rose Steen could convince Linda's parents to bring her for therapy.

$$\Omega$$

Linda was released from the hospital on Wednesday and her appointment at Barrows Neurological Institute was for the following Monday. Dell tried to talk Dorothy into skipping the appointment. He raged, "Who does this counselor women think she is to tell us what we have to do?"

"If we don't do it I know she will call child protective services. Is that what you want? A whole team of social workers coming to the house, going to the school. Linda took an overdose. This is serious."

"She was just trying to get attention, what I should do is take a belt to her."

"Oh great idea give her welts just before she sees a doctor."

"Dorothy I promise if you go through with all of this it's on you I'm against it I won't participate."

"Fine you stay out of it, it's probably the best thing you could do anyway. I don't want to talk about this anymore. Don't you have to get to appointments?"

Dell grabbed his briefcase gave Dorothy one last nasty glare and left the house with a slam of the door.

Ω

Linda listened to the whole tirade between them from her bedroom; she was scared to death that her father would take the belt to her. She was too old for a belt beating and she knew it. It made her sick to her stomach to think of it. Linda decided right then that if her father ever tried to belt beat her again she would stand up to him even if it meant getting beat worse. Linda slipped out of her room to use the bathroom. She heard her mother putting ice in a glass for another rum and Coke. Her mother would be asleep in a couple of hours and her father wouldn't be home for several after that—Linda would have some peace for a little while.

Ω

The following week was an active one for Linda; on Monday she spent the whole day at the Barrows Institute being examined by Dr. Udell. He first did a physical neurological exam then a technician came in to glue at least twenty electrodes attached to wires to Linda's scalp. Then they took her into darkened room, attached the wires to a machine. Linda lay down on a comfortable bed was told to go to sleep if she could. Linda had no problem dropping off into a deep sleep after a few minutes. She slept for an hour while the machine recorded her brain waves. They woke Linda up to record her brain for an hour while she was awake, looking at a multitude of images on a screen in the room. When she was done the technician used rubbing alcohol to remove the glue loosening the electrodes from her head. The technician told her that the rest of the glue would easily wash out when she shampooed her hair.

Linda and her mother went down to the cafeteria for a late lunch at about two o'clock to give the doctors time to evaluate the results of her tests, they were supposed to go back upstairs to Dr. Udell's office at four o'clock. They ate a leisurely lunch then shopped around in the hospital gift shop for a while take up the rest of the time. Dorothy was being very nice to Linda much to her surprise. Linda had expected her mother to be complaining about how long it was taking but she didn't. Dorothy kept asking Linda if she was doing "okay" Linda agreed that she was fine even though she was a little embarrassed to be walking around with her hair looking somewhat messy. Dorothy said, "Don't be self-conscious your hair doesn't look that different just a little puffier than normal no one will notice."

Finally, it was almost time to meet with the doctor again, they took the elevator up to the fifth floor, went to Dr. Udell's office. He waited for them, took them into the examining room—he surprised Linda by redoing the physical exam asking her to hold out her arms straight and resist as he tried to push them down. He then had her touch her nose with her finger from holding her arms out to the side. He rechecked her eyes and her speech in an exercise where she repeated words after he told them to her quickly. Linda performed all the tests as she had before only this time Dorothy was watching her. Finally, Dr. Udell sat down looked at a clipboard full of papers about Linda's other tests. Dr. Udell began to speak choosing his words carefully. First, he said that Linda had no evidence of brain lesions or damage. He added however that some of the results were not as expected. He explained, "Brain waves are determined to be normal by how 95 percent of individuals test when given an EEG—injuries and lesions show up in the testing process as well, they will show up as specific abnormalities. Your EEG was definitely not what we see in most of our testing, in fact it was what we see in about 3 percent of the tests we do."

Dorothy heard the word abnormal, she interrupted to ask questions "What do you mean abnormal? What is wrong with her?"

Dr. Udell held up his hand to stop her outburst. "I didn't say it was abnormal it is just simply different, Linda's brain has developed somewhat differently than 95 percent of brains develop. We have checked her out there are no lesions or injuries, her sleep issues I would say are psychosomatic in nature, in fact, she fell asleep very easily for us during the test. I think a psychiatrist will best deal with the sleep issues. I understand she is scheduled to see Dr. Durfee. I will forward the records of our exam to him."

Dorothy asked, "You mean she is physically fine, maybe mentally messed up?"

Dr. Udell was losing patience with Dorothy's negative attitude "No Mrs. Moore, Linda is not 'mentally messed up' in fact the difference may be the result of a higher than typical IQ. Dr. Durfee will test her for that first thing."

Dorothy shook her head in confusion. She was chastened out of asking any more questions. She stood and thanked Dr. Udell, said to Linda, "Come on let's get you and your unusual brain home." She laughed, Dr. Udell did not, he just patted Linda on the shoulder as she passed by. "If you have any other questions feel free to call me any time."

Ω

Dorothy and Linda made their way to the car where Dorothy immediately pulled out a small flask took a long swig of rum. Linda watched her with surprise it was the first time she had seen her mother drink rum without Coke. Dorothy snapped "Don't you dare look at me that way this has been a very long difficult day for me." She took another long gulp before putting the cap back on returning it to her purse. Then she started the car turned the radio on loud to preclude any conversation, then headed home to Scottsdale.

Linda was going to go to school tomorrow. She was glad she hoped she would have the chance to see Rose Steen to apologize to her for taking the pills. Linda felt very guilty about having done such a thing not because of her parents with their self-interested reaction, because Mrs. Steen had been genuinely worried about her. She truly hoped that her counselor would accept her apology.

Rose Steen was concerned about Linda. She was relieved to hear that she was sorry for having taken the overdose. Rose had continued to do research into what might be causing Linda to act out in such a way. One of the answers she kept coming to was some sort of physical or emotional abuse. This would be a difficult subject to broach with Linda she certainly couldn't count on Linda's parents to be forthcoming since if anyone was hurting Linda it was likely one of them. Linda didn't seem to have any obvious physical evidence of abuse Rose hadn't seen any bruises. She feared that the emotional abuse could be much worse. Rose Steen already had decided that Dell Moore was a bully, likely a mean-spirited disciplinarian—Dorothy Moore seemed more concerned about appearances than the reality of Linda's having attempted an overdose.

Linda and Rose had a long discussion about what her appointment with Dr. Durfee would be like later that day. Rose had known David Durfee to be one of the best child psychiatrists she had ever met. He worked very naturally with children had an innate manner that put them at ease. Linda asked about the tests that Dr. Udell had told her about. "He said something about an IQ test is that another test where they put wires on my head?"

"No IQ stands for Intelligence Quotient it measures how smart you are by asking you questions having you solve some puzzles and problems." Rose added, "Most of what you will do with Dr. Durfee is talk to him so that he can get to know you really well. I'm sure you'll do just fine with him he is a very nice doctor."

"My parents had a fight about me going to see these doctors—I usually only go to doctors that my dad knows from work."

"Why did they have an argument surely they want you to get better."

"My mom said you'd call child protective services that would be trouble."

Rose took a deep breath, "I'll do that if I have a good reason to but as long as you're seeing Dr. Durfee that won't be the case."

Linda had been seeing Dr. Durfee for about a month when Dorothy told Linda that she was pregnant again. Linda went into a deep depression began building her nighttime fortress of pillows every night. When her period came, her mother took her to the hospital to get her Demerol shot. Linda asked her mother why she had to get a shot anyway. Dorothy told Linda to shut up go to sleep before they got home. Linda was developing a tolerance for the sedative shot so she stayed awake the whole ride home talking nonsense, asking way too many questions that Dorothy didn't want to answer. At home in bed Linda passed out. Dorothy went to drink as much as she could before Dell got home.

The next time Linda saw Dr. Durfee she told him about the terrible recurring nightmares that she had been having all of her life. She told him about the volcano erupting while she rode her bike around on the semi-cool lava as the volcano never stopped erupting she could never stop riding or the lava would burn her up. Linda also told Dr. Durfee a story about a secret boyfriend, "who would come into the house at night, and get in bed with her even though she didn't want him to. When she tried to lock him out of her room, instead he locked her in." Lastly, she told the doctor about the most frightening dream of all "I'm riding in the backseat of my Grandpa and Grandma's car I have a bloody can opener in my hand. They are very angry with me because they say I have killed my parents. In my dream I wake up to go check to see if my mom and dad are still alive I find them in bed just fine. Then my grandparents tell me that I haven't done the deed yet. I am cursed to do it someday."

Dr. Durfee recorded his sessions with Linda. He had all the information about her dreams on tape so that he could analyze them. He also knew that Dorothy's pregnancy made Linda very upset. Linda had just turned fifteen years old was greatly embarrassed even frightened by the fact that her mother was having another baby. Dr. Durfee understood the embarrassment for a teen-ager. Linda's fear was visceral, once when she was talking about it she had hyperventilated passing out for a few moments. That was a shockingly strong over reaction. The doctor wanted to find the underlying cause of it.

The doctor had done all the usual tests including the IQ test. He discovered that Linda's IQ was 156, significantly above average and near genius levels. He had also given her the Rorschach tests for emotional and perceptive awareness she had done well on those tests also. He had studied the information from Dr. Udell considering the possibility that some sort of early childhood trauma had somehow affected Linda's brain development.

After several months of seeing Linda every other week Dr. Durfee had a fairly clear and certain perception of what was happening in the Moore household. He did not know how he could handle the situation without risking having to remove Linda from the home, which she would be able legally to do on her own in three years, hopefully to go away to college.

The biggest problem for the doctor was that Dell Moore was a so-called "Pillar of Society" in Scottsdale, a successful businessman and a civic leader of various business organizations—He also was known for his charitable works on behalf of the blind children through his association with the Civitan Club of which he was President.

Dr. Durfee decided to ask Dell and Dorothy Moore in for a conference on their daughter's progress in therapy. He had decided to lay out his concerns quite plainly.

Dell and Dorothy arrived for the appointment—Dell in his business suit looking very self-important and Dorothy in a shocking pink designer maternity dress complete with a matching pair of pink-dyed satin heels. Dell started the conversation before they were even seated "I hope this isn't going to take too long I have a meeting with the mayor and the city council this afternoon."

"No this shouldn't take any longer that you want it to take." Said Dr. Durfee sharply "Please have seats in my office."

"I hope Linda is doing what you want her to do not being any trouble." Said Dorothy.

"Linda has not been any trouble. I think she has some very troubling aspects to her life that I'd like to discuss in order to put an end to them."

"That child has everything she needs or could want I don't know what trouble you could be referring to." Dell was crossing and uncrossing his legs in an impatient manner.

"Mr. Moore I would like to suggest that you no longer go into your daughter's room at night in response to her nightmares. That would be a role best served by her mother."

Dr. Durfee's statement seemed to float over the room for a moment as if no one wanted to take it in. Dorothy whined, "I'm pregnant I need my sleep why should I be the one to get up, she has nightmares almost every night—I'd end up exhausted."

Dell Moore didn't make a sound until he roughly told Dorothy, "Shut up woman."

He rose from his seat "I think we are done here doctor if you have anything else to recommend I think you should contact my attorney."

The Moores immediately left the office slamming the door on the way out.

Ω

Two weeks later without her parents knowing Linda made her way to Dr. Durfee's office by bus, he happened to have an open afternoon. He welcomed the child with a hug. "Linda I am so glad to see you."

"I'm glad to see you too. This is the last time. My dad says I can't come anymore I wanted to talk to you one more time. I wanted to find out what happened when my parents came here. Were they mean to you?"

"No, not at all. Did you have any problems because of our meeting?"

"Dad just said I couldn't come here anymore that it was nothing, just a waste of time. I tried to tell him it wasn't he started to get mad. I just went to my room I cried because I knew I wouldn't be seeing you again." Linda paused and smiled "Then I came up with this plan."

"This was a good plan let's go sit in the office to talk."

Linda and Dr. Durfee talked for more than two hours that last afternoon. He shared as much wisdom with her as he thought she could handle. He didn't talk about his suspicions of her sexual abuse. He had realized that Linda had dissociated from any knowledge of what was happening to her. Now as her former doctor, he was not in a position to do anything about it that wouldn't cause more harm to Linda. If she ended up in the foster care system, he couldn't guarantee that she wouldn't be subject to even worse conditions. In their last meeting he did his best to build her up, to convince her that she could manage whatever she chose to do in the future with her life.

"Linda I want you to understand that you can handle the greatest heights you choose to achieve and that you can also survive the lowest lows that life may bring you. You are one of the smartest, kindest, and dearest girls I have ever had the pleasure to meet. I hope that someday as you look over your life you'll remember that you can cope with it all, the good, the bad, and especially the great. I wish for you to always seek the truth, no matter where the search leads."

"Thank you Doctor you've helped me a lot I didn't know how important it is to know yourself better. You've shown me how. I do know more about myself, what I'm capable of than I ever thought of before. It is a great gift I feel very special to have had the time I did with you." Linda started to tear up she gave him another big hug before she said, "I have to catch the next bus so they won't suspect anything—Thanks again." With that Linda dashed out of the office.

That was the last time Linda saw Dr. David Durfee.

11

"You will never find the real truth among people that are insecure or have egos to protect. Truth over time becomes either guarded or twisted as their perspective changes; it changes with the seasons of their shame, love, hope, or pride."
Shannon L. Alder

Justin Dell Moore was born on July 7, 1969, four months away from Linda's sixteenth birthday. Dorothy didn't do well after giving birth, she was sick in bed. Taking care of Justin fell on Linda's shoulders. Within a month of giving birth, Dorothy had to go back to the hospital to have a hysterectomy. Linda continued to be the primary caregiver for the new baby. While Dell was at work, one of his friends George Sloan spent many afternoons at the house talking with Dorothy, helping with Justin. Linda was going to be starting her junior year in high school. She was relieved that George seemed to be willing to help Dorothy. The day after Labor Day, Linda went back to Coronado High School, that day when she quietly entered the house not to wake

Justin if he was sleeping; she covertly discovered her mother and George Sloan locked in an embrace in the master bed.

Linda ducked back out of the house waited on the far side of the front yard until she saw George leave, when he was driving away Linda pretended as if she were just arriving home from school. Linda wasn't particularly surprised, she had heard many a fight over the years about either her mother or her father being angry over being "cheated on."

$$\Omega$$

Dorothy finally recovered from her ordeal when Justin was close to six months old. Dorothy told Linda that she had to start going to the Sloan's house to babysit their two boys who were in third and fourth grade at Hohokam. After school, Linda would walk the extra couple of blocks to the Sloan house and babysit George Sloan and his wife's sons. The boy's mother was home at the time. Linda soon discovered that she was passed out in bed with an empty vodka bottle next to her. Linda sat in the family room with the boys watching them as they watched cartoons, while their mom was blackout drunk in the room down the hall.

One day Dorothy called Linda to tell her that George Sloan would be home early so that Linda could run an errand. Linda had started driving when she was sixteen, she drove the 1960 Ford Falcon Station Wagon. Dorothy wanted Linda to drive to the Skaggs Drug Store to get some math flash cards for Deedee. Her teacher had sent home a note saying that Deedee was failing in third grade math. Linda asked why she had to go all the way to Skaggs when Smitty's Department Store was much closer. Dorothy said that her father told her to go to Skaggs that she'd better do what her father said.

Linda came home, got the money for the flash cards from her mother took the car, headed down Granite Reef Road to McDowell Road, to drive the five-mile distance to Skaggs Drug Store. Linda was coming to a stop at Miller Road when the brake pedal not only went to the floor it literally broke off the car. Linda had time to realize that she was going to be in an accident. She let go of the steering wheel covering her face with her hands. The Ford hit the car that was stopped, glanced off the rear end, hit another car in the next lane over and finally came to a stop after hitting a third car on the driver's side back door.

Linda's head flew forward with the first impact she hit the steering wheel face on, then with the second impact she was thrown to the side of the driver's door hitting her head again. By the last impact, Linda hit her lower jaw against the steering wheel. As the Ford came to a stop, she saw the blood on her hands and passed out.

Linda regained consciousness when police officers wrenched open her door and the sound of the ambulance pulled in close to her totaled car. Linda was bleeding from her forehead. Her mouth had two cuts in her bottom lip, one gash inside her cheek. Her jaw was hanging open slackly she couldn't attempt to move it without screaming out in pain. The ambulance technician told the police officer that she had a broken jaw and wouldn't be able to give any statement for some time. The ambulance rushed her to the hospital, Scottsdale Memorial where she went into the emergency room. They started to stitch the bleeding lips and inner cheek. Linda couldn't talk to the police officer; he used her driver's license to contact her home. Dell and Dorothy were at the hospital about an hour after Linda had arrived. The emergency room staff had already taken nearly a hundred ex-rays of her head looking for evidence of concussion, trying to find exactly where the left side of her jaw was fractured. When Dorothy heard about the number of the ex-rays, she became hysterical, she was forced to leave the emergency room. Finally, the radiologist found the break in the jaw joint declaring that Linda did have a concussion as well. The nurses began to get her ready for surgery. Her jaw would have to be set, then wired shut with wires inserted into her gums, around the roots of her teeth, and then attached to hooked metal bands, that could then be wired together to prevent Linda from opening her mouth. The surgery was done under general anesthetic. It took about two hours. Dell and Dorothy waited until Linda was out of surgery, out of recovery, in her hospital room, and then Dorothy went home to relieve the neighbor from next-door, Jewel Evans who had rushed over to watch the other kids when the call came in about Linda.

  Dell said he would stay with Linda until she woke up from the surgery. He could explain to her what had happened. Dell was sitting silently in the dark corner of Linda's hospital room; a nurse had just been in to check on her saying she would be back in about half an hour.

Just after she left Linda suddenly sat bolt upright in the bed started choking, a barely audible gurgling sound. Since her mouth was wired shut, no real sound could come out. She was obviously vomiting into her wired mouth. Dell rushed across the room instead of pressing the emergency call button, he grabbed it holding it out of Linda's reach. Linda's eyes grew wide as she realized what her father was doing. He wasn't going to call for help he was going to let her choke to death on her own vomit. Fluid began running out of Linda's nose, out of her mouth, it oozed through the barest of spaces between the wires, and her teeth. In moments, her nose was plugged she couldn't breathe at all. In a minute or two, Linda lost consciousness slumped down in the bed no longer making a sound.

Dell laid the emergency call button on the nightstand just out of Linda's reach. He slowly began to make his way toward the door. Once there, he opened it just a crack peeked out to see if the coast was clear for him to leave. It was so Dell walked out of the door down the hall to the stairwell and out of the hospital. He believed that Linda if not already dead would most certainly be dead before anyone found her. He would be home with Dorothy when they both got the call. His problems would finally be memories of the past.

$$\Omega$$

A few moments after Dell exited to the stairwell and was out of sight a young woman dressed in a Candy Striper uniform entered Linda's room turned on the light thinking that the room was empty. What she saw scared the daylights out of her. A girl was lying in the bed her face was oozing vomit. At the end of the bed was taped a pair of surgical wire cutters. The volunteer moved closer, realized the girl was still struggling for breath even though her mouth was wired. She grabbed the wire cutters and cut the wires holding the girl's mouth closed. Vomit poured out of the girl's mouth and nose. She started to shake as if she was having a seizure. This terrified the young woman even more she ran out of the room leaving the surgical floor without a word to anyone about what she had done.

    The nurse who had said she would be back in half an hour was caught up with another patient's emergency. She forgot about checking in on Linda. It was nearing dawn almost at the change of shift when a nursing supervisor found Linda covered in vomit with her broken jaw gaping open with little pieces of surgical wire embedded in her tongue and lips.

    She called for a code blue because Linda had aspirated so much vomit she was barely breathing. The surgeon who had done the surgery was called, he headed back into the hospital to find out what had happened to his patient, worried about a lawsuit for having failed to pump her stomach before having wired her jaw shut. The code team suctioned out her airway put her on an IV antibiotic drip. To help forestall the pneumonia that would most certainly set in from having vomit in her lungs.

    A call was placed to Dell and Dorothy to let them know about the emergency—telling them that

Linda would be back in surgery to re-repair her jaw. Dell answered the phone, he had been waiting for the call all night that Linda was dead. He was distraught to discover that she was in bad shape but alive. He remembered how she had looked at him when he was backing away from her bed he wondered how much she would remember.

Linda had her jaw reset and rewired without the benefit of anesthetic, which was a very painful experience to go through right after the nightmare of almost choking to death, while being left for dead. Linda had defense mechanisms of dissociation that took her away from the pain and terror of most of what she'd gone through. The Linda that saw the worried faces of her parents after she returned from surgery did not recall any of her harrowing experience. The only thing she could recall was that an angel had come in the night and saved her. She tried her best to speak. Linda wasn't able to say anything intelligible. The doctor gave her a new IV of antibiotics and a shot of Demerol so she could get some rest.

Dell and Dorothy went home again, Linda was left to sleep it off. She did end up getting a mild case of pneumonia spending two full weeks in the hospital before she was able to go home. The wiring of her jaw would last for two more months after she left the hospital. Linda's slim body would go down to flesh and bone by the time she could eat real food again.

Dell was issued a ticket for the accident and had to go to court, the police officer testified that he found the brake pedal to the car broken off and lying on the driver's side floor. The accident was ruled caused by preventable mechanical failure. Dell's insurance had to pay for all the other damages and he had to pay a $500 fine for allowing someone to operate a car with imminent mechanical failure. The Ford Falcon was totaled and Dell received no coverage compensation since the accident was ruled by the court to be his fault.

$$\Omega$$

That was the seminal event of Linda's sixteenth year between taking care of Justin, being hospitalized, and having to go to school with her mouth wired shut, Linda didn't recall much of that entire year. It disappeared taken in by one of the aspects of her shattered personality more capable of handling the crisis and the near death experience.

12

"It is easier to be a lover than a husband."
Honore DeBalzac

Austin was the first boy Linda dated after she recovered from her car accident. Evidently she was fashionably thin and attractive to him when he asked her to go to the junior prom in the spring of 1970. Linda was five feet five inches tall weighed all of 85 pounds after ten weeks without solid food. Finding a prom dress that she liked that could be altered to fit her was a task in itself. The prom was two weeks away when Austin had asked Linda. Dorothy went into high gear in trying to find a suitable prom dress in a junior size 1. Since Dorothy bought her clothes at the fancy Scottsdale boutiques that's where they began the search. After a whole weekend of shopping, Dorothy and Linda found a yellow with white eyelet ball gown that was a size 1 and only had to be taken in slightly in the top so it wouldn't hang off her bony shoulders. Dorothy went all out getting Linda matching shoes as well as a string of faux pearls. She also got her first girdle and stockings even though a girdle was ridiculous on her non-existent hips.

For the first time Linda had a curfew that was at two o'clock in the morning because one of Austin's best friends was having an after party at his house. That night Linda did enough making out with Austin for him to decide that she was worth some more of his time. He announced to everyone that they were going steady giving Linda his class ring. Austin was a senior, he was graduating so she didn't know if they'd last through the summer, he was handsome and had a cool car. Linda was willing to go along for the ride. She didn't know at the time how important it would be for her to have a steady boyfriend with what was coming in the future. Dell was very uncharacteristically pleased when Linda came home with a steady ring and a college bound boyfriend.

$$\Omega$$

Dell started stalking Linda and Austin almost right after they started dating. He would follow them everywhere. Linda would see him in the car around where they were, too many times for it to be a coincidence. She didn't understand why he was doing it, wasn't even sure he knew why either. Linda just decided it was one more way of being a control freak and a bully. However, by the end of the summer she had another problem Linda was having her nightmares much more frequently, not only when she had gotten a Demerol shot. Sometimes she would wake up in the morning dressed in one of Dorothy's revealing nightgowns instead of the cotton pajamas that she still wore to bed. It was making her feel crazy because she couldn't explain what was happening to herself; Linda couldn't tell anyone else it was happening.

In September after school started Linda got the Demerol shot. She did not get her period. She waited until October, still her period didn't come, there was no Demerol shot that month. On Halloween night, Linda decided to do something that Austin had been begging for since he started college. He wanted to have sex, she decided that the time had come for her to lose her virginity. They went to a Halloween party, he was Dracula, and Linda was a princess. At the house where the party was, the parents had left for a few hours. Linda was nervous that Dell might show up. Austin and Linda went into one of the bedrooms; he'd had a few beers sensing that she had made a decision to go ahead and have sex with him. They lay down on the bed, he was all over her right away taking off her clothes, removing his pants. Linda didn't know what to do but to lay there. He started but it wasn't working because she was too tense. He shouted at Linda to relax, she did because the shout startled her. A few minutes later it was over. He told her to go clean up before she got blood on anything. Linda went into the bathroom she wasn't bleeding. He asked when Linda came back out if she was bleeding badly, she lied said a little bit but claimed she had come prepared. He took that for an answer then asked if Linda had liked it—she said "Yes." They kissed to seal the deal. They went back to the party. Linda could tell by how he was acting that he was telling everyone. Linda told a couple of the girls that she knew and that was that.

Linda told Austin that she had missed her period by the middle of November. Austin and Linda were married by the end of the month. On the night of the wedding they stayed at the Rhode House Inn on the corner of Scottsdale Road and Indian School Road. Linda had started to miscarry three days before the wedding. When she told Dell and Dorothy, Dell told her to keep her mouth shut that she was getting married no matter what. He wasn't going to put up with her promiscuity.

After their wedding, Austin spent the night drinking until he passed out watching a football game. Linda spent the night in the bathroom having a bad miscarriage in the empty bathtub. She bled and cramped for hours before it was over, it was nearly dawn before Linda dared to leave the bathroom. She had scooped up the remains flushed them down the toilet. She did wonder for a little while why she hadn't had her period for a couple of months before she got pregnant. Linda rinsed out the tub, took a shower, and felt safe to put in a tampon for a couple of hours. The next morning they went to Denny's for breakfast. She didn't tell Austin or his family that she'd had a miscarriage for another month.

Ω

Four months later Linda was still bleeding and Austin was sick of her excuses. She told Dorothy about it, finally she took Linda to one of her doctors, not the ones that Dell always made her take her to see. Dr

Asadourian examined Linda. He grabbed Dorothy by the arm dragging her out of the exam room into his office next door. Linda heard him yell at her mom, telling her that Linda would be lucky if she could ever have a baby with all the damage that she had inside her. He put Linda in the hospital overnight did a D & C; put her on birth control pills immediately. Eventually, she healed enough to have sex with her husband. However, by that time Austin already had a couple of girlfriends in college, he didn't care one way or another about sex with Linda.

    The two things Linda could be grateful for was that she was away from Dell and Dorothy. The nightmares seemed to go away as well. Since she had always gone to summer school, she graduated in January from Coronado High School. She only had to go to school for two months while she was married. Linda was seventeen years-old.

13

"You are the bows from which your children as living arrows are sent forth."
Kahlil Gibran, The Prophet

Austin and Linda were married for two and a half years before they had their daughter Brandi Kae. Born on March 1, 1973, she weighed 7 pounds and 11 ounces. She was beautiful, perfect, and Linda was very eager to be a mother even though she was nineteen when Brandi was born. During her pregnancy, Linda had worked at a nursery school she had loved taking care of the babies. Since she was often responsible for at least eight babies at once, she felt like she was well prepared to take care of Brandi.

Austin had spent most of his college years working nights as a pizza cook for Gino's Pizza, a small shop that only did take-out or delivery. Austin often delivered pizzas on his nights off from cooking to make the most money he could. Before Linda got pregnant, she had worked at a downtown Scottsdale restaurant called the Sugar Bowl—it was an upscale ice cream parlor/luncheonette where Linda could earn $40 in tips in a four-hour shift.

Austin and Linda were not rich they earned enough money to cover their expenses. They had been lucky enough to get into a one-bedroom co-op apartment that only cost them $109 per month. Austin was graduating from ASU, Arizona State University, in May. Brandi's birth in March was good timing. Austin's mother Donna was delighted to have a granddaughter since she had always wanted a girl but ended up with three sons. Dorothy wasn't much into the grandmother thing since Justin was three and a half years old when Brandi was born. Dorothy still having a toddler of her own cancelled out the grandmother urge toward Brandi.

Linda had found a second-hand crib and a chest of drawers a couple of months before Brandi was born, she refinished them in her favorite color of Shamrock green. She bought some baby-styled decals decorating the crib to match the chest. When Brandi was born, she had a beautiful set of furniture that fit into the one bedroom with her parents just fine.

However not all was perfect in Linda's life. When Brandi was about two weeks old, Linda got a phone call from a young woman who claimed to be Austin's girlfriend. She didn't give her name, she told Linda that Austin wasn't going to stay married to her for very long. She claimed they were going to be together as soon as the divorce was final. Linda didn't care about Austin and his girlfriends she had always known that he was cheating on her. The idea of a divorce scared her, she didn't want to be a single parent, not when Brandi was just a baby. Linda got her revenge though, she called Austin's mother told her about the phone call after that Linda didn't have to suffer any more divorce threats from anonymous girlfriends.

When Austin graduated, he already had a job with Southland Corporation the company that ran Seven-Eleven stores. Austin's father was a regional director for the company and he had recently relocated the rest of Austin's family to Colorado. The plan was for Austin, Linda, and Brandi to move to Denver after school was finished.

Linda was very excited about the move to Denver she hadn't ever traveled out of Arizona. This was a big deal. Dell was not happy about the impending move he made a clumsy attempt to de-rail it by trying to get Austin interested in coming to work for Allstate. Austin was unenthused about being an insurance salesman even though Dell had been successful. Austin wanted a good management job like his father had, so nothing came of Dell's Allstate plan.

Once Linda left Arizona, Dorothy and Dell couldn't leave her alone, they were always calling with a family problem that only Linda could solve. Linda flew back to Scottsdale three times during the first year they were in Colorado. More often than not, it was to mediate her parents' marital problems. Dell was insisting that Dorothy get a job, she was resisting after all Justin was only 4 years old. Dell was insistent saying that Justin would be better off in daycare with friends to play with and get a head start on school. What Dell really wanted was a divorce, he wanted Dorothy to be working when he filed for one so he wouldn't have to pay alimony. Dorothy was completely ignorant to Dell's ultimate plan. She did manage to go find a sales clerk job at I. Magnin's a very exclusive store in the newest mall in Scottsdale. The store was upmarket so each sales clerk was allowed to pick out three outfits from the store to wear to work to be dressed appropriately for the clientele. Dorothy loved that part; she of course proceeded to spend her entire paychecks on more expensive clothes.

When Dell brought up the subject of divorce Dorothy quit her job, had a bit of a nervous breakdown—Linda made her second trip from Denver to try to talk Dell out of divorcing her mother. During that trip, Linda herself got sick. She fell asleep on the sofa bed in the guest room and had nightmares for the first time in four years. Linda woke up bleeding and it wasn't her period time. She called Dorothy's doctor, making an emergency appointment to see him. An hour later, she was in the hospital, diagnosed with a ruptured ovary. Linda had no idea how such a thing had occurred. The doctor asked her if she had rough sex recently. Linda of course said she hadn't had sex at all for at least three weeks. Linda became hysterical with all the pain, the strange questions, and had to be sedated.

A week later Linda was released from the hospital, she didn't go back to Dell and Dorothy's, instead she caught a plane to Denver without calling Austin to let him know she was coming home. She had left her car at the airport so she drove straight to pick up Brandi at her Grandma Donna's house then headed home to the apartment that she and Austin had rented.

When Linda walked in the door, a woman was standing nude in the kitchen. Linda asked her name, getting nothing but a blank stare. Austin walked out of the bedroom, his face turned white. He asked Linda to leave for fifteen minutes with Brandi. Linda turned around walked out. Half an hour later, she returned the woman and Austin were gone. He didn't return for three days, when he came back home he refused to talk about the woman or anything else for that matter.

Ω

Brandi was two years old. Linda knew that the whisper of a divorce would cause Donna, Austin's mother, to go off the deep end. She decided to wait out the latest affair to see what happened. Six months later the affair was still going on even more seriously. Brandi had to have eye surgery to correct one of her eye muscles, Linda went through that entire process alone without concern or support from Austin.

When Brandi was two and a half years old, Linda packed up her Ford Pinto hatchback with trash bags full of clothes and stuffed animals. She left Austin telling him to file for divorce. She had never driven more than fifty miles from home. She and Brandi set out from Denver to go back to Scottsdale to start a new life just the two of them.

While Linda's marriage was falling apart, Dell had made good on his promise to divorce Dorothy. She refused to participate for her own self-interest ending up with a smaller house, older car, older furniture, very limited alimony, and $600 a month in child support for three kids. Dorothy slipped into a deep depression that was on the rough edge of psychosis when Linda and Brandi showed up at the end of July 1975.

14

"By far the most fragile mother is the unmothered mother...psychically very young or very naïve."
Women Who Run With The Wolves,
Clarissa Pinkola Estes, Ph.D.

When Linda and Brandi arrived at Dorothy's house Linda had no idea what to expect. I was a large three-bedroom house in the "old" neighborhood where they had first moved to Scottsdale. Dell and Dorothy had upgraded a couple of times. Dell kept the new house in northern Scottsdale. He brought Dorothy back into the neighborhood where they'd started.

As it turned out Dorothy insisted that Linda and Brandi take the master bedroom, she had the habit of sleeping on the sofa in the living room since they moved in several months ago. Dorothy was divorced and ashamed; she refused to sleep in the master bedroom. Linda didn't argue with the idea of moving her and Brandi's clothes, belongings, and toys into a big bedroom with its own bath.

Justin had just turned six years old. Brandi followed him everywhere. Deedee was fourteen, Richard was almost seventeen, Linda was almost twenty-two. Dorothy had all her children back—didn't have any idea of what to do about it. In spite of her depression, she had gotten a job at Smitty's in the bakery. In the grocery store bakery world being slightly psychotic is borderline normal.

Linda however needed to find a job right away; she had left Denver with $220, a gasoline credit card, and a MasterCard. She figured that both the credit cards would be cut off shortly. Linda needed to work. However, she wasn't prepared to leave Brandi during the day. She focused her job search on night jobs. She found a cocktail waitress job within the week at a big new nightclub that was opening up in Tempe near the university. Dorothy and Deedee could watch Brandi at night putting her to bed. Linda got home around two o'clock in the morning then woke up with Brandi at eight. So far, things were going pretty well.

After the divorce, Dell had more or less disappeared except to take the kids out somewhere occasionally. He was already involved with another woman named Barbara who had a son and daughter. Dorothy or the kids didn't see him much. This was just as well; because she was living under the delusion that he was going to come back to her in the near future.

Once Linda was back in the picture, Dell started hanging around more insisting that Linda and Brandi spend time with him and his new girlfriend. Every week or so Linda and Brandi would meet Dell and Barbara for lunch in downtown Scottsdale. Linda was very uncomfortable around Dell even on his best behavior in front of Barbara. He still struck terror into Linda's heart. She tried to start begging off on the lunch dates saying that she needed to get some extra rest for her night job when Brandi took an afternoon nap. Then she just said she couldn't go because it upset Dorothy. It worked to blame it on her mother, the invites stopped.

Linda waitressed all weekend long. She had Mondays and Tuesdays off from the club. One Monday night Brandi wanted to sleep in Auntie Deedee's bed. Linda was alone in the master suite. On Tuesday morning, she woke up around five o'clock because she had a nightmare. Once she was awake she realized that she was injured. She was bleeding from behind and her abdomen was hurting badly.

As she continued to wake up, she grew more alarmed; she looked across the room saw a tennis racket that hadn't been there the night before. The handle was covered in blood. Linda struggled out of bed, finding several bloody towels were there to protect the sheets. They hadn't been there when she went to bed.

Linda went into the shower where large clots of blood dropped onto the shower floor. The blood clots seemed to subside she turned on the shower washing herself until the water ran clear. Then with the shower still running she ducked out, grabbed the tennis racket, took it into the shower, washed it clean.

What had happened to her Linda wasn't sure she wanted to know. This wasn't the first time she had awakened to discover strange injuries, those times had happened when she was younger. This was frightening because not only she had been hurt. The weapon had been left in the room for her to find. The more she thought about it the more upset she became. Linda fainted on the bathroom floor.

She regained consciousness a few minutes later she thought. When she looked at the clock in the bedroom it was almost seven o'clock, she awoke at five. What had she done in two hours of time? She looked down at her right hand she was clutching something. Linda opened her hand slowly seeing what she had in her grasp. It was hers now it would save her and Brandi.

When Linda went out of the master bedroom, she found her mother still sleeping, snoring on the sofa in the living room. The front door was unlocked, someone had walked passed Dorothy on the sofa. Linda went checked the other doors in the house they were all locked from the night before. The bleeding had stopped Linda snuck the tennis racket out of the house, putting it in her car—when she went to work she threw the racket in the club's dumpster.

Ω

On Wednesday, Linda also went to a pawnshop that was just down the street from where she worked. She had a large diamond cocktail ring that she had hidden in her purse that morning. Linda did not remember finding or taking the ring but she knew exactly what she was going to do with it. Linda sold the ring for enough money to get her and Brandi an apartment so they could move out of the house where Linda's nightmares had started again. She never knew what had happened to her except that a nightmare, one that she hadn't had in a long time had woke her up. That incident went deep into Linda's soul like all the rest of what she couldn't explain. Deep into the darkest recesses where her nightmares still lurked.

15

"To the immature other people are not real."
Harry Overstreet

    When Brandi turned three years old, Linda could put her in preschool. Her friend Shelley's husband happened to run one of the locations of one of the best preschools in Arizona. Linda had her fill of working in a nightclub, she definitely didn't want to live at Dorothy's house anymore. She'd found another job, a much better job, working for USLife Title Company in their Tempe office for a nice guy named Nick and his escrow officer Sherry. The job paid Linda enough money to pay for preschool, find a nice two-bedroom apartment, and if she was frugal pay the rest of her bills. Linda and Brandi were very happy she loved going to school. Linda loved her new job—instead of having drunken guys hit on her Linda was having single real estate salesmen asking her out. She had moved up fast.

    Brandi had a friend at the apartments; another three-year-old girl named Charity she and Brandi became inseparable on the weekends. Linda met Charity's parents, a young couple about her same age and they became friends. It was the spring of 1976, things were really going well for the two of them. Until one day on Linda's way home from work to go to pick up Brandi, she was rear-ended in her Ford Pinto by a huge Cadillac. The Pinto was totaled Linda was lucky that she barely had any gas in the tank or she might have burned to death. The blessing was that Brandi wasn't in the car. Linda came out of it unscathed except for many muscle aches for a couple of weeks. She had Allstate Insurance; they paid right away, so she had money to buy another car.

    The college boy neighbor next door to Dorothy's house happened to be selling a 1963 light blue MGB Midget convertible. Linda offered him all of her insurance settlement of $1,500 and he agreed to lower the price so she could buy it. It was a good deal for both of them—he got a couple of dates with Linda, she got a car that she just loved. Linda and Brandi looked cute driving down the road in the car with the top down, people would honk at them and smile all the time.

    It was the Fourth of July weekend of 1976 the bi-centennial. At the apartments, they had a big party at the pool and pool house for all of the residents. Linda had noticed that a couple of guys had moved in next door. She hadn't had the chance to meet them yet. One of them she thought was cute she hoped he'd show up to the party.

It was about ten o'clock; the girls, Brandi and Charity, already had a long day and were settled into bed at Charity's apartment for the night. Linda had been drinking Corona beer since noon, she wasn't used to drinking so much but she had eaten a couple of hotdogs, she was doing okay.

When the new cute neighbor walked by she noticed for the first time that he had a long ponytail that hung down his back. Linda decided right then that she wanted to meet him for sure. She followed him into one of the open apartments next to the pool. He turned around after a moment, "Are you following me?" Linda was flustered didn't know what to say when someone handed her a joint. Even though Linda had never tried marijuana before she did. It made her choke, cough, and then as fast as the smoke went in it made her high. She laughed at herself for coughing, then took another hit from the joint. The cute neighbor said, "You gonna keep that all to yourself Newbie?" He held out his hand for Linda to pass it on. She did so, he took a deep long hit passing it on himself. By that time he had hold of Linda's elbow steering her to a spot on the sofa. "My name is Dylan and I already know your name is Newbie. Was that your first hit ever?"

"Yes I admit it. My name is Linda and it's all I'll answer to from now on."

"Deal, nice to meet you Linda."

For the rest of the evening Dylan kept Linda amused and high he showed her how to inhale without choking or coughing, Linda confessed that she liked how she felt.

"This is way better than drinking, I never knew." Dylan said "And there's no hangover."

By the end of the long weekend, Dylan and Linda were the newest couple at the apartments. Dylan met Brandi he was great with her. He had her laughing and giggling within minutes. Linda was falling hard for this longhaired, pot smoking, construction worker, and once he saw her car he was pretty much on the hook too. He had an old Land Rover that was good for getting around to construction sites. The MGB was definitely for fun.

For the rest of the summer they were inseparable—a couple of his friends from Massachusetts came to visit and they stayed so it was a party, the more the merrier.

On August 1, Linda put Brandi on a plane to visit her Grandma Donna who had moved from Colorado to Texas. Donna had paid for the plane ticket insisting that since Austin was paying child support Linda had to send Brandi to see her father and grandparents for a month every summer. She was terrified that they would not send her back. She was also terrified that if she didn't send Brandi they'd come take her for good. It was losing situation from Linda's perspective she decided to trust they'd send Brandi back on September 1.

On the other side of the coin, Linda had a month of freedom, a new boyfriend to spend it with, and she was determined to have some fun like never before.

Ω

A big group of friends went to a concert in Tucson; it headlined Fleetwood Mac, Heart, and Kenny Loggins. They stayed a few blocks from the university; the concert was at the stadium. Linda and Dylan had a great weekend.

At the concert Linda had never been so high in her life. Even when she stopped smoking herself, the air all around would get her even higher. Several times she had to walk around the stadium track to keep from passing out. There were so many drugs at the concert. People were just passing out pills, pot, hashish, and cocaine Linda steered clear of everything but pot. However, Dylan was not so particular, he took some of whatever came his way, yet he seemed to keep it together. Linda was amazed, just a little impressed that he could handle himself in an environment of random drugs, huge crowds, and rock and roll. Linda was running with a new pack she never knew what to expect.

$$\Omega$$

When they all got back from the concert, Dylan suggested to Linda that they move into a bigger place. His apartment was always full night and day and he said they should be living together. Linda was excited by the possibility although she had never considered what it would be like to live with lots of roommates. She could see that communal living might have its advantages with everyone sharing the bills. Two other couples had come from Massachusetts—Dylan's two-bedroom apartment was over-flowing with people. For Linda it wasn't very hard for her to talk to a couple of real estate guys she knew getting them to find her a big five-bedroom house in Tempe not far from Linda's job.

Dylan and Linda both gave notice at the apartments within the month, they moved into a big house on a cul-de-sac lot about ten minutes from Linda's work and Brandi's preschool. Dylan and Linda took the master bedroom; Brandi had a small bedroom right next door. Tom and Tessa, Dylan's brother and his girlfriend, were across the hall, and Danny and Brenda were in another room. Dylan's best friend Ron had a small room to himself.

Tom and Tessa both worked in construction with Dylan. Ron got a job at U-Haul renting trucks. Danny and Brenda got part-time jobs in restaurants near the university. Everything was going great for the "Tempe Commune" as they all called it. Until Linda's younger brother Martin showed up.

Martin's life was a crazy mess Linda hadn't seen or talked to him since he'd gotten married and joined the army—he had a wife, two sons, was AWOL from his post in Colorado Springs. He'd been living with Dell until he totaled his father's van running over a guy on a motorcycle leaving him permanently paralyzed on one side of his body. The insurance was battling it out, Martin was trying to avoid going to jail. He had been high on heroin at the time of the accident. Dell had thrown him out. Martin had stopped into the U-Haul where Ron worked to rent a trailer to move his stuff to his mother-in-law's house. When Ron saw that Martin's last name was Moore, he mentioned that his best friend's girlfriend was named Moore too. It didn't take long for Martin to discover he'd found his long lost sister. Thanks to Ron's naïve stupidity Martin had a place to stay as well

When Linda came home from work that night she found Martin firmly ensconced in the family room smoking a joint telling stories about his drug dealing days in the army. The holidays were coming up Linda didn't want to seem like a shrew to her brother so she said he could crash on the living room sofa for a while. Dylan and Martin seemed to get along. What could be the problem—Linda thought, as she went to bed that night alone because the guys were up late getting high, telling stories.

Within the month, Linda regretted her decision to let Martin stay—to start with, she found out that he injected heroin, he had left a needle around where Brandi might find it. Linda also overheard Martin trying to convince Dylan to try heroin himself which up to that time he had steered away from any "hard drugs." Linda was not only upset that Martin was bringing all his problems to her doorstep. Linda had just found out that she was pregnant. She hadn't told Dylan yet. Linda would have to tell him in a day or two because she had stopped getting high. He had already asked her why, she lied saying that she wasn't feeling good and thought a break would help. He was cool with that. Would he be cool with a baby on the way? On the Sunday before Christmas 1977, Linda laid her news on Dylan. She was shocked and happily surprised when he hugged her, said it was great news. He also said the whole idea made him horny so they made love in bed right then. Linda was relieved but excited she had wanted another baby, this was as good a time as any, even though they weren't married had no plans to be. Linda had never felt more secure with her own circumstances—except for Martin's presence everything was perfect.

Two days later the police showed up looking for Martin. Linda told them where to find him—he was working the night shift at U-Haul with Ron who was the manager. Linda called Ron to warn him that the cops were coming for Martin. She made him swear not to tell Martin but just let him get picked up. Nevertheless, Ron spilled to Martin, he took off in a U-Haul truck before the police got there. Ron reported the truck as stolen Martin was picked up within an hour. He used his one phone call to call Linda to bitch her out for betraying him. Linda told him that they were all done with him. He was never to show up again, she could only hope to be lucky.

Martin went to jail for three months before he was bailed out by Dell. The insurance settled with the motor cycle rider, the criminal charges against Martin were dropped. The army gave him a dishonorable discharge, his wife filed for divorce. Out of all the trouble that Martin's own actions had caused the one person he blamed for his problems was Linda.

Linda was about four months pregnant. She needed to buy some clothes that she could wear to work. It was one thing at home to wear one of Dylan's rock concert tee shirts and cut-off jean shorts tied with a shoelace but she did have to look good at work. She had saved some money went shopping getting five outfits in one fell swoop. Linda had just arrived home from her shopping trip when Martin showed up, coming into the house through the garage door. He was furious with Linda; she was scared for herself and the baby. It was obvious that he was high, he admitted that he had just shot up some cocaine, which explained his level of agitation. Linda was home alone. Her purchases were laying on a chair next to the fireplace in the family room. Martin grabbed them up, began tearing the outfits then he threw them into the empty fireplace. Once all her clothes were torn up in the fireplace. Martin pulled out a lighter then with Linda watching set her new clothes on fire.

"I'm calling the police again." Linda screamed.

"Fuck you, you snitch."

"Get out of here." Linda moved toward the phone on the wall in the kitchen "I swear I'm going to call them you'll go back to jail."

"I'm gone you bitch." Martin walked out through the garage door.

Linda ran to close the door saw Martin pick up one of Dylan's toolboxes walking out of the garage with it. He called out over his shoulder. "You know Dylan tried the heroin—he'll never forget it."

Linda was shaking when she finally sat down next to the fireplace. Her clothes were ruined she didn't have any money to buy anything else. Suddenly she felt sick to her stomach and ran for the bathroom. She threw up then had the dry heaves for a few minutes. Linda didn't know if it was 'morning sickness' or just anxiety over what had just happened. How had Martin ended up being messed up on drugs, almost killing someone, and ruining his life in general? He was always the favorite son, taken care of and nurtured—so much for that working out.

16

"Your children are not your children. They are sons and daughters of Life's longing for itself."
Kahlil Gibran, The Prophet

On August 29, 1978, Robert Grey was born in Mesa General Hospital. Dylan was by Linda's side, well sort of, he was outside in the truck smoking a joint when Robert was born. Robert was healthy and weighed the same as his sister Brandi weighed 7-pounds and 11-ounces.

The worst thing that happened on the day that Robert was born was that Dorothy showed up at the hospital right after Linda had given birth. Dorothy was a mental, emotional wreck. Dell had her hospitalized several times in the last year for mental illness she was not in a good state of mind at the hospital. Linda had just given birth—Dorothy wanted Linda to get up off the delivery table to take her to the bathroom. "Mother

I don't want you here you are ruining everything." Linda wailed, "They can't bring the baby to me because you're here in the way. GO NOW!"

Finally, a nurse heard all the commotion in the delivery recovery room managed to get security to escort Dorothy out of the hospital. They gave Linda a shot to calm her down, she fell asleep without getting to hold Robert for a couple of hours.

Robert had a little bit of jaundice. The hospital had to keep him under special lights for a few days. Linda, because she didn't have insurance, had to go home leaving Robert at the hospital. She went to see him every day staying for the whole time that Brandi was in school. Brandi had started Kindergarten. She was in school for half of the day. Brandi was anxious to see her new brother she cried every day when he wasn't home yet. After a week Robert was released, he was fine.

Dylan was proud to have a son; he called his mother to tell her about it. He hadn't talked to her in about two years, it was a big surprise to find out that she was a grandmother. Dylan's parents were divorced, he called his dad the next day, and they had a good conversation.

Linda for obvious reasons did not want to talk to either one of her parents, especially not Dell. When he had found out Linda was pregnant, not going to get married, he disowned her. She thought that was a fine idea. Linda hadn't talked to Dorothy either because of her behavior at the hospital and Martin was living with her.

Ω

The birth drama was over. The new family came together. Robert went in a bassinette in with Brandi who of course slept in her own twin bed. They had already put up the crib in the room for Robert to switch over to in a few weeks.

The first two people to mention the end of the commune were Tom and Tessa they thought the kids would be better off without so many people around especially people that got high most of the time they were at home. Ron had been asked by U-Haul to become an on-site manager 24/7. He was going to move into a small studio apartment above the shop. Danny and Brenda had been getting homesick were thinking about having kids themselves, they were ready to head back to Massachusetts. It all worked out for the best. Dylan, Linda, Brandi, and Robert settled into a two-bedroom apartment in Tempe. Dylan was making good money working construction. Linda didn't have to worry about going back to work right away. Their lives were on track they had a happy little family.

Right after Christmas Martin was arrested again, this time for armed robbery. He had been living with Dorothy making sure his exploits kept her crazy as a loon. Deedee had moved out, she was living at Dell's house, she dropped out of high school found a job selling menswear at an upscale Scottsdale boutique. Dorothy and Justin lived at the house, but they wouldn't be there for long. Dorothy had lost her job at the bakery. She hadn't paid the taxes or the insurance on the house. It was being foreclosed on for back taxes—

the two of them were going to be on the street. Once Dell got wind of what was happening he contacted his lawyer in order to reclaim custody of Justin. He also managed to have Dorothy committed to Camelback Hospital, an expensive inpatient mental hospital in Phoenix. Dell called Linda guilt tripping her into being Dorothy's primary emergency contact. Linda was the one who had to go see her to sign the papers for her commitment.

Now with all the kids not living with Dorothy she didn't even have the little bit of child support she'd been living on—she was in the hospital but when she got out, she'd have to go somewhere. Linda could see that Dell was setting up that somewhere to be with her. She couldn't, not for a million dollars let that happen. Dorothy was a drunk; most of her "mental illness" was that she drank from morning to night every day. Of course, at the hospital they also discovered that she was psychotically depressed. The medications started, they began to dry her out.

Linda had to leave Robert with her neighbor a couple of times a week to go visit Dorothy, which was a futile effort if Linda had ever seen one. Dorothy just spent the time complaining about the hospital, that had a pool and fancy dining room for its clients—most of whom suffered from alcohol or drug related issues. After 30 days of sobriety, most would be sent home, a few thousand dollars less in their bank accounts, going right back to drinking or drugging. Camelback Hospital was a rehab mill; it wasn't going to help Dorothy recover or learn to take responsibility for herself. Linda damn well wasn't going to end up taking care of the mother who had never taken care of her.

  Dorothy's stay lasted longer than most; at least Dell had kept up her health insurance. She was there for nine months. When she got out she wasn't crazy as a loon anymore she was crazy like a fox. Dell bought her a condominium Justin moved back home with his mother. As for Linda, Dylan, Robert, and Brandi they rented a U-Haul truck from Ron and hit the road for Massachusetts where Dylan already had a job as a U-Haul manager waiting for him in North Hampton.

  Linda felt ecstatic she and her family were moving almost 3,000 miles away from Dell, Dorothy, Martin, Deedee, and Justin. Her responsibility was to her own little family she was a happy as she had ever been—Linda had a feeling she was leaving the nightmares behind for good.

Ω

  Linda, Dylan, and the kids arrived in Massachusetts in time for Robert's first birthday, which was celebrated like a family reunion. All of Dylan's family had been estranged from one another for reasons they no longer remembered. Dylan came home with a son all was forgotten, more or less, at least for a week or two. They settled in North Hampton which was a pleasant little college town, found an apartment about five minutes from Dylan's work. Everything went well for the family for a couple of years. Dylan grew some pot, made a little money. They were able to buy a small lot of land in Belchertown.

When Rob was three years old, Dylan and Linda got married in a civil ceremony with a couple of friends, Mike and Carla, as witnesses. They didn't even tell family until Dylan went to talk to his grandmother about giving him some money to build a house on the land they had purchased and already cleared for construction. His grandmother was not overly enamored with Linda but she was Catholic and relieved that her grandson wasn't living in sin anymore—she agreed to give Dylan the money. Two weeks later Linda got a job working for Pepsi-Co running the first Taco Bell Restaurants in Massachusetts. She got the job because she was the only applicant who had actually eaten Taco Bell food before. She could describe what a Taco Bell Restaurant looked like. Linda was a store supervisor; she went into training while Dylan got a new job working for the small construction company that was going to build their house.

Things were all sunshine and roses for them. Linda liked her job in North Hampton, which was about twenty minutes from where their house was being built. Dylan liked his job because they all got high in the morning with their coffee—had beers at noon with their lunch, and went out and drank whiskey for a couple of hours after they quit building for the day. They had good friends, good pot, and good times. The house was going to be finished on Thanksgiving of 1981, and they planned a big party, friends only, no family except for Tom and Tessa. Linda was twenty-eight and Dylan was twenty-five they were still in love, living well, and working hard. It seems that something always changes when you least expect it.

Ω

About six months after they moved into the house the building boom slowed down. Dylan and his construction buddies were having a hard time making a go of it. They even took a job out of town in Martha's Vineyard to do a massive remodel of a vacation house there. Dylan was gone for three months while they worked on the job. Linda had to pay all the bills on her own. She managed, it was tough even though Dylan called every weekend—it seemed like he was having a better time of it than she was. When Dylan came home they had a very romantic, sexually fulfilling reunion. The next day when Linda inquired about Dylan's paycheck, the whole day and evening went sour. Dylan acted as if he was offended that Linda would ask him about money, to prove it he went to the bar for the night. Not coming home until Linda had gone to bed because she had to work the next morning.

When Linda came home that next evening with the kids in tow Dylan and his buddies were down in the basement huddled around the table and chairs that were down there, doing lines of coke. Linda wasn't a prude about it she had done a line or two herself from time to time but pot was her drug of choice. She went outside up on the deck, smoked a joint and had a diet Coke. Then she went inside to be with the kids for a while before they went to bed. After the kids went to bed, the party downstairs was still going. Linda went in the bedroom turned on the television smoked another joint and fell asleep. The next morning Dylan hadn't come to bed. She went downstairs to find the place a mess. She also found something she didn't expect to find. A crack pipe— that's what Dylan and his buddies had gotten into while they were gone for three months. That certainly explained how mad Dylan had become when she asked him about money. Pot wasn't cheap but it wouldn't break your bank—it made you mellow, was a slow burn on a bank account. Smoking crack and doing coke was fast money going up in smoke or up your nose. Dylan had spent all his earnings on partying and who knows what else. Linda was pissed off—probably for the first time in their five-year relationship—Linda was truly angry with Dylan, her own anger scared her.

    Linda was no good at confrontation, what always happened when she got angry was she would do something self-sabotaging or self-destructive. Over the next couple of weeks, Linda and Dylan's relationship got worse and other than the drugs, she didn't know why. Dylan was staying out all night, Linda assumed he was crashing at his buddies' houses. One night after the kids went to bed she decided to take a little ride down to the Belchertown tavern to see if Dylan's truck was there. Not only was his truck there in the parking lot, Dylan was inside, parked under a lot light. Linda could see that he wasn't alone. He was in the truck going at it with the young girl that worked for the local insurance agency, as a receptionist. If she were a day over nineteen Linda would bet a hundred dollars and win.

    Linda parked, waiting across the street at Crystal Springs Dairy Bar she watched as they finished in the truck. The girl got out into her own car. Both vehicles left the parking lot together heading toward the only apartment complex in Belchertown. They parked next to each other, went into a downstairs apartment. Linda waited a little while. She had to get back home to the sleeping kids. Now at least she knew where Dylan was spending his nights—with his crack whore teen-age girlfriend.

Ω

The worst part of it for Linda as she drove home to her kids was that she knew that Dylan's secret was only secret from her. Linda was certain that the whole town had gossiped about Dylan's cheating on his wife. Belchertown was a small town in the woods; people liked nothing better than a juicy story about cheating wives or husbands. Linda had done it herself about neighbors or people she barely knew. Now it was her own problem—she knew what she was going to do, was it smart maybe not, would she feel better, she sure are hell hoped so. Linda went home smoked a joint and drank a half a bottle of red wine that was left over, it tasted like crap, she didn't care. Drinking helped keep her mad that's why she rarely drank more than a beer or two. Now things would change she needed to stay mad because the other alternative was sad and she was afraid that sad would kill her.

Ω

Linda made the decision to start looking for another job. If she was going to be a single parent again she needed to make more money. In the classifieds, she found an ad for a company called Management Search

Inc.; the ad said they were looking for people to train from the ground up as executive recruiters. Linda sent in a resume, they responded in a week setting up an interview. The office was in West Springfield about a forty-five minute commute. Linda was looking for any opportunity that would allow her to let go of her attachment to Dylan. A new job could be part of the fresh start that she needed.

Linda met with Larry Lopez and Michael Duvall the two partners in the business, she liked what she heard; they liked her as well offering her a position as a recruiter for $800 per month plus commission on every job placement she made. The salary was less than what she was making by a little bit. The commission upside was significant—$40K to $50K a year which was over three times her salary in the restaurant. She accepted the job agreeing to start training in two weeks.

Within two months Linda was adding $1,000 to her base salary. She had decided to see an attorney about her marital situation. Linda wanted to sell the house. She hadn't had any conversations with Dylan since he moved out. She didn't want to get into any hassles with his family. Since she had been paying all the bills for the past year she wasn't going to walk away empty handed.

She got an idea of what was ahead when the next week Kris, Dylan's mother, called to say that she wanted all the furniture she had given them as a wedding gift back. Linda told her to call her son, if he would put down his crack pipe long enough, he could come take whatever she wanted back. Linda hung up hard on that call.

Linda put off the divorce. She did get Dylan to agree sell the house—he wanted some money as much as Linda did. It took them four months to sell the house, they got full price, which meant that each of them got about $5,000 after Dylan paid back his grandmother.

Linda moved to Lowell Massachusetts, which cut her commute in half, the kids had to change schools. They liked the townhouse that Linda found to rent—as long as Linda was happy, her kids were happy. Once Linda was settled into a new place Dylan started coming around—it seemed all was not good living with a crack whore.

Linda made the mistake of sleeping with Dylan a few times and he started to think they could get back together if he only used Cocaine. Linda had some bad news that plan wasn't going to fly—alcohol and pot were the drugs of choice she was willing to deal with—anything else was out of bounds. That's when she discovered what happens when you tell an addict to stop *his* drug of choice. He used the bank debit card to clean out her checking account. Over a period of four days Dylan took $1,200 from her. That's when Linda decided that she could be a recruiter anywhere. She arranged to move from Massachusetts to Arizona. Dylan begged for forgiveness for taking the money, so she decided she would give Dylan one chance to go with her and the kids.

Linda had a big commission coming for over $6,000 it was enough to move and resettle. She got a new job with a recruiting firm in Phoenix by a phone interview, started arranging to leave as soon as school was out. Dylan insisted that he was coming with them that it was the best way for him to get a clean start. He moved into the townhouse for the last two weeks before the movers were scheduled. Brandi had flown to Texas to visit her grandmother for a month and would fly to Arizona in July. Linda had sold her car, she and Rob were going to fly to Arizona—three days before they left Dylan said he couldn't go right now, that he had gotten a construction job for the summer and wanted to make some money before going to Arizona. Linda foolishly believed him.

There was an emotional tearful goodbye for Dylan, Rob, and Linda at the Hartford Airport. Dylan promised to be in Arizona by Rob's birthday on August 29.

Rob was still sobbing when he got on the plane. Linda was glad when he fell asleep a little while after take-off. She had the feeling that they would never see Dylan again and that would almost prove to be true.

17

"The first sign of a nervous breakdown is when you start thinking your work is terribly important."
Bloom County Milo Bloom, Berkeley Breathed

Linda worked as a recruiter in Phoenix for about four months and then she recruited herself into a great in-house recruiter position for a company called Fairchild Data Inc., a subsidiary of Fairchild Industries. The company was a high-tech R & D communications manufacturer and Linda got paid $35,000 to recruit software engineers from all over the country. She did such a good job that after six months the company President Beau Harper fired his HR director, promoting Linda into the position. Linda was 31 years old and was a director of a 20 million dollar division, of a Fortune 500 company. She had to pinch herself to believe her luck. She was earning $50,000. It was 1984; she and the kids were going to have a great Christmas.

Dylan hadn't come to Arizona by Rob's birthday, by Christmas, or by Brandi's birthday. Linda stopped calling him to listen to his empty crack induced promises. They all had given up on Dylan; it was especially hard for the kids. Linda filed for divorce in Arizona it was final by the time she got her promotion. She had to by law, require some kind of child support, she had the lawyer put in $100 per month Dylan never even acknowledged getting the papers let alone paying any support. From Linda's perspective, he was nothing to her anymore.

Linda had decided that marriage was not a good thing for her. She didn't object to dating, not at all, and computer and software engineers most of whom were single because they were nerds surrounded her. She had also met two new girlfriends at the apartment pool, Shelley and Joanie. The three of them would go out to the clubs in town almost every Friday night. Brandi was eleven years old and had been babysitting herself and Rob since she was a latch key kid at age seven. Brandi would babysit when the women went out. The truth was that she was still too young to babysit at night let alone three boys and a toddler. That was how it was then, it was wrong, Linda did it anyway.

Ω

One Friday night the women went out together. Linda came home with a guy she'd met at the club. When they came into the apartment Brandi woke up, Linda told her to go back to bed. She and her friendly stranger had sex then he left at about two o'clock in the morning. Linda was up checking on the kids since Shelley and Joanie weren't home yet. There was a knock on the door. Linda answered it thinking it was one of her girlfriends. When she opened the door, everything went black. Someone grabbed her elbow steering her into the bedroom. Linda was thrown down on the bed, raped from behind, and then the nightmare was over. Her vison cleared—she began to cry without making a sound. Linda hadn't had one of her nightmares in a very long time. She was shocked into silence she couldn't speak. There was another knock at the door, this time Brandi answered—it was her grandfather Dell. He told Brandi to go back to bed while he went in to Linda's bedroom. Linda was catatonic, Dell nearly dragged her out of the apartment got her into his car and took her to the hospital. She never said a word, not to the doctors, not to Dell, not to anyone.

Dell proceeded to tell the story of how Linda and her friends had gone out clubbing, that Linda had come home with a stranger that she'd met who had raped and sodomized her. No one wondered how Dell knew the whole story since Linda was in a dissociative fugue not saying or reacting to anything. No one questioned his version of events at all. Not even Brandi.

Ω

Linda was referred to a psychiatrist after her hospital stay. The doctor prescribed Tofranil for depression and sent her on her way. Linda took it for about two weeks, hated how it made her feel so she quit taking it. Work was too important to have to be taking medication that made her feel out of it. Linda didn't remember what had happened that night other than the nightmare. She vowed not to put herself in a position to have any nightmares again. She stopped going out with

Shelley and Joanie instead stayed home and babysat with Brandi. Linda decided that if she were going to date it would be real dates with nerd engineers.

By February of 1985, Linda was dating Russell one of those engineers she had recruited to work for Fairchild. Their dates usually consisted of dinner out at Linda's favorite Mexican restaurant and then back home to watch television. Brandi babysat for only a couple of hours she got paid $5 bucks. She was happy with the new arrangement. The kids seemed to like Russell he seemed to like them. Early in the summer, he told Linda that all he'd ever wanted was to have a wife and kids. Linda thought, "I can do that." She was hooked. The two of them got married in November. Beau Harper was Russell's best man.

Linda and Russell bought an 'earth house' in northeast Phoenix everything seemed to be going well until Linda met Russell's mother. They both took an instant dislike to each other. Linda discovered what a "mama's boy" her husband really was. It put a strain on the relationship because his mother was brutal in her criticism not only of Linda, but of Brandi and Rob as well. Russell took his mother's side. Since she was visiting for an entire month it created a giant rift in Linda's relationship with Russell—they had been married for six months and Linda doubted that she had made the right decision not only for herself also for the kids.

$$\Omega$$

Linda's job was her major salvation she loved it. She was excited to go back to work on Mondays she could not sleep on Sunday nights. Even though Russell and Linda worked at the same place, they rarely saw each other at work. Most of the time drove in separate cars because they worked different hours. Linda was in the office by eight o'clock every morning Russell came in around ten. The engineers pretty much worked to their own inner clock as long as they got the job done it didn't matter. Linda was home by six o'clock had dinner with the kids then she would cook for Russell whenever he got home. It had turned out that Russell didn't like kids as much as he thought he would. Linda did her best to keep their schedules different.

Ω

In January, Linda began having menstrual issues and went to a gynecologist. She discovered that she had a severe case of pelvic inflammatory disease the result of years of untreated pelvic infections. The doctor said it was the worst he had ever seen. He immediately urged Linda to have a hysterectomy as soon as possible. Linda was only 32 years old it was a big decision. She'd had her tubes tied five years earlier the concern wasn't about having any more children. The surgery would mean she would be in menopause in her early thirties. Ultimately, the doctor's concerns convinced Linda that she had no choice; in March 1986, she scheduled the surgery with the caveat that if he could the doctor would leave one ovary. The surgery took four hours to remove all of the infection and scar tissue. Linda's recovery would not be easy.

Ω

The one part of Linda's job that she did not like was firing people. Even though she usually did it with the person's manager, it was always a high stress situation for her. Linda had been away from work for six weeks after having a hysterectomy. When she came back, Beau Harper called her into his office to tell her that he had been waiting for her to get back from medical leave. He and Ray Kinsey, the V.P. of sales, needed to fire a young woman employee who had been with the company for less than a year.

Linda was surprised that Beau wanted to fire Katy—before Linda had gone on leave, he was praising her work. Linda wondered what had happened in six weeks to result in a firing of a female sales engineer. She talked to Ray he agreed it had to be done. He said that Katy was a temporary success, wasn't meeting her sales numbers anymore. They agreed to sit down with her on Friday to give her the bad news.

The meeting seemed to be going smoothly Katy was taking the termination in stride she even added that she was going back to California to be with her boyfriend—it seemed to be a win all around. Linda and Katy left Ray Kinsey's office heading to Linda's office to finalize the paperwork. Katy didn't say a word to Linda as they walked through the hallways. When they arrived in Linda's office Katy took off the gloves she started berating Linda "You are all going to be sorry that you did this believe me, this is gonna cost you your job and other people too."

"Now Katy I know you're upset, let's just finish up the paperwork, get you out of here before you say something you'll regret."

Katy reached into her purse pulled out a Polaroid picture that she tossed across Linda's desk. It was a picture of Beau Harper with the sheets pulled up under his chin in a bedroom that was painted pink. Linda sucked in her breath "What's this?"

"Beau in my bedroom—we were sleeping together until I told him I was getting back with my boyfriend. Beau got furious and I'm fired. I think you as HR director catch my drift." She paused, "I've already hired an attorney I was just waiting for this day I knew it was coming. My sales numbers are fine I just didn't want to sleep with the boss anymore."

Linda watched as Katy reached for the photo "This is my whole case, Mrs. Harper isn't going to be very happy either."

Ω

Within the week, Linda had to tell Milt Deever, the CEO, Beau Harper's boss, about the major liability that they had as the result of Katy's firing. Linda spent three days on the phone with corporate attorneys back in Washington D.C. being deposed. On the third day one of the attorneys asked Linda what she wanted for severance. Linda didn't understand, "What do you mean I'm not leaving over this."

The attorney said, "I'm sorry no one has told you. You are leaving over this, a kind of 'shoot the messenger' situation. I'll call you tomorrow, let you have some time to think about it. I'd ask for three or four months' pay if I were you and you'll want to keep your insurance for at least a year."

Linda was too stunned to say anything else, "Thank you." She hung up the phone.

It had never occurred to her that she would lose her job. She thought this would all be on Beau and maybe Ray if he knew, she couldn't have imagined that it would be blamed on her.

Two weeks later thanks to having her insurance for a year Linda was in another psychiatrist's office this time, she was given a prescription for Klonopin. She went home and took them for a week then one day when the kids were gone on a camping trip with the neighbors, Russell had gone to play golf. Linda took the whole rest of the bottle of Klonopin-80 pills. Just as she was about to fall asleep she called Ray Kinsey to ask him why he hadn't told her about the real reason they were firing Katy. Linda's slurred words, nonsensical monologue alarmed Ray, even though he was 25 miles away on the other side of town, he called the police and reported a possible overdose.

When Linda woke up, she was in the Humana hospital a few blocks from her house. A police officer was standing guard at her door. After all suicide is a crime so is attempted suicide. Her throat was on fire a nurse told her it was because of the stomach tube they had inserted to pump her stomach. Linda asked how long she had been there the nurse said three days. "You nearly didn't make it; most of the pills were already in your system when you got here."

Linda almost didn't believe her, three days at death's door. Why had she called Ray? She didn't want to be saved she almost wasn't. Linda thought to herself that maybe once she knew what was going to happen to her she'd make a better effort next time.

When the doctor released Linda from the hospital Dell took it upon himself to pick her up. They went for a long ride. Linda had no idea where he was taking her. First, they went to a bridge that crossed the dry Salt River bed on Hayden Road between Scottsdale and Tempe. Linda knew it was where the son of one of Dell's friends had died in a car accident going over the railings and crashing into the dry riverbed. He had just been 20 years old. Dell mentioned the death as they drove over the bridge "I have to admit that I never believed that it was an accident. Mark was just too clever for his own good. It could have been suicide or foul play. In that kind of accident it's hard to tell, plus Mark had a drug problem."

Linda didn't understand Dell's point, she was tired, didn't feel well. The next place they went was to the back roads that led from Scottsdale to Tempe. Dell finally stopped on the side of the road near an overpass. He said, "This is where Ron Barr died—crashed his Corvette right into the concrete. They said he took this corner too fast, lost control. Ron of course was a big drinker, I think his alcohol test said he was over the limit when it happened. But what if someone cut his brake line, anyone who ever worked at a gas station could do that."

Dell had Linda's attention she realized that he was taking her to places where people he knew had died in what everyone assumed were accidents. However, Dell was casting doubt on that reality. Linda finally spoke up "You're saying their deaths weren't accidental. Do you know that for a fact?"

"All I'm saying is that if someone cut the brake line on their cars the crashes were bad, no one would ever know. Could be drugs, drinking, or suicide" Dell Paused "That's all I'm saying."

"Why did you bring me here?"

"I just want you to know how precious life is you almost lost yours—you could try again it could happen anytime. You could have a terrible accident or kill yourself either way your kids would be without you."

"Did you do something to Mark and Ron's cars?"

"I would have known how to; that's my point." Dell drove silently for a few minutes. "I'm taking you to Camelback Hospital."

"No you can't!"

"Yes I can, either that or the police are prepared to arrest you for attempted suicide you'll end up at the state hospital. It's not your choice."

Linda felt herself getting light-headed "No not now." She said in her mind before the blackness in front of her eyes swallowed her up.

Catatonic or not Dell made certain that Linda was checked into Camelback Hospital on suicide watch. If anything happened to her in the future she would be a known suicide risk and have been committed to a mental hospital—bad stuff happens to people with bad backgrounds.

Ω

Russell had bailed. He'd gone to Salt Lake City to stay with his mother. Dell and his fourth wife Cassandra were taking care of Brandi and Rob. Linda was going to be in the hospital for at least two months. On her second week there in her private room she pried up the metal flashing on the shower door, using the sharp edge to slit both wrists. A housekeeper found her on the shower floor unconscious and again Linda was rushed to the hospital this time for stitches in both wrists. One vertical slash required fourteen stitches plus a pint of type O- blood. Three days later Milt Deever, the CEO of Fairchild, showed up at Camelback Hospital to coerce Linda to sign an agreement that she would not sue for wrongful discharge. She signed the papers with bandages on both wrists.

Linda was put on medication, had extensive therapy while she was hospitalized. The turning point came when Cassandra brought Brandi and Rob to see Linda—she was sorry that she had tried to kill herself without thinking of the effect it would have on them. She cried for the first time since everything had happened. After the visit from the kids Linda began to improve quickly, the medication began to help.

The next hurdle she had to face was whether the police and district attorney would actually charge her for attempted suicide. It was rarely done Linda had made two very serious attempts that came close to succeeding the district attorney was ready to make an example of

Linda. Dell got her an attorney who convinced the authorities to back off. Linda went home from the hospital two and a half months after taking the pills. She had about two months of severance pay left then unemployment would kick it. Linda did not know if Russell was coming back or not—she didn't care. She went home to do her very best to try to make it all up to Brandi and Rob.

Russell did come back once Linda was home, they tried for about a year to make things work out, but it was an effort in futility. Linda found another job—once she did, the marriage was over for her. She and the kids found an apartment nearby. They could stay in the same schools. Russell and Linda officially separated.

Shortly after they moved into the apartment, Dylan showed up in Arizona and moved in with his friend Ron who had never left. Dylan of course thought they could pick up where they as a family had left off, Linda wasn't going to go for it. That's not to say that she didn't let the kids see Dylan or that she didn't sleep with him a couple of nights for old times' sake. The one thing they did do well together was sex. He'd ruined any love Linda had for him a long time ago and she wasn't going to bring back the possibility of that kind of hurt again.

$$\Omega$$

All Linda wanted was to work and try to make a good life for herself and her kids. She was determined to put the past behind her as best she could. It would be harder for Linda than most because much of her past was a blank slate. Linda knew she had been, she knew she had lived through days, months, and years. But didn't always know where, or what, or with whom. It is hard to feel like you are split apart by a darkness of being that you do not want to know about.

18

"I do not speak as I think, I do not think as I should, and so it all goes on in helpless darkness."
Franz Kafka

When Brandi turned thirteen Linda was not prepared for the change that came over her nor was she prepared to take the blame. She still smoked pot every day and of course, it came as a great shock to her when Brandi started smoking pot. Linda somehow believed that all the years of being open about smoking pot had somehow inoculated her children from doing it. Linda was wrong and that's when all the problems between her and Brandi started. In a fit of fear and hypocrisy, terrified that she was losing control of her daughter, Linda admitted Brandi to Camelback Hospital. Brandi was there for about two weeks. The doctors put her on tricyclic antidepressants set her up for weekly therapy then sent her home.

Three weeks later Brandi had unintentionally overdosed on her medication landing in intensive care at

Humana hospital for a week. Linda was living in the dark of what to do. She put Brandi back into Camelback Hospital for an undetermined amount of time. While Linda worked and switched jobs, Rob was lonely and confused. Brandi was inpatient for over a year and a half.

Ω

Linda worked in Chandler, Arizona for Coleman Spas, which was a 46-mile one-way commute to their apartment in North East Phoenix. She would go see Brandi at the hospital at least three days a week on her way home. She would get home to Rob who was still in grade school by about seven-thirty to fix him a late dinner if he hadn't already made himself Kraft Macaroni and Cheese. It was a very challenging time for the family. Linda was just trying to keep her head above water. Rob was raising himself. Brandi was at least going to school while she was in Camelback Hospital.

Ω

By the time Brandi was released from inpatient care there was no chance that she was coming home. She and some of her friends from Camelback were determined to live on their own. Which Linda had to admit in spite of all her concerns, she and her friends did better than Linda could have done at her age, which by the way, was sixteen. Brandi was on her own, happy, with no regrets about it.

Linda decided that it was time to concentrate on Rob. The first thing she did was move them both to Chandler, Arizona taking him away from his school and his friends but lessening Linda's two-hour daily commute. She could spend more time with him. By the time that Linda had completely upended Rob's life he was not much interested in spending time with his mom.

Of course, Linda took his disinterest personally, as she should and decided to start dating again another brilliant decision—NOT. It was about two months later, that Coleman Spas held their annual dealers convention. Linda was up to her ears in the planning and execution of the event and of course would be front and center doing her best HR/PR.

On the last night of the conference at the most exclusive hotel, The San Marcos, in Chandler, Linda had more than enough to drink and even snuck away for a toke or two. She ended up naked in one of the Coleman Spas that were placed around the hotel grounds for the guests to use. Linda was only partially decent because one of the guests had brought her down his complimentary robe from his room. Linda ended up joining that guest in that very room for sex, drinking whiskey, and smoking pot. By the dawn hours, he was trying to convince Linda he loved her and would leave his wife as soon as he got home to Colorado Springs.

Linda and he carried on a long-distance affair for three months until Rob's school was out. Then the plan was to move to Seattle, Washington. Linda bought the plan completely. She sent Rob to stay with Dylan for the summer while she made ready to make her great escape.

The man she was *mildly* in love with was named Dan Smith.

Book III

"When the walls came tumbling down, when the walls came tumbling down. Everybody ran as they screamed at the sound."
On Through The Night—1980
Def Leppard

19

"Abuse manipulates and twists a child's natural sense of trust and love...She can't afford to feel the full range of feelings...pain, outrage, hate, vengeance, confusion, arousal—so she short-circuits them and goes numb...the only recourse is to shut down. Feelings go underground."
Allies in Healing, Laura Davis

Linda had been in Seattle for about six months in 1990, she was living with both of her children and Dan Smith. Brandi had decided to try out the Pacific Northwest and so followed her mom to Seattle, mother and daughter were reunited.

Dan was in the process of getting his divorce. Linda was bugging him about their engagement. She was following her same pattern, find a husband, get married, and then take care of him and his problems. Dan was a high functioning alcoholic. Linda admitted that even though the two of then drank together almost every evening. She had no idea that he bought a six-pack every morning, drank it on the way to work, and polished off a pint of whiskey over the course of his workday.

Linda had finally found a good job in Human Resources; she was oblivious to anything that wasn't job related. Linda was the HR Director, Sales Staff Recruiter for a direct marketing company. Payroll reported to her, and the company employed about 200 people working two shifts. It was a marketing company that designed and did all of the print manufacturing for its clients.

The marketing and sales staff was essentially an advertising agency within the company itself. It was always a volatile environment because sales and marketing were more often than not at loggerheads.

Ω

Linda had been with LaserDirect for about a year when she invited a work friend Iona and her husband Paul and young daughter to join Dan, her, and the kids for a Labor Day barbeque. The margaritas were flowing the food was grilling. At about eight o'clock Dan and Iona insisted on going to buy more tequila. There were still plenty of margaritas, but they were determined to go—Linda was wary but went along with their idea. At nine o'clock, they still hadn't returned from a 15-minute trip. Paul and Linda were starting to worry. Paul had put their daughter down to sleep on the bed. Brandi and Robert had both left to go spend the night with friends. At nine-thirty Paul was about to head out in his car to go look for them when Dan and Iona burst through the door.

Iona had leaves, grass, and lawn debris in her long black hair—her tunic shirt was on inside out. Dan was in the same messy state, he had grass stains and mud on the knees of his jeans. Paul took one look at his wife made a judgment about why she'd been gone so long, what she'd been doing. Linda felt the same way he did. She was struck numb by the obviousness of the situation. Paul gathered up his sleeping daughter headed out the door without a word, Iona silently followed.

They were gone. Linda was alone in the apartment with Dan. He quickly tried to talk his way out of the situation. "I know it looks bad, we went for a walk instead of going to the store we slipped, fell down a hill, and got messed up."

"I guess the fall down the hill removed Iona's shirt putting it on wrong side out."

"I didn't notice that. Are you sure it looked the same to me?"

"Dan not only am I sure—one look at the knees of your pants makes it very clear that you just fucked my friend from work while her husband and I were waiting upstairs here in the apartment." Linda stopped to catch her breath "in fact this is my apartment, I would like you to start packing your things up right now. I don't want you here anymore."

"Come on you've got to be kidding we're getting engaged."

"No we aren't, you have a choice grab some of your stuff or walk out that door empty handed, because you're not staying here one more night." Linda turned around opened the hall closet grabbed an empty duffel bag. "Here take what you need for a couple of days, we can make arrangements for you to get the rest of your stuff later—I want you out."

Dan realized Linda was serious. He went into the bedroom to pack his bag. She sat fuming on the sofa until he came out. He tried to talk again but she waved him off. All Linda wanted was to hear the door close behind him. A moment later, she had her wish.

Iona and Paul stayed together but in the next round of layoffs at LaserDirect, she was gone. Linda made sure of it. Not one of Linda's proudest HR moments. It's just that sometimes a little bit of revenge is called for. Looking back, she got rid of Dan Smith an alcoholic philanderer, and Iona a marginal employee. Dan went back to his wife. Iona got another job. Linda had her sense again.

$$\Omega$$

Two weeks later Brandi was in an accident that totaled the Neon that Linda had kept after the split with Dan. Brandi was not hurt luckily, but the car was totaled Linda had no way to buy another one. Her mother had called one evening a couple of days after the accident to try and get Linda to send Martin a birthday card in prison—She said no that she had enough problems of her own dealing with trying to get a car. Brandi and Linda were both begging rides to work—that wouldn't last very long. About a week later Dell called saying he'd heard from Dorothy that they needed a car. He claimed to have one that he would drive up to Seattle for Linda.

Linda was very cautious, she and Brandi needed a car to work, warily, she accepted the offer. Dell said he'd be there for her 38th birthday October 7, 1991. Dell arrived on the day before Linda's birthday. He spent the day sightseeing on his own in the Silver Nissan Sentra that he had brought. Brandi was delighted with the car—Linda had the feeling it would cost her more than she wanted to pay. Sure enough that first night Dell brought up the car payments he expected it was $300 a month for two years. Linda had no choice except to agree, she was still waiting for another shoe to drop. That night the kids went to bed, Dell went to sleep on the sofa. Linda woke up several times during the night having been startled by Dell's loud snoring. The next day was Linda's birthday it was also Friday night. Dell insisted that they all go out to a nice dinner, the kids reluctantly agreed; they had plans for the evening but went to dinner at Linda's insistence. They ate at The Three Coins restaurant near the airport, all had fine steaks, Linda, and Dell had a bottle of Merlot. When they went back home both of the kids left, Brandi took the car, dropped Rob off at friends to stay overnight then Brandi went to her boyfriend's place to do the same.

    Linda and Dell were alone for the evening. He'd bought a bottle of Jim Beam whiskey on the way home. He started drinking right away, had two or three drinks before Linda finished a glass of white wine that she had left in the refrigerator. About eleven o'clock Linda claimed to be tired from a long day at work. Insisting she was going to bed. Dell stood up got undressed down to his shorts while Linda was putting the glasses in the sink. She came out of the kitchen shocked to see Dell lying on the sofa in his underwear. She said good night ducked into her room closed and locked the door. She regretted that she had ever agreed to take a car from him because being in debt to Dell felt like making a deal with the devil.

That night Linda had nightmares and night terrors all night long while she slept. She felt as if she were paralyzed. She tried to scream at the torments she was dreaming about, not a sound would come out. It was a terrifying night for Linda. When she woke the next morning, she was sore from head to toe. She went in to go to the bathroom and was brought to tears from the pain that urinating was causing. The toilet was full of blood. Linda didn't know what to do. She was bent forward in pain as she walked to the sink to splash water on her face that's when she saw the bruises and marks all over her body. There were bite marks on her shoulders and breasts. Linda got into the shower to let the warm water ease her injuries. She was completely lost to herself having no idea what had happened to her. Linda wrapped herself in a long terrycloth robe and went out to the living room. It was empty her father's travel bag was gone there was a note on the kitchen counter "I called a cab at five a.m. and my flight is at six. Hope you like the car—forget about the payments you need the money more than I do."

Linda waited for Brandi to come home she was still bleeding, on her back in the area of her kidneys were big blue bruises. When Brandi came home, Linda said she needed to go to the hospital that she thought she was having kidney stones. Brandi took her mom to the hospital said she'd go pick up Rob then be back. In the emergency room, the nurses and the doctor started examining Linda's injuries, the doctor said to one of the nurses "We need to do a rape kit."

"No I haven't been raped I don't know what happened, it couldn't be that."

One of the nurses said, "Well you sure like it rough if you don't believe you've been raped."

"I just have a kidney infection; I used to get them all the time when I was a kid. Just give me some antibiotics let me get out of here." Linda's voice was bordering on hysterical when the doctor decided to take charge.

"Okay antibiotics it is, how about I give you a little shot for the pain?"

"Yes that would be good. My daughter is coming back for me."

The doctor ordered a Demerol shot wrote out a prescription for two weeks of antibiotics. By the time they were done with Linda, Brandi was back to pick her up.

Brandi or Rob never said anything about the incident to their mom; they just took her at her word that it was a kidney problem.

Linda was scared to death because she knew it wasn't but had no idea what it was.

In the next week Linda went back to work doing her best to forget what had happened. She threw herself into her job. Three months later after two mostly drunken affairs with sales employees and Brandi's announcement of engagement to someone Linda found unsuitable. She had a breakdown that started one afternoon at work. She started crying, couldn't stop, and a work 'friend' took her to see the doctor. He promptly had her admitted to the psychiatric floor of the same hospital she had been to after the "kidney stone" issue.

Linda spent three weeks in the hospital under the care of Dr. Gutiérrez, a psychiatrist. He called in an endocrinologist who determined that not only had Linda had a serious breakdown; also her thyroid had ceased to function. The doctors put her on thyroid replacement medication, anti-depressants, and anti-anxiety pills as well. Linda stayed on the thyroid, went off the other medications the first time she was invited to happy hour once she was back at work.

Ω

Linda had met Ian at LaserDirect when he was hired three months after she was. He was brought onboard as the Creative Director for the advertising and promotional department. Ian seemed to connect with Linda as a friend from the very beginning, they had the occasional lunch together where he would complain about the sales staff just as all marketing people do. He was dating a woman. He and Linda exchanged information about dinner dates where the good restaurants were, etc. Nothing but a very straightforward business friendship developed.

Ω

Two years later, her sexual harassing boss Saul Wham handed Linda her walking papers. He had proposed that they have an affair saying he was good at not being caught—Linda said no. Five months later, he said goodbye and good riddance to her. Just before

Linda was let go he had given her a $5,000 raise so that she could not claim discrimination against him.

Linda was dating Ian by this time; they had started a dating relationship about two weeks before she was fired. Actually, technically, she was laid off with three months of severance pay so Linda wasn't complaining. After she took a two-week vacation to Mexico, she returned to move in with Ian. Linda started looking for another job only to discover that the son-of-a-bitch, Saul Wham, was giving her bad references, which were the result of having turned down his sexual advances. Linda lost two job opportunities because of his bad-mouthing her, and by the time her unemployment was ending Linda had a lawyer and was suing him for sexual harassment and defamation. Ian was still working at LaserDirect, he decided to propose marriage a couple of days after they met with John Costo, Ian's friend, and attorney. It was October 7, 1993, when Ian made it official with an engagement ring. Linda was happy and anxiety-driven at the same time. For human resources executive to sue for harassment and defamation pretty much closed off all employment opportunities in her career field. Linda wasn't going to be able to find a job unless she stopped Saul Wham from his campaign against her.

Ian and Linda got married on January 2, 1994, and John Costo served Saul Wham with her lawsuit the next day. John met with Wham within a week negotiating an exit package for Ian complete with severance, unemployment, and written letter of recommendation. Ian had a new job within a couple of months—they were just waiting for the lawsuit to proceed. Depositions were the next step. Linda would have to be first. As it turned out John discovered that LaserDirect Inc. was in both Saul Wham and his wife's name so that she would need to be present for all the legal proceedings. Linda knew the things that she would be testifying to in her deposition; if she were the wife of the defendant, she wouldn't be very happy hearing what Linda had to say.

    Saul Wham and his attorney decided to use stall tactics, the lawsuit just started to drag out. His attorney played dirty getting a copy of Linda's medical records from her LaserDirect breakdown. It showed that she had smoked pot. They thought they could use that against Linda and they got information about her kids two fathers, preparing to try to intimidate Linda with something to do with her fitness as a parent. She was getting more nervous. She was drinking so that she would stay mad enough to want to go through with the lawsuit.

    Ian was set on it. When he had first gone to work at LaserDirect, Saul had told everyone that Ian was probably gay. That had made Ian pissed off when he heard about it. Now he was just glad that our attorney was gay and happened to know that Wham's female attorney was a lesbian, something Saul didn't know. Any way there was plenty of animosity to go around in this whole deal it was weighing heavy on Linda.

    In late March, Linda heard about a job for a Personnel Administrator at The Bush School, a very exclusive K-12 independent school in Seattle. The school was about a ten-minute drive along the shore of Lake Washington. Linda sent in her resume got a call the next week. She interviewed twice told them about the lawsuit, got the job anyway. She started on April 4, 1994. It was a great job she loved working at the school, the setting looked out over the lake, the grounds were beautiful, it was a peaceful charming place to work. One of the kindest places Linda had ever had a job.

Ω

Ian and Linda weathered the lawsuit; she gave her deposition about how Saul Wham had propositioned her and then fired her for saying no right in front of Saul's wife. She jumped up from the deposition ran out of the room—Wham and his attorney excused themselves. John Costo and Linda just sat there waiting for someone to come back into the room. Wham's attorney returned after fifteen minutes or so telling John she'd be contacting him about a settlement. The lawsuit was over except for negotiating the price. Linda ended up with about a year's salary after the legal fees. John was happy how it had all turned out he'd taken a particular dislike of Saul Wham, called him a vulgar man.

By the winter holidays, Ian had changed jobs again. He found a position at Attachmate, a company for which he had always wanted to work. He and Linda had a great holiday season and their lives were looking like everything was going their way.

20

"What's past is prologue."
William Shakespeare, The Tempest, Act 2, scene 1

It happened on March 4, 1997. I drove home from The Bush School where I had just spent the morning processing payroll for 150 teachers, other staff, and administrators. Three years earlier I had gone to work as an employee, the Personnel Administrator; now I worked as a consultant, except for a monthly payroll, a couple of hours a day, all week I worked from home. It was a typical day, rainy and in the mid-forties—I was in my mid-forties as well and was nursing a day in day out kind of depression that I refused to blame on the weather. I actually liked the rain, the gray skies; it meant I was not in Arizona.

I pulled into the parking lot of the Safeway that was at the bottom of the hill from my home. I just needed to grab a couple of items for a quick weeknight dinner. As I walked into the store, I felt a bit light-headed reached for the grocery cart to steady myself. I headed toward the produce section thinking about the fact that all I'd had in my stomach was several cups of black coffee. I stepped away from the cart to grab a couple of plastic bags suddenly, my vision dimmed. I thought for a moment am I having a stroke. I grabbed the cart for dear life—next everything before my eyes faded to black.

I heard a rhythmic pulsing sound in my ears the sound of blood rushing to my head, my face felt like I was blushing, on fire at the same time. My heart was pounding wildly in my chest. I thought again, am I having a heart attack. My head felt like it was spinning I strained to regain my vision by opening my eyes wide. I was stunned at what I saw; I was looking down at my own body standing like a statue next to the tomatoes; my hands gripping the cart. I watched myself take a few slow, shuffling steps as I moved passed the lettuce. My view was becoming more distant as if I were rising away from myself. The blackness returned then there was a pinpoint of light—then an image appeared it barely registered in my mind's eye, it was me as a small child then there was another image and another I was watching a horrific slideshow inside my brain. Compelled to focus on the dreadful images, the memories I had buried deep within a crypt inside to keep myself from going mad. My senses were overrun by acrid smells, dissonant sounds, bitter tastes, and abusive physical and sexual contact. I was experiencing panic, pain, a desire to flee, but unable to do so. I felt a flood of emotions—shame, betrayal, fear, and white-hot anger. I was lost to my past it was erasing any sense of my presence. The nightmare flashbacks continued to rush through me…

I jumped when I felt a hand on my shoulder, I choked back a scream—a man stood next to me and asked "Ma'am I'm the manager are you alright?"

"Yes." I whispered trying to understand where I was. I was standing in the corner of the dairy aisle gripping the cart so hard that my knuckles were white and my fingers had turned blue. My cart held a dozen items that I didn't remember selecting. "I have to go home." I said letting go of the cart, praying I could stand on my own. I slipped passed the manager moving as quickly as I could manage I walked out of the store.

I made it to my car door before I started to shake—struggling to get the keys from my shoulder bag; finally, after fumbling with the door lock I was seated in my car. My heart was still pummeling in my chest. I experienced a wave of nausea threw open the car door just in time to get my head out to throw up bilious coffee. I dry heaved a few times before the vomiting shudders stopped. Sweat ran into my eyes I slammed the car door shut for the second time pushed the keys into the ignition, started my Subaru. I looked at the clock on the dash…it was three o'clock; I had gone into the store at noon, *three hours had disappeared*. Tears sprang to my eyes, a loud sob burst from my throat. I wiped my eyes with the back of my hands, gripped the steering wheel putting the car in gear. I took a deep sucking breath as I backed out of the parking lot.

I thanked God silently for the recollections I believed had come from a spiritual initiation—the fragments of me that had spontaneously come together. I looked up the hill seeing my home a couple of blocks away. My next thought was what I would do when I got home—everything in my life had changed. I decided that the first thing to do was to take a long hot shower to try somehow to wash away the filth that felt attached to me. I always knew deep down that something was very wrong but all this was beyond my grasp…that I knew all that had happened to me in my childhood and as a woman how could I ever get over the horror of it—how could I tell anyone, I didn't even want to tell anyone. I'd have to ask my daughter and son if anything had ever happened to them, after all, they had been around the monster he was their grandfather. However, telling Ian seemed impossible his reaction would be bad. We had been married three years he often talked about other women he had broken up with because they had too much "baggage." I was sobbing in the shower when I asked myself the hardest question of all. How could I continue to live?

21

"Life can only be understood backwards but it must be lived forwards.
Soren Kierkegaard

I was drunk on vodka gimlets by the time Ian got home from work. I told him I was sick, had taken a shower, and going right to bed. Ian said he was going to the golf store for a little while. He would try not to wake me when he got home. That ruse had bought me a night's sleep, at least another day before I had to tell him about what had happened. In truth, I was close to a nervous breakdown the last thing I needed was the additional stress of telling my story. That night I suffered the first of scores of flashbacks that were destined to be in my future. I woke up in a cold sweat with my heart beating out of my chest. I quietly went up to my office on the third floor of the condominium. I sat at the top of the stairs looked out at the floating bridge that crossed Lake Washington. I loved the home that Ian and I lived in with its modern multi-story floor plan, beautiful views of the city, and the lake. I was terrified that once I told Ian about my history my whole life would be lost to the past that had reached out to drag me backward toward a darkness I could not escape.

I thought about my children "Oh God" I shuttered "had anything ever happened to them?" How would I ever be able to ask them when I was afraid of the answer? I knew that Brandi and Rob were the least of my worries. I knew that I had to confront Dell and Dorothy and find out if my brothers and sister had lived the same fate. With all that was before me, telling Ian seemed a little less daunting. He loved me certainly he wouldn't blame me or hold my, unknown 'til now, past against me.

The next day I went to work for a couple of hours in the morning to finish the payroll processing waiting for the checks to be delivered. Once I was done I went home called Brandi at work telling her that I wanted to meet with her and Rob about something important. Her response on the phone caught me off-guard. "You're divorcing Ian because he's gay."

"No what would make you say such a terrible thing?"

"I've just always thought he was. Sorry I didn't mean to piss you off."

"I just need to see you guys okay. I'll be by tonight I'll bring money for pizza."

"Cool. I am sorry about what I said."

Considering what I wanted to talk about I couldn't afford to be mad "Don't worry about it just don't say it."

"Okay Mom see you tonight."

As I drove to Kent, a Seattle suburb, where the kids shared an apartment I wracked my brain to think of any signs that either of them had ever been molested or abused. I couldn't believe that they had, yet here I was going to ask them about it—to tell them in vague terms what had happened to me. That I was ill prepared was an understatement; it hadn't occurred to me that my first call should have been to a therapist. I was running scared was the simple truth. I had to find out how deep my fears truly were.

Brandi and Rob were waiting for me. Rob ordered the pizza the second I walked into the apartment. The look on my face must have been grim because Brandi said, "What's wrong you look like someone died."

"No one has died. I do have something kind of difficult to talk to you about."

Rob said, "Okay cut the drama tell us what's up."

I just blurted it out "I was molested, sexually assaulted by Dell as a child, as an adult."

Brandi sat down hard on the sofa. Rob just stood there. "Why are you telling us?" Brandi asked with a tremor in her voice.

"Because my memories all came back a few days ago I've always known something was wrong. I didn't understand until it all came flooding back."

"Do you mean he did this when you were a kid?" Rob asked.

"Yes, when I was grown too." I added, "Something happened in my mind to make me forget it all like I blocked it out."

"Okay, again, why are you telling us?"

"Because I want to make sure nothing ever happened to either one of you. You were both around Dell sometimes; he didn't ever do anything did he?"

Rob said "No fucking way Mom you can't be thinking he did."

"Mom I would have had a fit even as a little kid, you know I never liked Grandpa Dell. I always thought he smelled bad." Brandi shook her head in disgust. "Now I wouldn't be surprised if he did something to Cassandra's daughter Lori she got weird at one point it could have been something like that."

"Well all I can worry about is you guys and me. I'm relieved that you're okay."

"Are you gonna be okay Mom?" Rob put his arm around me.

"Yes somehow I think I will be I don't know about right now, I guess it's better to know the truth than be confused."

The doorbell rang it was the pizza delivery— Brandi held out her hand for the money I dug into my purse for a twenty-dollar bill. Rob came out of the kitchen with three bottles of Corona. Brandi had just turned 24, Rob was almost 19, I wasn't going to quibble about him having a beer with his pizza. We ate pizza Brandi asked me what I was going to do now that I knew. I told her "Well at some point I'm going to confront Dell and Dorothy with what happened. First I have to tell Ian he isn't going to be easy to tell."

"Why will he have a problem?" asked Rob

"He doesn't like baggage from the past."

"Well maybe he should explain why everyone thinks he's gay." Brandi chimed in.

"I told you not to say that, who thinks that anyway?"

"All I know is that all the guys working in the printing department at LaserDirect seemed pretty sure about it."

"Well we're married so that should take care of the stupid rumors started by Saul Wham, I did win a lawsuit because he's a liar and a jerk."

That ended the conversation about Ian. I talked to Brandi about possibly going to Arizona with me when I decided I was ready. I said she could hang with her old friends while I dealt with family issues. She agreed to the future trip.

When I left the apartment, I was so relieved I felt better than I had in a very long time. This led me to believe that the return of my memories had been percolating inside me for some time. Even though it was traumatic, it was also as if a weight had lifted, something split inside of me had come together. I was trying to work my way up to telling Ian hoping that his reaction would mirror the kids.

$$\Omega$$

When I got home, there was a message on the kitchen counter Ian had gone out to dinner with a friend from work. That was just as well I needed a good night's sleep, a couple of days off work to lay out the story for him. I went to bed, had a night of flashbacks that woke me up several times with a pounding heart and hyperventilation. I managed to fall back asleep deciding, this was the price to pay to get all my memories back intact.

Ω

The next morning I decided to broach the subject with Ian as we had our morning coffee with a weekend joint out in our courtyard patio. I started telling him about the experience at the grocery store then got to the point of what the memories had been. I thought I was prepared for any reaction but the one I got. Ian stood, "This has nothing to do with me nothing at all. I am sure you feel affected by it. I do not want to have anything to do with this. If you need to see a therapist feel free just don't expect me to go."

I was stunned "How can you feel this way?"

"I told you I didn't want to marry someone with baggage I meant that." He paused "You're telling me you just remember. How do I know that? Especially with some story about you wandering around the Safeway it sounds like crap to me."

I was starting to get angry; I didn't want to cry, "You think I'm making this all up what would be my motivation? Certainly not to gain your comfort and support."

"No, maybe you have your reasons. I just don't know them yet you're a hard woman to trust."

"I'm hard to trust, everyone who has ever met you thinks you're gay, you say I'm hard to believe." I regretted it as soon as I said it. It was too late.

"Fuck you bitch."

Ian walked in the condominium and slammed the door I heard him getting his golf clubs together I knew he was leaving. I went into the downstairs bedroom to wait for him to leave. The day could not have gone worse.

Ω

The next day I arranged for Brandi and me to fly to Arizona for a long weekend. Easter fell on March 31, 1997, we arrived in Phoenix on Good Friday. I had called Dorothy two weeks earlier telling her I was coming to Scottsdale "to talk about some things from the past." On March 25, I got a call from my sister to tell me that Dorothy had a mild heart attack was going into surgery on Thursday. Deedee suggested that I not come at all. I told her nothing she could do or say would stop me.

Brandi and I rented a car went to the hotel in Scottsdale near the hospital, the very same hospital where I had received many Demerol shots. I dropped Brandi off and went to see Dorothy—I knew if she was afraid of what I was going to say she would go into confession mode that is exactly what I wanted from her.

Dorothy was alone in her room when I arrived she looked like she was sleeping until I got to the end of the bed she opened her eyes. "Deedee said you would be here today she told me not to talk to you until she gets here."

"I don't care if you talk to me or not but Deedee can't keep you from listening, if I start talking right now Deedee won't ever know what I've said."

"I've always known that you and Martin were smart I never had to worry about you two. But Deedee and Justin I've always worried about them."

"All my memories came back I remember everything from age four."

"How did that happen? Did some therapist put ideas into your head?"

"No I haven't seen a therapist. The memories came back because it was time. It's time for me to do something truthful about the pit of lies that you like to call your family."

"You are all my family I made you!"

"NO! You didn't you helped to break me but I'm back together I'm going to fill you pit of lies with the truth."

"There are parts of the truth that you can't possibly know."

"Then start talking…"

Dorothy did talk, so did I. A couple of times she almost lost consciousness because she was using the morphine pump to calm herself.

My mother confessed many things to me—about Chester being my biological father, about Dell always suspecting something was not right about me being his daughter. She told me about what had happened to cause me to have to wear a leg brace when I was a toddler. She believed that since I was Chester's daughter that what Dell did to me was not actually incest. She revealed that all four of us siblings had different fathers. Martin was Dell's only child. Deedee's father was a neighbor from across the street, Robert Knowlton, a tall, blue eyed, blond man. Of course, George Sloan was Justin's father. Dorothy was a tragic figure, even knowing that—forgiveness remained very hard for me. Nevertheless, she did help me to be able to tell this story by telling me some of the truth and those bits of truth led to the research that filled the black holes in my life.

$$\Omega$$

I confronted Dell in a letter that I wrote about his filthy deeds in a professional executive style. I explained to him that all of my memories of childhood and adult sexual abuse and assault had come back. I told him that I would do whatever was necessary to make sure that he never hurt another child again—however I told him I did not think he was a pedophile; I thought he was a sociopath who had no regard for any life but his own.

I told him that I went to the hospital after he brought me the car. I threatened him with the fact that the medical records of my condition after the assault still existed. I reminded him that both Brandi and Robert knew he had been there alone with me.

Overall, it was a very serious, moderately threatening letter. I sent the letter on April 7, 1997, and indicated that I provided my attorney with a copy. On April 14, I got a terse response—"Send anything else you have to say to my attorney." A business card was enclosed.

By early November, I got a phone call from Justin who I hadn't talked to since I was in Scottsdale. He said, "Dad has been diagnosed with mid to late stage Alzheimer's disease. I just thought you should know." I hung up without as much as a goodbye.

I knew how the deal was going to work—I got my memories back. Dell lost his, how fucking convenient.

In mid-December I answered the phone and recognized Dell's voice "Linda is that you?" I said nothing. "Can we talk?" I still said nothing. "How can I apologize for that which I cannot recall?"

I finally found my voice "I know you remember every beating and rape—you enjoyed it too much to just let it slip away from you." I paused, "If you truly are sick I hope there comes a time when all you can remember is my name tied to the depravity of what you did." I hung up the phone.

Ω

I hoped that Ian's shock would have abated that he was prepared to be more understanding. However, nothing about his attitude had changed I was devastated, determined never to mention my memories to him again. That of course would prove impossible to do but I did try for many years. Our relationship was a sham after that, no sex, separate vacations, separate lives. I tried to write several novels—came close to being published but then something always fell through. I went to writing seminars Ian went to visit old friends to play golf. We moved from Seattle to Issaquah, Washington and bought a smaller condominium. I walked every day at Lake Sammamish Park. Ian telecommuted to a company in Portland, Oregon. We didn't have mutual friends or mutual interests. Why we stayed married for so long I can only guess. I didn't feel I had the right to ask for a divorce since the problems were entirely my fault. He didn't want to give up any money or possessions to me in a divorce settlement. I never thought that he was having an affair because he had male friends or married couples as friends. He played golf every weekend when he got tired of the rain in Washington he decided to move to Las Cruces, New Mexico right on a golf course. The move was good for him he was still telecommuting. For me it was isolating. We didn't have pot anymore so I began to drink which as I've said before keeps me mad not sad.

$$\Omega$$

All together we were married for almost eighteen years during which time I did very little healing and lots of drinking, self-pitying, and self-destructing. When we got divorced, we had been living as roommates that did not get along very well for about fifteen years. It was brutal it cost us both dearly in different ways.

Ian had to pay me $85,000; I had to walk away from all of my possessions other than clothes and a few items I could ship to Florida. We signed the separation papers on July 1. I was gone by July 3, heading out alone for the 2,000-mile trip to the Florida coast. I drove to El Paso that first afternoon stayed at a hotel so I could have a peaceful dinner and night's sleep. I left the next morning at dawn. I was in my Subaru packed to the gills with trash bags, space bags full of clothes, a few precious boxes of books, and a flat screen television that I insisted on taking at the last minute. I was off on my great adventure at 57 years-old, adventure, or misadventure I admit I did not know.

22

"Our spirit is mightier than the filth of our memories."
Quintana of Charyn, Melina Marchetta

I arrived in Florida on Friday, July 8, 2011, to be near my daughter and son and their families. Nine months later to define those relationships as estranged would be a diplomatic description. I found myself more anxious about leaving my apartment for necessary errands I was isolated in my shrunken world.

I was in trouble knowing I needed help. When I had either tried to get therapy in the past I had been turned away when the therapist realized my issues stemmed from childhood sexual abuse—or been told I would have to get over it, or be medicated.

The week after I spent Mother's Day alone I was depressed I decided to do something. It was a clear cry for help when I found a therapist on-line, dug up the courage to contact her. Kate Wertz was a certified Jungian counselor with a strong background in trauma therapy. I called her left a short message. "I was a victim of sexual abuse. I need some help." I left my phone number quite honestly never expected to hear from her. Kate called me back that same day to set me up for an appointment that very week.

Going to the first appointment caused me such anxiety I almost decided to cancel. Her office was in Jupiter, Florida about thirty miles from where I lived in Jensen Beach. I hadn't driven that much in the last 6 months let alone considering the round trip would take me about two hours in traffic. I was terrified that I would have a panic attack while driving so I ill-advisedly drank a couple of glasses of wine before I left for my two o'clock appointment—a crazy thing to do yes, but I was on my way to a therapist.

When I met Kate she was not what I expected. She was very soft-spoken in her late fifties like myself. At the first session, I was determined not to cry I decided just to give her the facts about my current life situation. If she asked me about the abuse, I would stay in control not share too much too soon. I didn't want to scare her away.

My best-laid plans didn't work out. As hard as I tried I was in tears within ten minutes. Just talking about the current lack of relationship with my daughter and son had me wiping my eyes—blowing my nose. About half way through the hour session, I lost track of my thoughts for a few minutes. When I spoke again I heard my own voice sounding like a frightened child as I quietly told her that I had been sexually abused by my father. Her soothing response caused me to relax I felt very childlike for the rest of the session. Kate suggested that I come back for another appointment within a few days she indicated that she would like to see me twice a week if I agreed. I said I could then asked, "Are you okay I mean what I told you didn't upset you?"

Kate shook her head "I'm fine you don't have to worry about me—I promise that I can take care of myself."

I saw Kate regularly after that for the first time in my adult life I was in therapy that was constructive. To tell another person for the reality of the scope, the duration of the abuse I had endured was extremely challenging. At times during our sessions, I dissociated into one or another of the fragmented aspects of myself. The wounded child was often present, as well as the unmothered mother, the scholar who had studied psychology in an effort to heal herself. In spite of Kate's reassurances, I continued to make sure she was all right dealing with all I had disclosed.

For the first time out loud, I told about the incestuous attacks and rapes that had occurred when I was an adult. This was very hard for me to admit because I feared the questions about how as an adult I failed to defend myself. Kate stuck with me recognizing that the viciousness of the assaults had created the perfect storm of helplessness and dissociation. In many of the adult instances, I had ended up in the hospital suffering from being beaten with internal injuries, no nurse or doctor had ever tried to dig deeper into what had happened to me at the time I would have had to admit that I didn't remember.

I continued to see Kate. I didn't realize what she most certainly knew—as I was unearthing, the darkest parts of my life that I remembered, even more disruption would start to plague me. I was having nightmares and flashbacks to a degree I hadn't ever experienced. Physical symptoms began to assert themselves I had headaches, digestive issues flared. I was exhausted my levels of anxiety kept climbing.

One day after a particularly difficult session for me, I thought about everything I had told her all the way home. At around four o'clock, I pulled into the parking lot of my apartment, parked in my regular spot. I suddenly saw a man dressed all in black in my rearview mirror. I had just driven through the open lot without seeing anyone I could not imagine how he had abruptly appeared. I jumped out of my car ran up the three flights of stairs to my apartment certain that the stranger out of nowhere was chasing me. Once locked inside my apartment I lost all control. I was sobbing feeling waves of nausea as I broke into a full body sweat. I ran to the bathroom closed the door locked myself inside. I vomited, lost control of my bowels and bladder all at once. My nose started bleeding I was shaking almost as if I were having a seizure. I felt like I was about to lose consciousness. I was a mess and the bathroom floor was covered in urine, diarrhea, vomit, and blood. I got into the bathtub fully clothed turned on the shower and cried as I watched the blood from my still bleeding nose run down the drain. I stripped off my soiled wet clothes in the tub put them on the floor. I curled in a fetal position in the end of the tub experiencing flashbacks which mirrored by current loss of bodily control. Waves of shameful stigma flooded my mind the sense of mortification and humiliation were painfully visceral cramping my body to the core. I stayed in the shower until the hot water ran out. I turned off the shower used my wet clothes to mop the mess up off the floor. I was still shaking unsteadily as I grabbed my robe from the back of the bathroom door. I picked up the wet dirty clothes, forcing myself make it to the washer in the kitchen.

I went into my bedroom grabbed my pillows, quilt, and crawled into the corner of the closet where I passed out into a deep dreamless sleep. When I woke up it was dark outside. The only light in the apartment was the one light in my bedroom that I always left lit. I forced myself to get up go turn on the rest of the lights in the whole apartment. I sat down in my upholstered rocking chair. My cat Lili cautiously crept on to my lap. I just rocked while I thought about all that had happened wondering why.

About an hour later I called Kate's cell phone, she answered. I told her in hushed tones what had happened about the man in black, about running away then getting full body sick. She talked to me for about an hour. By the end of the conversation, I wasn't sure the man I saw was real. That could only mean one thing I had hallucinated the man—the danger.

Kate and I agreed to meet in two days I was to call her if anything else happened. This was my first full-blown terrors attack it would not be my last. Delving into my own psyche was like enduring a deep descent into an abyss. To heal it needed to be done. That night I doubted if I had the faith or endurance, it would take. It was late September I had been seeing Kate for five months even though she had reassured me as my state of mind worsened that it was part of the process of intense therapy I felt closer to the grave than ever. At least I had emptied myself of the worst of my memories they weren't stuck inside poisoning me from the inside out. I instinctively felt that the haunting after-effects were just beginning.

I spent my first Christmas alone except for my cat. Not a word from family, the space and time was past explanation, it could not easily be overcome. I continued to see Kate at least once a week—a couple of times she mentioned adding a psychiatrist who could prescribe medications I resisted. I was drinking a bottle of wine a day in misguided self-medication. I didn't want to admit to it so I just continued to repel her suggestion.

After the first of the year 2013, I knew my money wasn't going to last much longer. I talked to Kate about finding a job with much more enthusiasm than I felt—not fooling her one bit. Spring came and went, I talked about going back to Seattle, the idea gave me comfort, the execution was impossible. At the beginning of June, I told Kate that my money was running low I would have to end my therapy. She had already put me on the lowest end of a sliding scale payment I felt guilty about it. It was obvious that I was more than deeply depressed in one of the last few sessions we had. She asked me if I thought about hurting myself. I fudged the answer and said that I often imagined just disappearing; I couldn't do anything that would hurt my kids.

At the end of July, I had my last session with Kate. I had invented a possible consulting job in Jacksonville so that I could leave on a better note than where I was. Two weeks later I got the news that my mother had died earlier in the year I was glad that I no longer lived on a planet where she and I breathed the same air. I wrote Kate an email telling her of the death, of my lack of sorrow. I was alone left to my own devices by my own choice.

I hadn't seen or spoken to my daughter or son in over two years—the youngest of my grandchildren had gone from age three to five and the oldest from age eleven to thirteen. The thoroughness of my alienation was stunning even to me. I was coming upon another holiday season alone and only had enough money and credit to get me past the New Year 2014.

Psychologically, I was broken, shattered really—depression so deep I saw the face of it in the mirror; I had stopped looking out of disgraceful guilt. I was in a constant state of high anxiety. The fear was manifested within me. Even locked in my third floor apartment I spent hours, days with my heart pounding in my chest. The effort to go outside took every ounce of energy I could muster I could only be out for thirty minutes before I would begin sweating like a stuck pig, feeling as if consciousness and control would escape me like air from a popped balloon. Since I had quit therapy, the eighteen months of digging into the moldering trauma packed deep inside me—I'd avoided the process of bringing much to light but I had dug an extensive network of tunnels into the depths of my psyche. I had quit therapy because I was suicidal, caring more about sparing my therapist than sparing my own life.

I was planning the event for several months—suicide was the only way I could stop the painful fear that was devouring me. It was as if I were being consumed by the great scavenger of my past. Horrific memories relived in my dreams every time I slept. I slept a lot. When I was awake I found solace in knowing I would soon end it. My plans, preparations to die were my last comfort, my final vestige of control, my flailing effort to stave off the talons and teeth of my own inner predator.

My physical condition was failing—my weight had soared to 266 pounds I was certain that my blood pressure was ascending with my poundage. I was numb in parts of my body a visceral symptom of the emotional numbness that had taken away all but the barest of shed tears that accompanied my choking rages at myself.

Agoraphobic was an understatement for the condition of my psyche. After over three years of visits to the same store I was acknowledged by the clerks rarely had to speak, they would get my packs of cigarettes; ring up my wine, and frozen dinners with a smile that I woodenly returned. I was grateful to be able to get out of the store before the flop sweats began. By the time I made the round trip, when I was safely locked in back at home, I would be dripping with perspiration heart-pounding out of my chest too often I was ashamed to admit I had wet myself in my size XXXL yoga pants—just another day in my life of panic, anxiety, and indignity.

Today was different; I had been planning. A month earlier I had convinced my cat Lili's veterinarian to adopt her. I lied while crying explaining that I was very ill, had to go away for treatment. She accepted my lies, my tears; I certainly looked ill or maybe just shitty and unkempt. The point was I found a good person to take my cat. I wept all the way back to the condo weaving my car through the Publix parking lot only having to cross one actual road before I could cut across Loew's lot make one right turn back inside the community gates. I sobbed up the three flights of stairs, once locked in at home barely made it to the bathroom in time to throw-up. I went to bed at 4 p.m. slept for twenty hours straight—a marathon of nightmares with a side of flashbacks.

After Lili was gone, I was alone. I started throwing things away. My balcony, which used to be her favorite domain, became the final resting place for a pile of black trash bags that I filled with clothes, important paperwork, photos, and personal items. I would stare at the television for hours—a break between the energy sapping purging of my belongings or a few fitful hours of wine-induced sleep.

Clearing all the files from my computer was one of the last efforts I undertook. I had kept a diary since I'd lost contact with my world. The journaling consisted of a jumble of self-pity, recriminations, apologies, rants to God, and just the barest bits of personal insight into my problems to keep me writing—according to my plan I wiped the digital slate clean.

On February 5, the eviction notice was rolled up, stuck in the knocker of my apartment door. I heard the maintenance man put it in place even though I imagined he was trying to do the task stealthily without risking a possible confrontation with an irate non-rent paying scofflaw. The truth was I didn't have the energy to be irate or confrontational; I was fully occupied with a level of anxiety that consumed even the potential of a response or reaction to another human being. I stuck my head out of the door after dark snatched the eviction notice inside. The notice gave me ten days to pay up. My money was almost gone and I had one credit card left that I could use; there was certainly not enough left for rent, electricity, or cable. Having never been evicted before I holed-up in my condominium for the last days; I prepared for the wait by buying a full carton of Salem Silvers, two oversize bottles of cheap Pino Grigio, a frozen pizza, and four boxes of frozen Stouffer's macaroni and cheese. I had not been able to go outside any further than the 7-11, which was so close to home I had to drive my car through one short left turn lane after exiting the condominium community gates to reach the convenience store parking lot.

On February 7, I gathered up a few mismatched clothes, some pillows, and blankets, a cold front was coming through. A few cold days in Florida is no real weather challenge nighttime lows in the forties I was going to be living in my car—a 1996 Subaru Outback. I stuffed two cloth grocery bags of books including my oversize American Heritage Dictionary, my Thesaurus, The Eagles Complete Songbook, and a dozen paperback crime novels, oh, and my copy of The Portable Jung just to make sure I had psychological support. I took my jewelry box and its less than impressive contents. I had the idea I could pawn it for the cost of a tank of gas for my car.

After packing my car at 11 p.m., I returned upstairs to take a final shower in my apartment. For months I had been showering maybe once a week if I could muster up the motivation. Tonight before I took up my final residence in my car it just seemed right to have shampooed my hair to be wearing clean underwear. After my hour-long shower, I finished off the last bottle of Pino Grigio shed a few tears as I took the apartment keys off my key ring to leave on my desk in the unlocked apartment.

The last thing I took with me was the loaded 38-special revolver in its gray plastic case that I had bought six weeks earlier at the Lotus GunWorks one block from my apartment. To get there all I had to do was go out of the community gates make one right turn and a second right turn into the gun store's parking lot. My first trip there was to pay for the gun and fill out the background check paperwork. There were no questions about my mental health I had no criminal background. I claimed to be concerned about living alone, the female clerk who helped me said she understood. After satisfying the 3-day waiting period, I picked up the gun on Christmas Eve.

Ω

It was midnight when I made my way into the Loew's parking lot where I found a spot under a lot light that was surrounded on three sides by car window high hedges. I kept the car locked, engine running, heat, and radio on. I felt innocuous enough that first night to fall asleep for a couple of hours. The next day I had to drive at least a mile to the *We Buy Gold* pawn shop in Jensen Beach to trade-in my bobbles for a little bit of cash. I had looked the store up on my phone it opened at ten o'clock.

At six o'clock I drove three blocks to the McDonald's to use the restroom, to get some coffee. I parked in the outskirts of the huge parking lot of Treasure Coast Mall. I read until it was time to make my big excursion to the pawnshop. I entered the shop expecting to get about forty dollars for everything including the jewelry box I was shocked when after taking 45 minutes to examine the jewelry that seemed worthless to me mostly because it was mine, the store owner offered me $540. I tried my damnedest not to betray my shock, concerned that my disbelief would make him rescind his offer. I left with money for gas and more. I drove directly across the street to Barnes and Noble bought another dozen books for $140, used the restroom again.

For the next couple of days I stayed in the Loew's lot dozing for an hour or so during the day and staying up all night reading. I never turned off my car's engine except when I went into McDonald's to use the bathroom or get coffee. I had no appetite so I hardly ate

I was worried about needing more frequent excursions to restrooms other than first thing in the morning and at the end of each day. I did however make a stop at the 7-11 to stock up on cigarettes—no wine or food.

On the third morning in the Lowe's lot, I began to get very concerned that a red Taurus with a middle-aged man driving had seemed to drive around in my distant unoccupied corner of the parking area in a not so random manner. It suddenly struck me that my phone had GPS that someone if they wanted to, could track me down. Even though my battery had been dead for at least a day I panicked, jumped out of the car, put my phone under my rear left tire, and left Lowe's with my crushed phone laying on the blacktop. My Lowe's refuge had been blown so I had to find another spot for my car to go unnoticed. I also had to be close to a gas station because keeping my car running twenty-four hours a day was using lots of gas.

The Publix Grocery Store became my next hiding spot. I don't exactly know when I started thinking that I was hiding out. It seemed to me to be a natural organic thinking process. After all, I was a 60-year-old woman alone in her car—it was important for my instincts to kick in. Especially since my plan was still in the forefront of my mind. In the far corner of the Publix strip mall was a BP gas station even though I had boycotted them since the Gulf oil spill I decided that proximity trumped my environmental consciousness.

My first night at Publix I found a bright spot under a lot light with two sides surrounded by hedges with close access to an exit to the street. I also found out that I was not the only car or van with people inside spending the night at a grocery store. Police cars drove slowly through the lot at least a couple of times a night. Neither the fellow car dwellers nor the police were of any comfort, in fact I sat up reading all night with my interior light on just so that I would not look aimless or lost nor up to something I shouldn't be. It worked because no one ever approached me.

    In the mornings after my run for coffee, facility relief, and a fill-up for my gas tank, I would move my car to the shade of a planting of trees in the furthest corner of the lot. I would be overcome by the need to sleep by about eight o'clock and wakeup two or three hours later shaking and sweating from some daytime nightmare that I couldn't quite remember. That day I suffered sitting in the car with my heart pounding and my mind racing. I counted my money and with gas being nearly $4.00 a gallon, I was down to $200 bucks—ten twenties was all the money I had left. By late afternoon I decided that I needed to clean up a bit I had water and a washcloth to clean my face. I brushed my teeth and brushed my tangled hair smooth and into an oily, tight ponytail. Under the cover of a blanket, I changed into my last clean set of clothes. I was almost out of bottled water, which I'd been drinking sparingly, I hadn't eaten anything, I decided against my lack of hunger that I should eat something anyway.

    I was still shaky when I went into Publix to buy crackers and cheese, a couple of bottles of water; I added an orange juice for good measure. The only words I had spoken in days were to assure the checkout clerk that I had found everything I needed. Thanking God that I got out of the store before I broke out in a cold sweat could hear the sound of my blood pounding pressing its way through the veins of my neck. Back in my car locked in engine running, again I swabbed the rivulets of sweat from my face holding the damp cloth over my closed eyelids to soothe them from the salty drops that had burned my dry puffy eyes.

    Bit by bit in my compact car agoraphobic haven I pulled myself together ate a couple of cheese and cracker sandwiches drank my orange juice. By the time I finished it was starting to get dark. I needed to move to a different spot in the parking lot. I found a new place under a good light, started to read. It was eight o'clock when I looked up from my book a, Michael Connolly, Harry Bosch crime novel. I saw a young woman walking toward my car in some kind of waitress uniform; I tossed my cigarette out the crack in the window and started to close it up tight when I saw that she seemed to have a peacock, tail fully unfurled, walking on a leash alongside her. My head started pounding as I stared out of my window into the dark—the girl was coming toward me I was sure. My neck cramped for a moment, I was forced to lean my chin to my chest to quell the pain in my neck. When I looked back up the girl, the peacock on its leash was gone. I twisted around in my seat looking behind me; the area surrounding me was empty. I had seen it, a peacock strutting on a leash, tail feathers glinting turquoise, gold, and green in the street lamp—the waitress in her uniform. I had seen it....

I lit another cigarette cracked the window beside me. What should I do whom could I tell about this strange sighting? A name leaped into my mind, as the pounding in my head began to subside, Kate Wertz I could tell her about this, she would listen she'd believe me. Her office was in Jupiter I was in Jensen Beach at least thirty miles away. What the hell, I had driven down there sometimes twice a week for eighteen months. I could go tonight stay in the parking lot of her office, it would be quiet I could probably sleep, it was Sunday night she'd be in her office tomorrow morning. I put the Subaru in gear, pulled out of Publix lot onto Highway 1, heading south for Jupiter.

It took me an hour-and-a-half to make the drive through Stuart, Hobe Sound, and Tequesta before I made it to Jupiter. I admit I have trouble with night driving, sixty-year-old eyes are just like that. I pulled into the two-story medical office complex parking lot, it was empty. I drove all around the lot just to be sure then settled into a space where I had often parked for my appointments. I got situated with my pillows, blankets, and books in the back seat—the lights in the office lot were not bright enough to read by and the drive had exhausted me further than how tired I already was. Considering the nights I had gone without sleep, I closed my eyes I slept without dreaming.

I woke up with the first bare light of morning my car was covered surrounded by cats, every feral cat in the area had been drawn to the warm hood or roof of my running heated car. I had more than a cat problem…I needed to pee so bad that the idea of driving anywhere to find a restroom was simply not possible. I thought about the cats how would a gang of cats react to me opening the backseat door sticking my bare butt out to pee on the ground. Nature crowded out my hesitation I opened the door just an inch or two. Like lightening, the cats bounded off the car hood two or three thumped from the roof to the ground several others dashed out from under the car. They seemed to disappear as I watched but I was watching I did see them. I couldn't think about it any longer as I opened the rear door slipped down my yoga pants and relieved myself on the gravelly asphalt. Luckily, my car was still the solitary vehicle in the complex. I felt a little guilty for peeing outside Kate's office, when I talked to her, I was sure we'd end up laughing about it. I wondered if she had any idea about all the cats.

I climbed into the front seat checked the gas gauge less than half a tank; I'd have to get gas, water, and coffee. I looked up to the second floor where I could see the door of Kate's office. There was a sign of some sort on the window. I got out of the car climbed the stairs walked down the balcony hallway to her door. The sign said, "We are closed on Monday for Presidents' Day."

My spontaneous idea had been foiled I wouldn't be telling Kate Wertz about the peacock on a leash or the gang of cats or even about pissing in her parking lot. My original plan came back sharply as I returned to my car. Once inside I reached under the passenger seat felt the hard plastic gun case securely hidden there. I put my car in drive heading north back to Jensen Beach. I looked at myself in the rearview mirror I looked sick. Bags under my eyes were overlaid with dark circles, the creases from my nose to my mouth were depressed into my face, and my eyes were bleary and tired but also blank. My graying hair was a tangled oily mass surrounding a face with skin that was dismally dull.

"Who gives a fuck what I saw." I muttered, "I need a shower."

I thought about my plan it was time to go through with it— I didn't want to die filthy. I had one last clean tee shirt and one pair of clean underwear. The yoga pants I had on would have to do. Where could I get a shower? Did I dare go back to my apartment; no way surely, they had changed the locks by now. I could use a bathroom with just a sink; still, I needed some time without fear of being interrupted. McDonald's wasn't going to cut it.

As I made my way toward Jensen Beach, I remembered the last conversation that Kate and I had. She told me about a church she went to in Jupiter. If I could find a church, surely they would let me clean up, an old woman living in her car—I drove randomly around the neighborhood of North River Shores in Jensen Beach and lo and behold I found a Presbyterian Church. Yes, that's where I'd go....

23

"Whoever fights monsters should see to it that in the process he does not become a monster. And if you gaze long enough into an abyss the abyss will gaze back into you."
Frederick Nietzsche

I was stunned to discover that the pastor at the church I found knew a therapist and said her name was Kate Wertz. Pastor Joanne wasted no time getting her on the phone to talk to me. During the conversation, I admitted to Kate that I had a gun in my car was intending to suicide as soon as I could clean myself up a little bit. Kate insisted that she had a place for me to get some help asked me to wait at the church for her to call me back with some arrangements—a plan. I reluctantly agreed thinking that whatever the plan was it might involve a shower. My gun was hidden in the car the car was locked so it was still in my possession.

Kate called back in about 15 minutes said that she had called New Horizons had arranged for my admission as an inpatient there for mental health treatment. She told me that if I went today that I could go in voluntarily, leave whenever I wanted. That part sounded good she promised me I would be able to take a shower right after I checked in. I agreed. Kate was on the phone with Pastor Joanne making plans for her and her husband to drive me to New Horizons.

I had no idea where I was going. I was dirty, tired, and I had given in. Pastor Joanne and her husband got my purse, me with ID, two packs of Salem Lights, and $40 into the back seat of their car. We headed north from Jensen Beach to New Horizons. While in the car, I realized that I was allowing literal strangers to take me to a place I didn't know based on a phone call with Kate Wertz. Maybe I was crazy. I was becoming more scared as the drive went on. It seemed like we were going a long way passed any part of town that I had ever ventured out to. Of course, for my agoraphobia and me that wasn't saying much.

By the time we made it to New Horizons, I was having a full-blown anxiety attack I was close to losing control of my bladder in the Pastor's car. I got out of the car walked through a door that said emergency then had to go through a metal detector like at the airport with my purse going through a search. Then the guard took my purse put it into a container said I could have it back later. I was put into a room alone, it was a few minutes until Pastor Joanne was allowed to join me. While we were waiting in the room, a couple of men came in. One was bleeding from a wound across the bridge of his nose. The blood frightened me even more I began to cry, to yell that I needed to get out of the room. Finally someone came got me, said she was going to interview me. I thought to myself, "Good Luck with that."

I went through the interview process for about an hour with several different people. Pastor Joanne came in to say that she and her husband were leaving. No matter what happened I was here, this was starting to feel less voluntary and more like "no fucking choice." When they took me into a room made me strip down to my underwear so they could make note of any injuries that I might have I started shaking because I was terrified about what I had agreed to do. It felt like I was going to jail.

The last thing they did was to check my vital signs pulse, respiration, and blood pressure. They checked my blood pressure three times seeming to get more alarmed each time. The technician called in the manager of the screening department told her that my blood pressure was 239/130 she called an ambulance immediately. Before I knew what was happening I was being loaded on a gurney taken with sirens blaring to a hospital I didn't know from Adam. In the ambulance they tried to put in an I.V. but couldn't because my blood pressure was too high. The techs were talking about me "stroking out" before we made it to the hospital.

Once at the hospital it was clear I was in emergency condition, they rushed me into a room even though people were waiting on gurneys in the hallway. Several nurses, two doctors started working on me. They had me on two separate I.V. drips within a few moments of my arrival. A heart monitor and automatic blood pressure cuff were on me within minutes. The nurses asked if I had a headache. I said, "Yes, for a couple of days." With my response they put a needle syringe into one of the tubes going into my arm gave me some other medication then put me on oxygen.

The emergency room worked on me for several hours almost non-stop to try to lower my blood pressure. When it was down to 160/90, they decided it was safe for me to be admitted to a room. Before they wheeled me out a nurse asked me why I was being admitted to New Horizons she asked if I was suicidal. I answered "yes," not thinking of any possible consequences. The nurse immediately said she was going to "Baker Act" me, with that, I had a police officer enter the room to stay with me until I was taken to my hospital room. It seemed very ironic to me even in my confused unstable condition that they put a guy with a gun in charge of a woman who was going to kill herself with a gun.

I found out that I was at Lawnwood Hospital in Fort Pierce, Florida. I was getting a room on the psychiatric floor. That first night was like being in the movie 'One Flew Over the Cuckoo's Nest' it was downright bizarre. To start with, my blood pressure was very high I was still having a non-stop anxiety attack so they prescribed 5mgs Valium every six hours. I could have taken twice that amount every couple of hours still been in bad shape. Then there were cops with their guns everywhere guarding the psychiatric patients. Then to top off the first evening the door to the adjoining room burst open, a stark raving, buck-naked, bald, and otherwise hairless eighty-year-old man burst into the room, grabbed the end of my bed, began to shake it and me.

I screamed for help a couple of police came in to drag him back though the door to his bed. A few minutes later before I had half a chance to calm down the old guy does exactly the same thing again. This time I start yelling for the police, when they come I insist that the adjoining room door be locked so he can't keep coming in. At first they refused, saying it had to be unlocked for safety reasons—I screamed that I was the one who was unsafe that I wanted the door locked. I asked to talk to a floor supervisor then they agreed to lock the door.

Ω

The next day I found out what being 'Baker Acted' meant. I was no longer a voluntary admission to any psychiatric facility—if I resisted I could be court-ordered for whatever time the court thought was appropriate. I felt betrayed. I was too sick to put up a fight. I decided that I did not have any other choice than to call Brandi—hers was the only phone number I could still remember. I called her on the morning of February 18, 2014, and told her I was in Lawnwood Hospital in the psychiatric wing. I hadn't talked to her in more than two years. This was the call I finally made. I told her I'd been living in my car for ten days. The first question she asked was where Lili my cat was. I told her that the veterinarian had taken her a month ago. She asked about my furniture. I said I left everything in the apartment. She asked why I hadn't called before. I didn't have an answer. The conversation was short I don't know to this day if I told her about Kate Wertz or if she found out about her from someone else. I know she said that they, meaning her and Brian, Rob and Jennifer, would go try to get my stuff from the apartment. I told her I'd left it unlocked. It was a miracle to find out me that everything was still there. I don't remember when I found out I still had my stuff.

Ω

    I stayed on the psychiatric floor for three days then I went by ambulance to Lawnwood Pavilions the acute care facility for mental illnesses, extreme substance abuse. While I was there, I saw Brandi for the first time. She was very angry, very distraught at the same time. I remember thinking how I felt like a child who was in deep trouble. Brandi was the angry scared parent. It was a bizarre reversal of roles. I am sure Brandi felt the same sense of discombobulation.

    I was in Lawnwood for ten days. Marlene Price from New Horizons SRT came to interview me for a possible placement there—she said at first that she didn't think she'd accept me but after meeting me in person, she changed her mind. I am very thankful that she did give me a second chance. Again, in an ambulance I went from Lawnwood to New Horizons SRT, I arrived at SRT on March 3, 2014.

Book IV

"A chief event in life is the day in which we have encountered a mind that startled us."
American Transcendentalist, Ralph Waldo Emerson

24

"Scars have the strange power to remind us that our past is real."
All the Pretty Horses, Comac McCarthy

SRT stands for Short-term Residential Treatment. At New Horizons, it is the facility that you arrive to once your basic health and psychiatric conditions have been stabilized. Marlene Price was the program manager I had met her at Lawnwood she was the first person I saw when I came to SRT. One of the second people I met was the Senior Social Worker, Therapist, Lauren Odell.

Lauren interviewed me on that first day since I was indigent she got the paperwork started for my SSI/SSDI application. Kristen Wieser the recreational therapist also interviewed me. I felt as if I had boarded a ship on which I would be held far off shore out in the ocean of healing until I was ready to be on land again. Since I had spent 18 months in therapy with Kate Wertz, I felt like I had some idea of what I needed to do. SRT was different there were other people here, people like me with serious mental health issues or severe addiction problems. For the first few days I kept my head down, read a couple of books. I was happy to discover that I could smoke outside on the screened-in patio there were several designated smoke breaks a day. They even sold cigarettes in SRT. Some of my first acquaintances were fellow smokers, the comraderies of nicotine.

My second roommate was one of my first friends. She became my friend after about two weeks on the unit. She was a co-occurring patient meaning that she had both severe addiction problems with mental health issues. I was just considered to have mental health issues; my diagnosis kept growing as my therapy sessions occurred, the treatment team met to discuss my case. I met with a psychiatrist at least once a week, he worked to fine tune my medications to the growing list of diagnosis. After a few weeks my treatment team which was made up of the psychiatrist, the staff nurse Nicki, my therapists Andrea and Lauren, and the program manager Marlene Price. It was determined I had severe depressive disorder, severe anxiety disorder, PTSD post-traumatic stress disorder, and DID dissociative identity disorder.

My depression was so deep that I exhibited aspects of depressive psychosis, including delusions with hallucinations. It was at times difficult to have the energy or wherewithal to stay connected to reality. For me severe depression felt like living in a very dark empty space without the motivation even to look for the light or a different perspective. It is sometimes posited that depression is anger turned inward. After having gone down into the depths with Kate Wertz, I had to admit that I had built the nadirs of my depression with anger that was like red-hot lava that had hardened to a glassy black stone. My depression scared me; it was the killing kind.

    The anxiety disorder was severe including fainting, loss of bodily functions, incontinence. I had experienced agoraphobia for nearly two years during which I rarely left my home for fear of fainting or losing bodily control. Anxiety isn't even an adequate word for the silent terror I had lived with for years. I always knew that something was terribly wrong with my life. All I could conclude was that something was terribly wrong about me. This sense of wrongness easily translated into badness, for most of my life, I felt as if dire consequences for my wickedness were just waiting to become my fate. I expected something bad to happen at any moment, my anxiety made perfect sense to me.

    Post-Traumatic Stress afflicted me with flashbacks both waking, sleeping, and exacerbated my anxiety disorder; it also fueled my suicidal ideation. For me I'd had amnesia of the years of trauma, when the memories resurfaced it was as if I had to relive all the violence, pain, and fear. The same trauma would run repeatedly in my mind like a loop of film it was threatening all of my relationships and my sanity. I couldn't live with myself with what I knew had happened, it was like having the past overtake me, swallow me whole like some kind of devouring marauder.

The most difficult aspect of my diagnosis was Dissociative Identity Disorder formerly referred to a Multiple Personality Disorder. As someone who has experienced the effects of this mental illness, I can only do my best to explain it trying to dispel the doubts of those who think it is like the portrayal of "Sybil" the movie with Sally Fields. It is not like that at all. Dissociation is what happens when a traumatic event is so severe, so chronic that my mind literally blocked the event from my awareness. My mind captured the trauma holding it in place at the stage of development as a victim at the time of the trauma. This was my mind, body, and spirit's most powerful defense mechanism against the kind of suffering that might otherwise have destroyed my sanity. Over years of trauma, several aspects of my character were developmentally stalled. Then to protect me became a part of my self-preservation instincts. Various developmental identities function either individually or in concert to protect my collective sanity. Each of these identities has varying levels of consciousness with recognition of the other fragmented parts of me. The variation in consciousness of the identity fragments is what accounts for the "lost time and out of body" experiences I've had with DID.

As you can imagine all of this is very difficult if not flat out impossible to explain to my family although I did make some effort.

Brandi, Rob, and Jennifer came to visit me together one day. I gave them all copies of my diagnosis, listed the medications I was taking. I admit that I was still in rough shape. I was trying to make my family less afraid of me. Brandi and Brian had gotten my car. I asked Brandi to wash or bring me the clothes that I had. She agreed to do so, Brandi was still very angry with me. I think her anger scared me more than anything that I had to face from the other clients at SRT and some of them were scary.

Somehow, after a couple of months I slipped into a delusion that New Horizons was a place where everyone was actually dead just hadn't figured it out yet. I started having suicidal thoughts again, had a plan, the means—a pair of small very sharp surgical scissors. I decided that I wanted to move on from this way station for the unknowing dead. I thought that to kill myself would be the final solution. Before I decided when to do it, I had pangs of guilt about Lauren and my roommate. In a moment of weakness or strength I did not know which at the time, I told Lauren of my delusion and my plan. I immediately signed a safety contract, of course, had to give up my weapon. I slipped into a bout of guilty depression after that as I worried that my daughter would somehow find out that I had thought of killing myself once more. I couldn't stand to hurt her again—it is hard for families to understand that the illness does take hold of you until you do everything you must to break its hold. The SRT routine is part of that process.

$$\Omega$$

On SRT, clients had assigned chores to do every morning the assignments would rotate every week. The clients got paid $17.50 per week for doing their chores properly. This money could be used to buy cigarettes or to buy personal items on weekly outings to Walmart or the Dollar Store. You had to be on the unit for 30 days before you were eligible for outings and you had to attend 90 percent of the group therapy sessions that were held. After successfully achieving the goals, clients could get passes to go out with family for several hours then return to SRT at a designated time. Once you could go out on passes you had to take a drug screen test when you returned. If you failed the drug screen, you didn't get passes anymore.

The group therapy sessions were one of my favorite things at SRT, it was intellectual stimulation, and to be honest it was an opportunity for the high-functioning clients to show off how smart or insightful they could be. In particular, I liked the groups that discussed boundary setting because it became clearer to me that my history of childhood and adult sexual abuse had left me with very poor instincts for boundaries or protecting my own territory, meaning my body and myself.

My other favorite group activity was recreational therapy—I found my inner artist who helped me finally bring my partitioned aspects of myself into one whole being. Art is a powerful thing. I can never thank Kristen Weiser enough for helping me to believe I could heal myself with art. The self-portraits were a painful cleansing process—of course; I drew enough trees to populate a small forest to ground myself forever.

I also benefited from being able to complete my half-finished therapeutic process that I had begun with Kate Wertz. I was working through it with Lauren

Odell. We discussed that the effects of having been drugged, raped, neglected, and beaten hundreds of times in my life, had split my character into individual shards of functionality. I had my wounded child, my scholar, my nurturer, my executive, and my inner soul self that had somehow kept me from flying apart into a million pieces. I took to journal writing about my history finding tremendous relief, hope, and resiliency within myself.

Ω

When I had walked into that grocery store in March of 1997, it was as if the walls of a prison had collapsed in on me. It took me nearly two decades to dig my way out of the rubble of my lifelong captivity not unlike many prisoners at times I ached for the obligation of those penitentiary walls, I didn't know how to be free because I had been interred for so long.

Dell died eight years after I got my memories back in June of 2005, in a nursing home in Sun City, Arizona on a street called Dusty Lane. He was born in dust he died in dust, ashes to ashes, dust to dust. He haunted my life like an inescapable malevolent spirit in my nightmares; I would feel the pressure on the edge of the bed where he used to sit next to my sleeping body. My flashbacks still included his rough touch and his unforgettable smell. All of those things that I had dissociated from in the years they were actually happening were stored in my nerves, muscles, bones, skin, and senses. I didn't simply remember what had happened. I had to relive it all, every act, every painful attack, every gagging taste, every lash of the belt, and punch of a fist. In order to heal I had to go through it all. But to heal I did not have to forgive the unforgiveable I had to recollect and accept what had happened to me. Because while dissociation had saved my soul, the not knowing all that had happened nearly killed me.

Ω

I have weathered many a storm in my life, for much of my life I felt buffeted about by unseen unknowable forces of terror, at SRT I began to make peace with my own life. I learned to let go of unearned guilt, to apologize for the guilt I rightly felt. I learned that I am not perfect nor was I ever meant to be, neither were my one mother, two fathers, three siblings, four husbands, and two children.

SRT helped me reclaim my instincts from the depths of my soul where they were kept safe and sound. SRT was an institutional reckoning for me at the time in my life where only that could save me....

25

"When you are in doubt be still and wait; when doubt no longer exists for you then go forward with courage. So long as the mists envelop you be still, be still until the sunlight pours through and dispels the mists—as it surely will then act with courage.
Ponca Chief White Eagle, 1800s-1914

Authentic forgiveness is an act of courage forgiveness follows death and grieving.

I had to grieve the death of how I believed life should have, could have, or might have been. I grieved the death of the facade that defined who I thought I was or needed to be. I was grieving the death of loving relationships that failed due to guilt, desperation, obligation, or all three. I pushed myself to grieve the death of those who betrayed me the deepest, hurt me the longest, and unrelentingly shamed me. In the end I had no grief for them only relief at their passing.

Dorothy died in February of 2013, in the midst of my nearly terminal breakdown. She died of kidney failure except for Deedee and Justin, no one cared that she was gone. I didn't even find out until months afterwards; what I felt was relieved. The fact that she was abused, abandoned as a child and young woman was a factor in her irresponsibility as a mother; it is not an excuse for her collusion. She insisted that she had been abused but it didn't affect her negatively. She claimed that since Dell wasn't my biological father it wasn't really incest. I argued that she knowingly let a predator have his way in the home she claimed to be making for her children. In the last conversation, I had with her she attempted to recant her awareness of all that had happened. Saying she didn't know what was going on as she had previously told me. I tried to explain that it was my own memories that revealed what had happened that she had simply offered lame explanations. The truth was that Dell had promised her money to live out the rest of her life in a modicum of comfort. She wanted that more than she wanted a daughter who knew the truth. Dorothy had lived her entire life in the pursuit of security and comfort; I should have always known that she would never give that up. Finally, there was simply nothing more to talk about we didn't speak for the last 19 years of her life.

$$\Omega$$

I had to grieve the death of my sense of violation, outrage, and injustice that had split my spirit into fragments that felt lost to me forever. For forgiveness to happen I had to die to false expectations, embrace with unflinching acceptance, the grace of yielding in humility to the truest experiences of my life—then only then could genuine forgiveness recollect my broken spirit from the lost places allowing me to courageously reclaim my whole self.

The processes of reintegration of my multiple selves had begun spontaneously that day in the Safeway Grocery Store in Seattle. It was a confusing incomplete re-collection; some aspects of my mind seemed to hold my literal ability to function as an adult. While another aspect of my personality was a Revenant of my earliest childhood traumas. Yet another ghost-like presence held the keys to my adolescence and young adulthood. Since I had spent 18 months with Kate Wertz, digging through my psyche it was time to put everything from the last 60 years into some kind of perspective. I used my own desire to reclaim my soul as whole, to fuel the reconciliation of my parts; it was different from just knowing they existed to have them re-united, maybe not as one self but at least as cohorts.

I spent six days writing my abbreviated history for my social security supplemental income application. I doubt that anyone at social security had ever read an account as raw as the wounds I revealed. I also provided my full work history of course so one of my adult portions had to have some say. Much of the handwritten material was in a childlike or youthful voice. My therapist at New Horizons Lauren Odell even commented on the changes in my handwriting as different aspects of the partitioned me told their version of my life story. When I was finished, I had added 28 pages to a one-page section of the benefits application.

I was wrung out after completing my task. Because of going through the memories in writing, I had a flare-up of the symptoms of my DID, Dissociative Identity Disorder experiencing several lost time incidents and out of body issues. I found these to be very upsetting because after they would happen I would have the sense that I had been missing for a period. The clocks on the walls at New Horizons were my proof. I would miss groups that I meant to attend not knowing what had happened to the time but remember seeing others coming out of the group sessions but never saw them going in.

Lauren insisted that my partial awareness of the lost time was a sign of healing I wasn't sure. Sometimes "healing" made me feel crazier than ever. I was to the point where I had no other way to go than with the flow. I had been at New Horizons for about three months. My medications were doing their designated jobs well. I was feeling less depressed somewhat less anxiety-driven the flashback nightmares were coming less often.

Through the process of therapy, I was starting to have a better perspective about the estrangement from my son and daughter. My son's wife I knew was going to be a problem in that she has a very strong opinion about mental health. She works in the substance use recovery system, her perceptions of recovery apply to addiction. When it comes to mental health, she doesn't consider recovery in at all the same light. My son pretty much goes along with his wife when it comes to most conflicting situations—Robert is very conflict adverse.

My daughter on the other hand seemed to be coming around after her original outrage at the idea that

I was going to kill myself. One of the things she told me in one of our early visits was that she hoped that I was going to learn to have some humility. I was of course upset by her statement because at the time I was feeling about as humbly humiliated as I could ever imagine—my take at the time was that she was being mean to make up for how much I had scared her. Her husband Brian didn't know what to think other than he didn't want a crazy mother-in-law to disturb his happy predictable home. Brandi and Brian were very involved in running a Celebrate Recovery chapter at their church and were both in recovery—I think it might have been easier for them to handle if I had been a drunk or a druggie instead of mentally ill. Although from their convictions, either addiction or mental illness required a lot of prayer, church, and Jesus. I didn't disagree; however, my spiritual needs are far more introverted than the two extroverts, my daughter Brandi and son-in-law Brian.

I began having family therapy meetings that included Robert alone, Brandi alone, and then finally Brandi and Brian. I was to the point where I had earned the right to go on outings they all cautiously agreed to pick me up spend some limited time with me. Things started to improve with Brandi and Brian once we were out of the New Horizons locked ward setting as one might expect to be the case.

However, with Robert and Jenn, it didn't go so smoothly—I am to this day still at a loss as to what the difference was, ultimately nothing has been able to end the estrangement. I haven't seen or talked to my three grandchildren since a few months after leaving SRT. For a while, I kept making innocuous contact with my son he never responded. I have decided that the only way to live with this is to forgive myself for however I offended them, also to forgive them for being offended. Do I think they have forgiven me, no, I think they decided to forget me. Forgiveness isn't easy sometimes it doesn't always change the circumstances of the relationships, mostly it is a relief like clear cool water on a hot day. Exactly what every person involved needs.

As I continue to work toward recovery in New Horizons, I am coming to terms with the aspects of my life of which I am not proud. I guess that might be some of the humility my daughter has insisted upon coming into play. I regret how unkind and uncaring I have been toward myself in my adult life—it was as if I took over for Dell and Dorothy after they should have no longer had any hold over me.

The other patients are the ones who are helping me to see this aspect of recovery. I can see how they treat themselves sometimes with distain, sometimes with anger, sometimes just behaving in their worst possible interest. I can see myself in them. It helps me to not only find those parts of myself that need to be healed but to want so much to help them to see that there is another way to live with yourself. I used to think I was a compassionate person. I understand the meaning, the power of compassion especially compassion for oneself. I would go as far as to say that until you can have self-compassion you don't have the capacity to give compassion toward others. Luckily, at

SRT, there are staff people who have learned this lesson already or maybe they were born knowing. They do have compassion to give in abundance, especially Lauren Odell.

It is said that compassion is the ability to put oneself into another's shoes. Well until you learn to care about your own walk down your own path, it is almost impossible to take in someone else's trials.

I have been at New Horizons for four and a half months and with a new medication an atypical anti-psychotic I am no longer living with delusional thinking and the new medication is giving my anti-depressant a boost in efficacy. I am starting to feel good. I realized it one day when I went to Brandi and Brian's home for an outing. We were going to spend the day at the pool and as I changed into a makeshift bathing suit, some yoga shorts, and a camisole top, I saw myself in a mirror for the first time since I left to go live in my car. I was in shock. I came out of the bathroom laughing and crying and told Brandi that I was seeing myself for the first time. I meant I was seeing myself for the first time in my life. It was about not seeing the terrified, traumatized, depressed, and incongruent woman that I was used to seeing.

Ω

Unfortunately, during my fifth month in SRT a new client joined the ranks, a 57-year-old man who developed a degree of infatuation with me that I of course ill-advisedly reciprocated. I was ripe for the flattery. I was developing a hopeful attitude that made me feel very attractive as a person. When you've lived a significant portion of your life without hope when it begins to grow inside of you it is a powerful feeling. It rose to a sense of desire without much prompting in my case. Now it is never recommended that two clients develop anything more than a friendship, it is also difficult to tell two adults over fifty in my case over sixty what they should be doing with their personal life. My man friend shall remain unnamed due to the privacy of an inpatient environment; however, we made plans to see each other once we were both out of SRT. He left a month before I did, not because he was in recovery because New Horizons had done as much for him as he was willing to accept. An aspect of his illness made him prone to a stubborn streak that was not working in his best interests.

I decided that if we didn't get together it would be okay. I wrote about hope feeling like long-lost desire in my journal. But, once he left I never thought anything would come of it. I was surprised when he began calling every day suggesting that I move in with him in Vero Beach when I got out of SRT.

My treatment and discharge plan had me moving in with Brandi and Brian. I kept any other plans quiet I didn't want to affect my discharge date. I did talk to Brandi about it she was at least open to the possibility of me eventually moving in with my "boyfriend" once they had a chance to meet him to approve.

I was discharged on August 11, 2014. I went home with my daughter to a bedroom that she had ready for me. I had my medications with me, as well as a full set of prescriptions, appointments with my outpatient psychiatrist, and my therapist. I had been smoking up to three packs of cigarettes a day while in New Horizons SRT. When my daughter picked me up, she had a new electronic cigarette for me to use as a tool to quit smoking. Ultimately, by the time I left New Horizons I felt better about myself than I had in years. I had not had any wine in over six months my medications were working well, I felt as if I had a new lease on my life.

    I was a bit nervous about moving in with Brian and Marley. I was a mother-in-law, a three-year absent grandmother. From the beginning, they made me feel like part of the family. With such good prospects for a happy future, you might have thought that I would give up on the idea of moving to Vero Beach. Once I got my phone I was making and getting calls several times a day from my "boyfriend." Boyfriend is a silly word for a sixty-year-old woman to use let alone share with others but I admit that I was smitten.

    It took less than a month for me to move to Vero Beach, less than six months for me to realize I had made a terrible mistake. While I was taking my medications every day as prescribed, I came to understand that my housemate didn't hold the same attitude about staying well as I did. He stopped taking some of his meds, started to behave in a way that I recognized as severely bipolar and schizophrenic. He was a good person but without his correct medications, there was no match to be made. I did my best to try to care for him to get him back on track. If there was one thing I learned is I first had to take care of myself.

I left Vero Beach in January leaving much of my furniture and belongings with him. He had nothing when I came; he had a comfortable house that I was leaving. About a month after I had left, I got a phone call from a Vero Beach police detective wanting to know if I knew his whereabouts. I, of course, did not. The detective told me that he had started a fire in one of the bedrooms in the apartment we shared. They were looking for him for arson charges. I never spoke to him again. I hope he is somewhere safe, not in jail, and not homeless. I learned that recovery is a precious rare thing it must be treasured, nurtured, or it will be lost. Recovery is not a destination it is an unending path to walk in health and well-being.

I have lived with my daughter and her family for several years, we are all recovering more every day.

26

"No one saves us but ourselves. No one can and no one may. We ourselves must walk the path."
Sayings of Buddha, Gautama Buddha

  Being with my daughter Brandi, son-in-law Brian, and granddaughter Marley is a joyful state for me. I am grateful to be living in their home as an appreciated member of their family.
  I have a son Robert, daughter-in-law Jenn, and three more grandchildren Alec, Mackenzie, and Mckayla. I am still hoping to reconcile these relationships. It is my heart's desire—that I will someday be Grandma Linda to all of my family.
  Here at Brandi and Brian's home I have a cozy bedroom suite. My bed, my office, and a comfortable sitting area that is roomy enough for my upholstered glider-rocker. I am content with a small closet. I share a bathroom with Marley. It doesn't sound like much. I am happy. I don't miss the few belongings that are in storage. I gave away most of my furnishings lightening

my footprint of possessions, letting go of a heavy load, releasing my psychological need to be dispossessed.

Now maybe for the first time in my life I am focusing on taking care *with* myself. Taking care with my health and well-being—taking care with relationships of those that I love, who love me back. In sharp contrast for almost the entirety of my life, I tried to take care *of* myself, which for me was an exerting, exhausting, self-sufficiency that bordered on rabid detachment. I lived within a wall of inner isolation that I built stone by stone a veneer of pride, compulsion, and estrangement to hide the desolation, anxiety, and shame. Slowly by taking care *with* myself, my own worth is tempered with hard-earned perspective. Humility leads me to write it all down, to no longer be haunted by the past to accept and reflect the value of the whole journey to be willingly able to hold in reverence this Present.

Ω

My daughter Brandi has grown and matured into a remarkable woman—I don't take much credit other than for her work ethic. She is by far one of the most authentic people that I know or have ever met. With Brandi, what you see is what you get. Considering the façade creation that I spent most of my adult life trying to perfect, I would say she saw what I was doing wrong decided to do the opposite. I applaud her insightful integrity. Brandi has discovered the luxurious pleasure of being herself 100 percent of the time. Her sense of inner authenticity and well-being is the direct result.

My son-in-law Brian I have only known for six years, he is one of the most open, honest men I have ever come to know. He is the perfect mate for my daughter he loves her immensely and obviously. He and I have enjoyed many conversations on far ranging issues. My favorites are when we talk about spirituality. We come at the subject from the side of the introvert (me) and the extrovert (Brian) deep down we are both spirit-filled—to talk spirit to spirit is a great gift he has bestowed on me.

Last but not least is my granddaughter Marley; she is a beautiful child, smart, funny, clever, and quick with a perceptive quip. She is as remarkable as my daughter is in her own way. She is still young enough to be a clown or a goofball at home while making the honor roll every grading period at school. She is fearless with the dogs, Jake and Tanner, but afraid to put her head upside down. Marley is loving, sensitive, a normal happy healthy young girl.

Ω

My primary goal upon leaving SRT was to reconcile with my family. I also wanted to give back to the organization that in my estimation had saved me. After I had been in recovery, out of SRT for two years and two weeks, I called New Horizons to inquire about volunteering. I checked on the possibility of becoming a recovery peer specialist; I knew it required 500 hours of volunteer internship. I first called Marlene Price asking her if she would let me do my hours on the SRT unit, she enthusiastically agreed. Then I applied as a volunteer. By the middle of September 2016, I was in orientation volunteering at New Horizons on my way to SRT. In addition, even though I walked through the doors of the locked unit I had lived on for six months I had keys. During my first month of volunteer interning, I took a 40-hour class specifically designed to train and inform recovery peer specialist of their unique combination of lived experience with mental health issues and/or substance use problems. When combined with the natural development of empathy shown for others on their own recovery path. I learned about motivational interviewing, Relapse Preparedness Programs. During the six months of my part time internship I learned slowly how to use my lived experience to connect with, mentor, and advocate for SRT clients.

    I, of course, had a few missteps, revealing too much to a client who had asked a simple question. However, I had experiences that are more positive while I learned to share my story from a position of compassion for myself and for my clients. I started listening to my intuition and knew to talk about being homeless in my car to a young man who had been homeless in his car. I listened to the young transgender person who told me about the sexual abuse he had suffered as a young girl and I talked about my own sexual abuse as a child.

    In SRT, I did one-on-one sessions with peer clients, facilitated group sessions that focused on the steps and attitudes of a successful path to recovery. Because of my own experiences during the first two years of my recovery I could share that the path is not straight, the destination is not in sight, recovery is a path walked in a unique way for each person as individual as fingerprints. Sharing our stories with one another is fundamental to our journey. I have told many peers that no matter what was going on in my life I have never missed a day of my medications. Many have asked why I still take them if I am doing well. My answer is that I am doing well because I still take my meds. I have not had a drink of wine or any other alcohol in several years. I do not regret it a bit. I used to self-medicate with marijuana. My medications do a much better job—they don't give me the "munchies."

I still consider that I am in recovery from depression, anxiety disorder, PTSD post-traumatic stress disorder, and DID dissociative identity disorder. I no longer live imprisoned by my diagnosis I am free to be healthy, whole, and well that is the choice I make every day—I hope my daily choice encourages others to do the same.

I considered myself to have been in recovery for over three years yet my heart and mind are still opening to a degree I could never have imagined or have achieved. My peer clients draw me out letting me share their stories. Peer recovery is a compassionately intimate relationship requiring honesty, desire for wellness, and a willingness to be vulnerable enough to give solace to another.

To make my new skills and vocation official to complete the requirements for Recovery Peer Specialist to finalize my state certification requirements; I took a test at Florida Atlantic University. I passed with a B grade, which was good for a 63-year-old grandmother who hadn't taken a test in a few decades.

I returned to New Horizons began applying for open positions. The peer specialist position in the New Health Primary Care Clinic seemed like a good fit for me. My recovery had been based on my whole health, physical, mental, emotional, and spiritual. That was Will Joyce PA-C, integrated medicine philosophy to a 'T'. He was also my primary care physician at the time. I knew him to be a straight talking, kind, and caring person. I wanted to work in the kind of environment that he was creating at New Horizons.

I have celebrated yet another year's anniversary of my discharge from SRT. I am working at the New Health Primary Care Clinic with a great boss and wonderful teams of professionals who all make working here a dream come true.

I tell my story of my life in different ways to different people, depending on where they are on their own personal path of recovery. Some people are willingly able to hear the whole story, some only want to know about the happy conclusion, and either way is okay by me—I am doing what I was born to do, be a good little healer. I healed myself repeatedly using every physical and psychological instinct that I had. Looking back at my life, I know that God didn't give me anything I couldn't handle that he was with me all the time good and bad. Grace is given to be received one day at a time.

I look at my life this way—in my middling sixties I am doing what I know in my soul I was always meant to do—I am damn good at it too. The fact that my life's work took me sixty plus years to achieve must say something about my determination because I always knew that I wanted to help people be whole. Maybe I knew that because I had been broken and split apart, wholeness was always my goal. I believe that everyone desires the same.

While I have been very content to live with my daughter and her family, I have to admit that I still have a bent for independence. I am hoping to get a place to call my own in the near future. I live in the present moment, it is as it usually is, a darn good moment.

Afterword

The title of my autobiography is informed by a government statistic from the National Institute for Mental Health. At a minimum, since the crime is under-reported, in the United States 25 percent of female children or 1 in every 4 are molested, sexually abused, or sexually exploited before the age of eighteen-years-old. Sixteen percent of male children or 1 in every 6 faces the same damaging fate.

According to Diana E.H. Russell in her 1999, research book *The Secret Trauma Incest in the Lives of Girls and Women* the statistics become even graver. Biological fathers victimize one in twenty or 5 percent of daughters. In addition, stepfathers violate one in seven or 14 percent of stepdaughters.

In a study done by the National Institute for Mental Health in 2004-2005 it was determined that the act of rape, knowing the perpetrator, and the higher frequency of the abuse are associated with increased odds of psychiatric disorders. For example abuse involving a father or stepfather is associated with greater long-term harm. In that same NIMH study, 47 percent of all childhood onset psychiatric disorders and 26 to 32 percent of adult onset disorders are the result of childhood sexual abuse.

Every Fourth Girl is my life as I have lived it. Those involved and identified by actual names that were guilty or culpable are no longer living. In the cases of some of my other relationships with those still living I have changed names in order to respect the privacy and dignity of on-going lives.

Now over sixty-years-old I flood the darkness of trauma and dissociation with the illumination of wholeness and recollection. I am healing from the trauma that haunted my life like an ever-present ghost. It is my hope that my story will bring focus to the epidemic of child sexual abuse. It is my prayer that my truth can help others find their own path to healing as well.

About the Author:

Linda Dell Moore spent her adult life raising two children of her own and working in human resources management. When Linda was 43 years old, she experienced an extended dissociative episode during which she recovered the majority of her lost memories. After suffering for the next 17 years under the knowledge of her traumatic life and losing all of her family relationships to confrontation or estrangement. Linda's mental health was on the verge of suicide. She ended up hospitalized, in therapy, and on medication for the first time in her life. Slowly but surely over the next six months as an inpatient in New Horizons of the Treasure Coast, a mental health facility in Florida. Linda began to reclaim her sanity and her ability to relate to her loved ones. Now several years later Linda works as a Certified Recovery Peer Specialist in support, mentoring, and advocacy of peers with mental health and substance use issues. Many of her clients are recovering from their own life traumas and Linda's empathy and understanding of the experiences are helpful and healing. Linda has shared her life experience in her memoir "Every Fourth Girl" and is working on two mystery novels that have been created based on Linda's rich life experiences. Those titles are "Nicki Rose, Memoir of Murder," and "Killings on Laurel Lane."